THE INVINCIBLE

THE MANY ARMORS OF IRON MAN

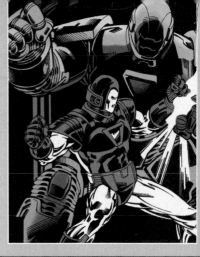

THE INVINCIBLE
IRON MAN
THE MANY ARMORS OF IRON MAN

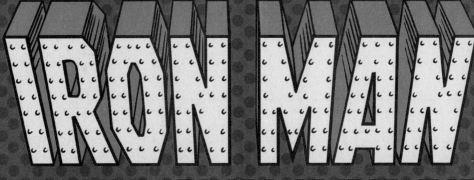

Iron Man #47
Writer: Roy Thomas
Artist: Barry Windsor-Smith
Inker: Jim Mooney
Letterer: Art Simek
Editor: Stan Lee

Iron Man #142
Writer: David Michelinie
Penciler: John Romita Jr.
Inker & Co-Plotter: Bob Layton
Colorist: Bob Sharen
Letterer: John Costanza
Editor: Jim Salicrup

Iron Man #143
Writer: David Michelinie
Penciler: John Romita Jr.
Inker & Co-Plotter: Bob Layton
Colorist: Bob Sharen
Letterer: John Costanza
Editor: Jim Salicrup

Iron Man #144
Writer: David Michelinie
Penciler: John Romita Jr.
Inker & Co-Plotter: Bob Layton
Colorist: Bob Sharen
Letterer: John Costanza
Editor: Jim Salicrup

Iron Man #152
Writer: David Michelinie
Penciler: John Romita Jr.
Inker & Co-Plotter: Bob Layton
Colorist: Glynis Wein
Letterer: Joe Rosen
Editor: Jim Salicrup

Iron Man #153
Writer: David Michelinie
Penciler: John Romita Jr.
Inker & Co-Plotter: Bob Layton
Colorist: Bob Sharen
Letterer: Joe Rosen
Editor: Jim Salicrup

Iron Man #200
Writer: Denny O'Neil
Penciler: Mark Bright
Inker: Akin & Garvey
Colorist: Bob Sharen
Letterer: Rick Parker
Editor: Mark Gruenwald

Iron Man #218
Writer: David Michelinie
Artist & Co-Plotter: Bob Layton
Colorist: Bob Sharen
Letterer: Janice Chiang
Editor: Mark Gruenwald

Front Cover Art: Luke McDonnell
Front Cover Colors: Frank D'Armata
Back Cover Art: Gil Kane
Back Cover Colors: Chris Sotomayor

Collection Editor: Mark D. Beazley
Assistant Editors: John Denning & Cory Levine
Editor, Special Projects: Jennifer Grünwald
Senior Editor, Special Projects: Jeff Youngquist
Senior Vice President of Sales: David Gabriel
Color Reconstruction: Jerron Quality Color
Production: Jerron Quality Color
Editor in Chief: Joe Quesada
Publisher: Dan Buckley

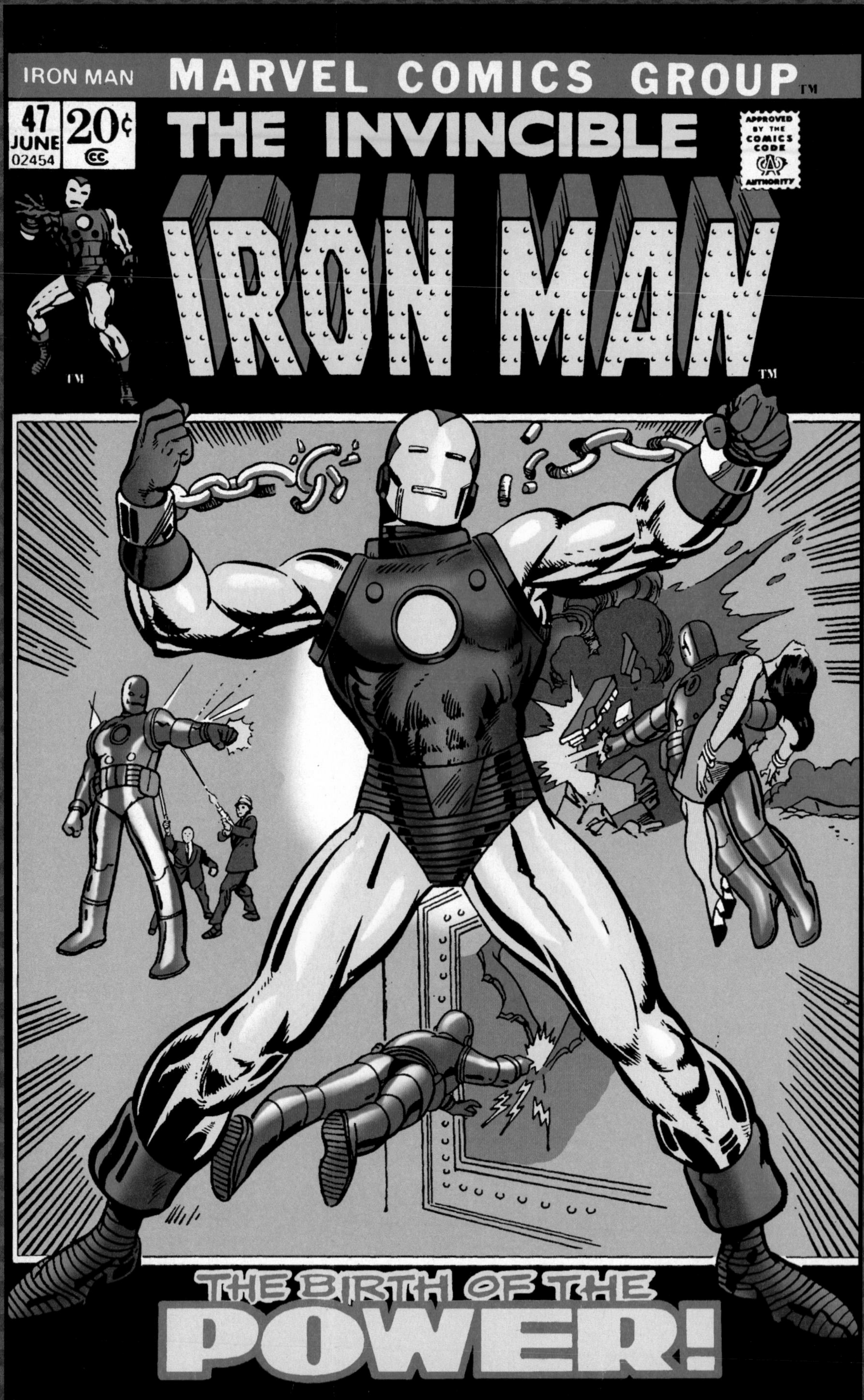
IRON MAN
MARVEL COMICS GROUP
47
JUNE
02454
20¢
THE INVINCIBLE
APPROVED BY THE COMICS CODE AUTHORITY
IRON MAN
THE BIRTH OF THE
POWER!

THE INVINCIBLE IRON MAN

YOUR NAME IS ANTHONY STARK, AND YOU LIVE TWO LIVES: ONE, AS THE MILLIONAIRE INVENTOR AND MUNITIONS-MAKER WHO IS THE ENVY OF MEN, THE SOUGHT-AFTER PRIZE OF WOMEN...THE OTHER, AS THE GRIM ARMOR-CLAD AVENGER WHO STREAKS THIS BLEAK MARCH MORNING THRU SAD AND RAIN-SWEPT SKIES.

BUT THAT IS MERELY THE BAREST BEGINNINGS OF THE REASON WHY, IF ANY HAD EARS TO HEAR, THEY WOULD HEAR YOU CRY--ALOUD AND IN ANGUISH--

WHY MUST THERE BE AN IRON MAN?

BUT THE GRIEF-STRICKEN MOURNERS IN THE LONG ISLAND CEMETERY BELOW DO NOT LISTEN... DO NOT HEAR....!

AND SO, YOU'RE LEFT ALONE IN YOUR TORTURED SORROW...

....MORE ALONE, PERHAPS, THAN ANY MAN HAS EVER BEEN...!

STAN LEE EDITOR * ROY THOMAS WRITER * BARRY SMITH ARTIST

JIM MOONEY INKER   ARTIE SIMEK LETTERER

BASED IN PART ON A STORY BY STAN LEE AND LARRY LIEBER FOR TALES OF SUSPENSE #39.

NOW, YOU STRIDE LIKE A GREAT, INSENSATE *ROBOT* THRU THE HUMAN THRONG THAT RINGS *KEVIN O'BRIEN'S* GRAVE...

AND YOU WISH, IN SILENCE, THAT YOU *WERE,* INDEED, A THING OF UN-FEELING *METAL*...

...INSTEAD OF ONLY A VERY VULNERABLE *MAN,* INSIDE AN ARMORED *SHELL.*

MR. GILBERT --I'M SORRY I COULDN'T MAKE IT UNTIL THE *LAST MINUTE* THIS WAY...

BUT... WHO'S THAT *MAN* BY KEVIN'S GRAVE?

THAT'S... KEVIN'S *FATHER.*

HE FLEW IN THIS MORNING... FOR THE *FUNERAL.*

GO TELL *HIM* YOU'RE SORRY YOU'RE IRON MAN-- AND WHILE YOU'RE *AT* IT...

...TELL HIM YOU'RE SORRY YOU *KILLED HIS SON!*

GILBERT! IN HEAVEN'S NAME, *STOP IT,* MAN!

AS YOUR FELLOW BOARD MEMBERS, *WE'RE* IN THIS THING JUST AS DEEP AS *YOU* ARE.

BUT, IN THE NAME OF HUMAN DECENCY-- *SHUT UP!*

IT DOESN'T REALLY MATTER, DOES IT, AVENGER? FOR, YOU ARE *OBLIVIOUS* TO ALL SAVE THE FALLING RAIN...THE TOO-FAMIL-IAR *DRONE* OF THE MINISTER'S WORDS...

"ASHES TO ASHES, DUST TO DUST..."

...**A**ND SUDDENLY, INTERRUPTING YOUR SOMBRE BROODING, THE VOICE OF *MARIANNE*...THE VOICE OF THE GIRL YOU LOVE...

...**T**HE GIRL WITH POWERS OF *EXTRA-SENSORY PERCEPTION*....!

TONY... I... I WARNED YOU *NOT* TO COME.

THERE IS *DANGER* FOR YOU HERE. I CAN...*FEEL* IT.

MUST YOU TWO *MUMBLE* AT EACH OTHER?

BAD ENOUGH, STARK HAD THE POOR TASTE TO SEND YOU AS HIS *PROXY*, INSTEAD OF COMING *HIMSELF!*

LOOK, GILBERT--YOU KNOW HOW *UPSET* HE--

GENTLEMEN, *PLEASE*--THIS IS NO TIME FOR THE AIRING OF *PRIVATE* QUARRELS.

SORRY, REVEREND. YOU'RE RIGHT. I'LL WAIT UNTIL--

SCREEEE

UH OH! THERE'S *TROUBLE!*

ALL RIGHT, IRON MAN--HOP IN WITH *US!*

THEY WANT YOU FOR *QUESTIONING*, IN CONNECTION WITH O'BRIEN'S *DEATH.*

CAN'T IT *WAIT*, OFFICER?

NEGATIVE! NOW DO YOU COME *QUIETLY*, OR-- *YEEOW!*

--OR NOT AT *ALL! ISN'T THAT* MY SECOND CHOICE?

STAY BACK, JOE! THOSE REPULSOR RAYS OF HIS COULD *TEAR* US APART!

KZAPT

SURRENDER, IRON MAN! THE *AUTHORITIES* COULD MAKE BETTER USE OF STARK'S PRECIOUS ARMOR THAN *YOU* EVER DID!

ALL *YOU* EVER DID WITH IT--WAS--*DESTROY!*

MAYBE GILBERT'S RIGHT ABOUT *ONE* THING, AVENGER.

WHY MUST THERE BE AN IRON MAN? *WHY??*

YOU *TOO*, MARIANNE!?

AND YET-- MAYBE YOU'RE *BOTH* RIGHT.

IT WAS ARMOR LIKE MINE THAT DROVE KEVIN *MAD*--AND CAUSED HIS *DEATH!*

AND NOW-- I'VE EVEN MADE A FARCE OF HIS *FUNERAL.*

STOP HIM! SHOOT TO *WOUND* HIM, SAM!

HOW? HE SHRUGS OFF BULLETS LIKE THEY WERE *CHICLETS!*

TRUE ENOUGH, TONY! YOU HARDLY *FEEL* THE STEEL PELLETS RICOCHETING OFF YOUR SKINTIGHT ARMOR...

...*BECAUSE* YOU'RE HEARING, OVER AND OVER AGAIN IN YOUR BRAIN, THE QUESTION *YOU* HAD FIRST VOICED...

...*AND* MARIANNE, OF ALL PEOPLE, HAD REPEATED:

"*WHY* MUST THERE BE AN IRON MAN?"

3

LIKE SOME BRUTAL, BLUDGEONING *TRIPHAMMER*, THE QUESTION POUNDS WITHIN YOUR SKULL....SO THAT YOU SCARCELY *NOTE* THE RISING NORTHERN WIND, THE DRIVING RAIN WHICH PELTS YOUR RUSTPROOF ARMOR...

MY *ARMOR!* MAYBE SIMON GILBERT IS RIGHT! MAYBE I *SHOULD* SURRENDER IT AND MYSELF TO THE AUTHORITIES--TELL THEM WHO I REALLY AM----LET THEM TRY *IRON MAN*--AND TONY STARK--FOR MURDER.

WHAT GILBERT DOESN'T KNOW IS KEVIN O'BRIEN WASN'T THE *FIRST* MAN TO DIE BECAUSE OF THIS METAL SHELL THAT KEEPS ME ALIVE.

BUT *YOU* KNOW WHO WAS FIRST, DON'T YOU, AVENGER?

YOU KNOW ALL *TOO* WELL....!

SLOWLY, ONE BY ONE, THE WALLS YOU'VE BUILT AROUND YOUR MIND BEGIN TO CRUMBLE--AND YOU RE-LIVE IT STILL AGAIN...

OH, *COME* NOW, MR. STARK...

WHAT YOU CLAIM FOR THAT CRAZY GADGET OF YOURS IS *IMPOSSIBLE*.

THINK SO, GENERAL? THEN WATCH.

WE'RE ALL *EYES*, FELLA.

YOU HAVE SO *MANY* LABORATORIES, TONY STARK. AT WHICH ONE DID THE FATEFUL DEMONSTRATION TAKE PLACE? CAN YOU TEAR DOWN THAT *FINAL* WALL AND REMEMBER? AND DOES IT TRULY *MATTER....?*

THERE! I'VE SWITCHED IT *ON*.

NOW, IT'S ENER-GIZING THIS COMMON, GARDEN-VARIETY *MAGNET....!*

THE *DOOR* OF THAT LOCKED VAULT--IT'S STARTING TO BUDGE--!

CLIK!

URRRRHHH

NATURALLY! MY TINY TRANSISTORS ARE SO POWERFUL--

--THEY CAN INCREASE THE FORCE OF *ANY* DEVICE--A *THOUSANDFOLD!*

LOOK OUT, GENERAL! *THERE SHE BLOWS!*

KRAKK

NOW DO YOU BELIEVE MY "CRAZY GADGETS" CAN BRING AN EARLY END TO THE BLOODSHED IN *VIETNAM?*

STARK, AFTER WHAT I'VE JUST SEEN...

...I'LL BELIEVE *ANYTHING!*

AND THERE WAS STILL **ANOTHER** SIDE TO YOU THEN, WASN'T THERE, STARK? YOU WERE A **SOPHISTI-CATE** AS WELL AS A SCIENTIST... A MILLIONAIRE **PLAYBOY** AS WELL AS A PHENOMENONALLY GIFTED INVENTOR... AS MUCH AT HOME IN **HIGH SOCIETY** AS IN A CLUTTERED LABORATORY...

WHAT DID YOU KNOW THEN OF-- WONG-CHU?

HAH! ANOTHER VILLAGE BROUGHT TO ITS **KNEES!**

STILL, I SHALL BE GENEROUS! IF ANY PRISONER CAN **DEFEAT** ME IN FAIR COMBAT...

...THE WHOLE VILLAGE GOES **FREE!**

THE VILLAGERS WERE ALWAYS AS **DESPERATE** AS THEY WERE HUNGRY AND WAR-WEARY...

AND SO, THERE WAS ALWAYS SOMEONE TO **ACCEPT** THE GUERRILLA TYRANT'S CHALLENGE...

...**SOMEONE** WHO INVARIABLY, INEVITABLY **FELL!**

I AM **STRONGEST** OF ALL! NEXT TO **WONG-CHU**...

...ALL OTHER MEN ARE **FLEAS!**

IS **ENOUGH** SPORT, GREAT ONE?

YES, NOW, LET US **PLUNDER** THE TOWN.

FOR **NONE** CAN STOP THE VICTORIOUS **WONG-CHU!**

WHO WOULD HAVE **DREAMED** THEN, TONY STARK, THAT BEFORE LONG YOU AND THAT MURDEROUS MADMAN WERE FATED TO **MEET**...

...**IN** THE STEAMING **JUNGLES** OF SOUTH-EAST ASIA?

OUR HEAVY **ARTILLERY** COULD CLEAN OUT THE ENEMY, MR. STARK.

BUT WE CAN'T TAKE **TANKS** AND **CANNON** THRU THIS FOLIAGE.

THAT'S WHERE **MY** MIDGET DEVICES COME IN, EH?

RIGHT! THANKS TO YOUR TRANSISTORS, OUR MORTARS ARE NOW NO LARGER THAN **FLASHLIGHTS.**

UH OH. **MOVEMENT** AHEAD! HERE'S WHERE YOU SEE YOUR GUNS IN **ACTION.**

THAT'S WHAT I'M **HERE** FOR--TO SEE IF THERE ARE ANY **BUGS.**

BUT THERE **WEREN'T** ANY BUGS, WERE THERE, AVENGER?

WTHOM! WTHOM!

AND, PUT INTO MASS PRODUCTION, YOUR WEAPONS MIGHT HAVE **SHORTENED** THE WAR...

BUT, THE JUNGLE HELD A **THOUSAND** PERILS... SOME OF THEM **MAN-MADE.**

STARK-- **WATCH** IT!

HUH--?

A STRING--! **BOOBY-TRAP!!**

BAROOOOM!

CIVILIAN IS STILL *ALIVE.*

MAYBE HE IS *IMPORTANT.*

I SHALL TAKE HIM TO *WONG-CHU!*

*L*ATER, THRU STILL-RINGING *EARS,* YOU HEARD...

...HOW *IS* OUR HONORED GUEST, DOCTOR?

BAD! MUCH *SHRAPNEL* NEAR HIS HEART, GREAT ONE.

IMPOSSIBLE TO *OPERATE.*

IN A FEW DAYS THE SHRAPNEL WILL REACH HIS *HEART*-- AND HE WILL *DIE.*

THEN, BECAUSE YOU SAY HE IS STRONG ENOUGH TO WORK *UNTIL* HE DIES, WE SHALL *USE* HIM.

WE SHALL TRICK HIM INTO SPENDING HIS LAST DAYS ON EARTH WORK- ING FOR *US.* AWAKEN HIM.

YES, GREAT ONE.

...WE KNOW YOU ARE FAMOUS AMERICAN *INVENTOR.* IF YOU WILL DESIGN POWERFUL NEW WEAPONS FOR *WONG-CHU...*

AFTER- WARD, I SHALL HAVE MY *SURGEON* SAVE YOUR LIFE.

LYING THRU HIS TEETH! I KNOW I'VE ONLY GOT *DAYS* TO LIVE.

BUT, IF IT'S THE LAST THING I DO-- I'LL FIND A WAY TO TAKE THIS SMIRKING TERROR- IST *WITH* ME.

ALL RIGHT, WONG- CHU. IT'S A *DEAL.*

YOU WILL *NOT* BE SORRY IN YOUR OLD AGE, MR. STARK.

HERE IS THE ROOM WHERE YOU WILL WORK.

WHAT WILL YOU *DESIGN?*

PLENTY OF *SCRAP IRON*-- PLENTY OF *TOOLS.*

THIS I *PROMISE* YOU-- I'LL BUILD THE MOST *FANTASTIC* WEAPON OF ALL TIME.

SLAM

I'LL *BUILD* IT, ALL RIGHT-- BUT FOR *ONE* PURPOSE ONLY--

--TO KEEP MYSELF *ALIVE!*

EVERY TICK OF THE CLOCK BRINGS THE DEADLY SHRAPNEL *CLOSER* TO MY HEART.

GOT TO WORK *FAST,* CAN'T AFFORD A SINGLE *MISTAKE...!*

6

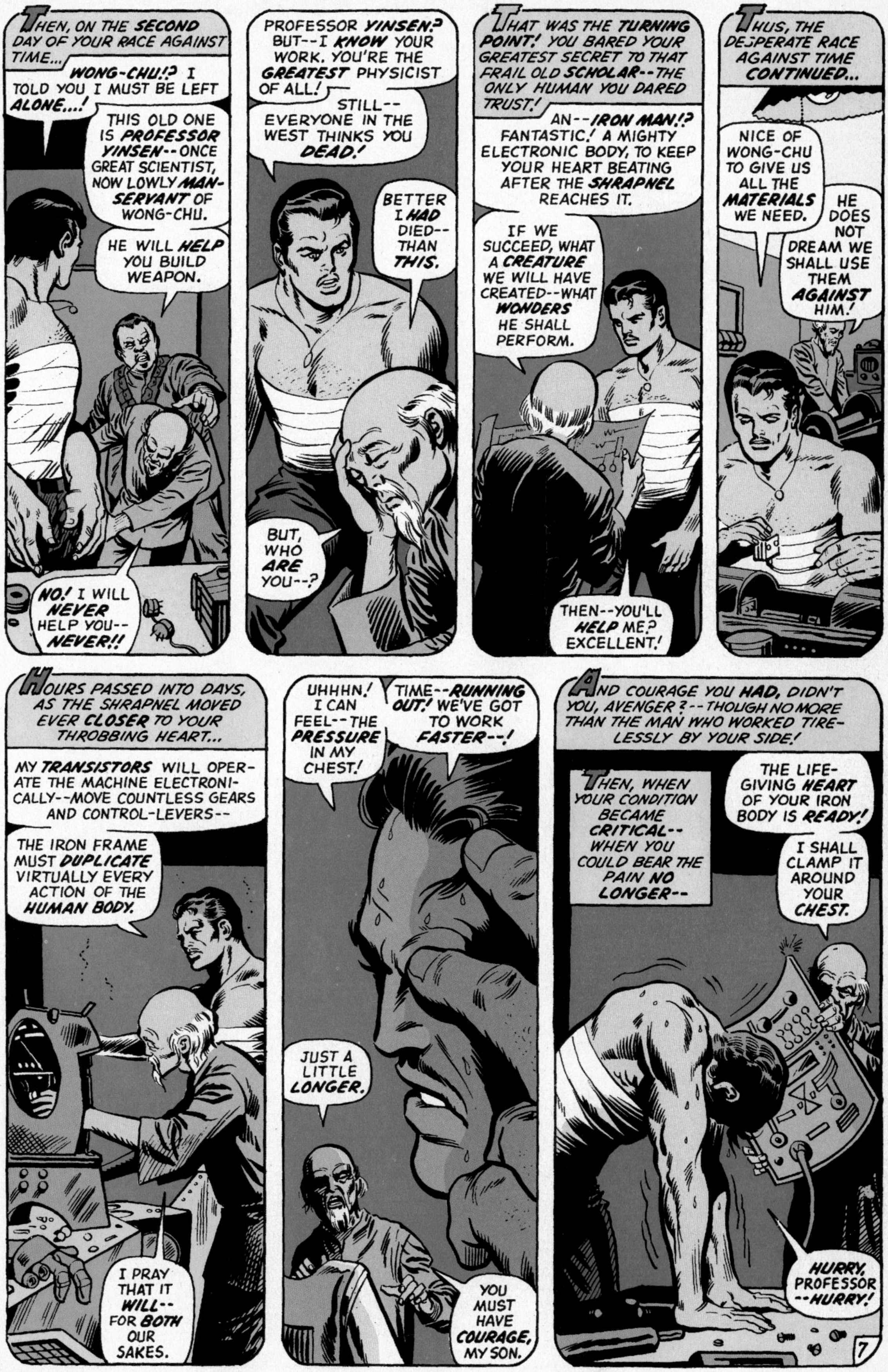
THEN, ON THE SECOND DAY OF YOUR RACE AGAINST TIME...
WONG-CHU!? I TOLD YOU I MUST BE LEFT ALONE...!
THIS OLD ONE IS PROFESSOR YINSEN--ONCE GREAT SCIENTIST, NOW LOWLY MAN-SERVANT OF WONG-CHU.
HE WILL HELP YOU BUILD WEAPON.
NO! I WILL NEVER HELP YOU--NEVER!!
PROFESSOR YINSEN? BUT--I KNOW YOUR WORK. YOU'RE THE GREATEST PHYSICIST OF ALL!
STILL--EVERYONE IN THE WEST THINKS YOU DEAD!
BETTER I HAD DIED--THAN THIS.
BUT, WHO ARE YOU--?
THAT WAS THE TURNING POINT! YOU BARED YOUR GREATEST SECRET TO THAT FRAIL OLD SCHOLAR--THE ONLY HUMAN YOU DARED TRUST!
AN--IRON MAN!? FANTASTIC! A MIGHTY ELECTRONIC BODY, TO KEEP YOUR HEART BEATING AFTER THE SHRAPNEL REACHES IT.
IF WE SUCCEED, WHAT A CREATURE WE WILL HAVE CREATED--WHAT WONDERS HE SHALL PERFORM.
THEN--YOU'LL HELP ME? EXCELLENT!
THUS, THE DESPERATE RACE AGAINST TIME CONTINUED...
NICE OF WONG-CHU TO GIVE US ALL THE MATERIALS WE NEED.
HE DOES NOT DREAM WE SHALL USE THEM AGAINST HIM!
HOURS PASSED INTO DAYS, AS THE SHRAPNEL MOVED EVER CLOSER TO YOUR THROBBING HEART...
MY TRANSISTORS WILL OPERATE THE MACHINE ELECTRONICALLY--MOVE COUNTLESS GEARS AND CONTROL-LEVERS--
THE IRON FRAME MUST DUPLICATE VIRTUALLY EVERY ACTION OF THE HUMAN BODY.
I PRAY THAT IT WILL--FOR BOTH OUR SAKES.
UHHHN! I CAN FEEL--THE PRESSURE IN MY CHEST!
TIME--RUNNING OUT! WE'VE GOT TO WORK FASTER--!
JUST A LITTLE LONGER.
YOU MUST HAVE COURAGE, MY SON.
AND COURAGE YOU HAD, DIDN'T YOU, AVENGER?--THOUGH NO MORE THAN THE MAN WHO WORKED TIRELESSLY BY YOUR SIDE!
THEN, WHEN YOUR CONDITION BECAME CRITICAL--WHEN YOU COULD BEAR THE PAIN NO LONGER--
THE LIFE-GIVING HEART OF YOUR IRON BODY IS READY!
I SHALL CLAMP IT AROUND YOUR CHEST.
HURRY, PROFESSOR--HURRY!
7

WHEN I ACTIVATE THE MACHINE, YOUR OWN AMAZING *TRANSISTORS* WILL FURNISH THE POWER TO KEEP YOUR HEART BEATING.

IT IS *DONE*.

YOU SHOULD *LIVE*--JUST AS LONG AS THE *IRON BODY* OPERATES!

AND *NO LONGER!*

THE GENERATOR WILL SOON *BUILD UP* ENOUGH ENERGY TO FURNISH ALL THE POWER YOU'LL NEED TO *MOVE* AGAIN. THEN--

THE *WARNING LIGHT* WE INSTALLED! SOMEONE *APPROACHES!*

IT CAN ONLY BE--*WONG-CHU!*

IF HE ENTERS NOW--ALL OUR WORK WILL HAVE BEEN IN *VAIN*.

HE MUST BE *KEPT AWAY*-- UNTIL THE MIGHTY ELECTRONIC BODY GIVES YOU POWER TO *WALK*--TO *STRIKE!*

AND THUS-- *FAREWELL*, TONY STARK!

THEN, BEFORE YOU COULD GASP AN ANSWER-- BEFORE YOU EVEN REALIZED WHAT WAS HAPPENING--

SLAM!

DEATH TO WONG-CHU! DEATH TO THE *EVIL TYRANT!*

THE OLD ONE HAS GONE *MAD!* HE IS OF NO FURTHER *USE* TO ME.

END HIS MISERABLE LIFE--*NOW!*

YOU HEARD IT ALL, STARK: THE SHARP RETORT OF THE RIFLE...THE THUD OF A FALLING, LIFELESS BODY...EVEN AS THE LIFE-SUSTAINING MACHINE BUILT UP MORE AND MORE POWER BEHIND THAT LOCKED DOOR.

AND--

THE TRANSISTORS HAVE SUFFICIENT *ENERGY* NOW!

MY HEART IS BEATING *NORMALLY* AGAIN.

THE MACHINE IS KEEPING ME *ALIVE!*

ALIVE!

8

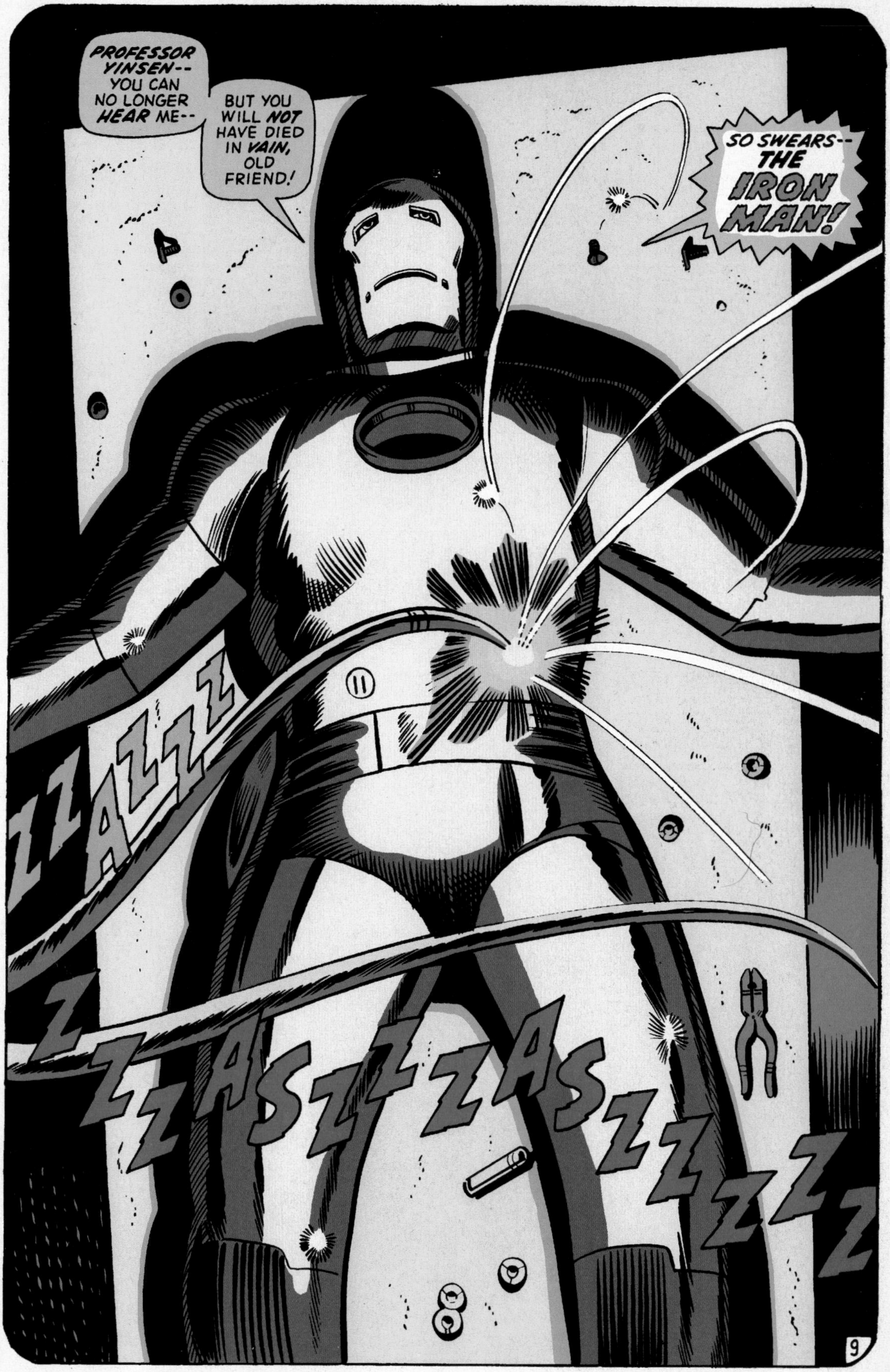
PROFESSOR YINSEN-- YOU CAN NO LONGER HEAR ME--
BUT YOU WILL NOT HAVE DIED IN VAIN, OLD FRIEND!
SO SWEARS-- THE IRON MAN!
ZZZAZZZ
ZZZASZZZZASZZZZZ
9

ALL THE SAME, YOUR *CONTROL* WAS STILL *CONSIDERABLY WEAKER* THAN YOUR *WILL*. AND SO, AS YOU BEGAN TO *STIR*...

HARD--TO *MOVE*. WELL, I *EXPECTED* THAT.

THIS ARMOR'S CIRCUITS ARE COORDINATED WITH MY *BRAIN WAVES*, JUST AS ANY LIVING HUMAN'S BRAIN CONTROLS HIS BODY.

BUT--I'M *LOSING*--

--MY--

--*BALANCE*--!

I'M LIKE A *BABY*--LEARNING TO WALK ALL OVER AGAIN.

BUT--I HAVEN'T *TIME*. I'VE GOT TO GET THE KNACK OF MANIPULATING THIS MASSIVE IRON SHELL BEFORE *WONG-CHU* BREAKS IN--

--OR ELSE I'LL BE *AT THEIR MERCY*!

GOT TO GET UP! *GOT TO.!!*

*A*ND, WITH A RESURGENCE OF *WILL*...

I--*DID* IT, I'VE GOT THE *FEEL* OF IT NOW.

I CAN STAND--MOVE--EVEN *WALK* WITHOUT TOPPLING!

BREAK IT *DOWN*! *SMASH IT*, YOU FOOL!

I MUST LEARN WHAT HAS *HAPPENED* IN THERE!

Y-YES, GREAT ONE! I AM *TRYING*!

WHAM WHAM

14

THEY'RE COMING! THIS IS MY FIRST, MY GREATEST TEST.

CAN THE THING I HAVE CREATED SURVIVE?

THIS THING WHICH IS LESS THAN HUMAN--YET SOMEHOW, FAR MORE!

THIS THING WHICH NOW IS-- TONY STARK!

AND YET-- AM I TRULY TONY STARK ANY MORE--

--WHEN, IN ORDER TO REMAIN ALIVE, I MUST STAY FOREVER IN THIS WALKING IRON PRISON??

COMMON-SENSE WAS ALWAYS YOUR STRONG SUIT--AND SO, YOU SUDDENLY SNAPPED BACK TO REALITY--

THEY'LL BE THRU THE DOOR IN A MINUTE.

AND MY METAL ARMOR'S STILL BUILDING POWER....!

SO, I'D BETTER CONCEAL MYSELF--TILL I CAN PLAN MY NEXT MOVE.

LUCKILY, YINSEN AND I EQUIPPED MY IRON BODY WITH PLENTY OF EXTRAS...

...SUCH AS THESE SUCTION CUPS WHICH FASTEN TO MY PALMS-- AND MY TRANSISTOR-POWERED AIR-PRESSURE JETS--

--WHICH GIVE ME THE POWER

SLAP!

--TO SOAR INTO THE AIR--

CHINK

--LIKE SO!

THEY DIDN'T LOOK UP, DID THEY, TONY....?

THE YANKEE IS GONE!

AND HE HAS BUILT US NO WEAPONS!

FIND HIM AND DESTROY HIM--AS YOU DID THE OTHER!

"THE OTHER"! THAT'S ALL PROFESSOR YINSEN HAD BEEN TO WONG-CHU--JUST ONE MORE HUMAN BEING TO WIPE HIS BLOODY BOOTS ON!

YOU MADE A VOW AT THAT MOMENT, DIDN'T YOU, STARK?

A VOW TO MAKE WONG-CHU PAY-- AS NO MAN HAD EVER PAID BEFORE!

STILL, YOU HELD BACK--UNTIL THE RAGING BUTCHER AND HIS LACKEYS HAD LEFT--

AMUSE YOURSELF WHILE YOU CAN, WONG-CHU.

JUDGMENT DAY'S A-COMING!

11

15

BUT, WONG-CHU ALREADY HAD *OTHER* THINGS ON HIS MIND-- THE ROAR OF A FEARFUL CROWD, THE APPLAUSE OF SOLDIERS CURRYING FAVOR...

HAH! I WIN AGAIN!

HAVE I NOT SAID-- *NONE* CAN DEFEAT WONG-CHU!

AND *I* SAY WONG-CHU IS A SNIVELING *COWARD!!*

WHAT? WHO DARES SPEAK THUS TO *WONG-CHU?*

SHOW YOURSELF! LET ME SEE THE *FACE* OF THE ONE I AM ABOUT TO DESTROY!

AS YOU *WISH,* TYRANT....!

WHY DO YOU *STARE,* WONG-CHU?

HAVE YOU NEVER SEEN AN *IRON MAN* BEFORE?

NOW, PREPARE TO *PAY* FOR YOUR MISDEEDS--FOR ONCE AND FOR *ALL!*

BAH! YOU STARTLED ME FOR A MOMENT-- BUT *NO MORE.*

YOU ARE BUT SOME CLUMSY *ROBOT--* A *MACHINE--*

I WILL *SMASH* YOU--AS I WOULD SMASH A *MAN!*

I SHALL-- *UNNGHN!*

THUD!

YES, WONG-CHU?

YOU *WERE* SAYING?

BOP!

YOU ARE NOT FACING A *WOUNDED, DYING* MAN NOW...

12

16

--OR AN *AGED, GENTLE PROFESSOR*--!

THIS IS *IRON MAN* WHO OPPOSES YOU, WONG-CHU--

--YOU, AND ALL YOU *STAND FOR!!*

YOU MAKE ME *LOSE FACE.*

BUT, EVEN *YOU* CAN BE SLAIN. *EVEN YOU!*

GUARDS! OPEN FIRE! DESTROY THIS-- *IRON MAN!*

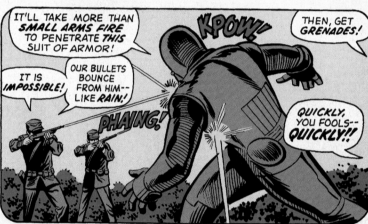

IT'LL TAKE MORE THAN *SMALL ARMS FIRE* TO PENETRATE *THIS* SUIT OF ARMOR!

IT IS *IMPOSSIBLE!*

OUR BULLETS BOUNCE FROM HIM-- LIKE *RAIN!*

KPOW!

PHAING!

THEN, GET *GRENADES!*

QUICKLY, YOU FOOLS-- *QUICKLY!!*

NO HURRY, NOW. *I'M* NOT GOING ANYWHERE.

I JUST WANT TO REVERSE THE CHARGE ON THIS MAGNETIC *TURBO-INSULATOR...*

...AND USE A *TOP-HAT* TRANSISTOR TO *INCREASE* ITS REPELLING POWER...

...ONE THOUSAND TIMES!

THERE! REVERSE MAGNETISM! OR, AS I MIGHT CHRISTEN IT-- --MY *REPULSOR RAY!*

AIEEEE! NOTHING CAN STOP THIS DEVIL! *NOTHING!!*

FLEE! FLEE!

NO, YOU SWINE-- *STOP!!*

BUT, THE GUERRILLAS WERE IN NO MOOD TO LISTEN TO *REASONED* ARGUMENT ABOUT HOW *NON-METAL* WEAPONS COULD DEFEAT YOU...

13

UPSTAIRS THERE IS A *LOUD-SPEAKER!*

WHEN I USE *IT* TO COMMAND THEM, THEY WILL *LISTEN* TO ME. THEY WILL *STOP* RUNNING!

THE IRON DEVIL WILL NOT STAND LONG AGAINST THE SHEER WEIGHT OF *HUMAN NUMBERS!*

HEAR ME, MY WARRIORS!

TEN THOUSAND YUAN TO THE ONE WHO *DESTROYS* IRON MAN!

AWWKKK BRRK

IT WAS *EASY* TO CREATE ELECTRICAL INTERFERENCE TO DROWN OUT HIS WORDS WITH *STATIC*, WASN'T IT?

FOR THE FIRST TIME EVER, YOU KNEW THE MEANING OF *TRUE POWER!*

PERHAPS --TOO MUCH POWER?

YOU PLAYED WITH HIM, LIKE A CAT WITH A MOUSE--SWITCHED YOUR *OWN* ARMOR-REVERBER-ATED VOICE ONTO THE LOUDSPEAKER...

DESERT THE CONWARD WONG-CHU!

FLEE INTO THE JUNGLE-- AND *NEVER* RETURN!

WHAT--WHAT IS *HAPPENING?* THOSE ARE *NOT* MY WORDS!

NONE CAN DEFEAT THE ONE CALLED IRON MAN!

FLEE--FLEE, BEFORE HE SLAYS YOU *ALL!*

SO MUCH FOR THE *FAITHFUL SIDEKICKS!*

NOW TO SETTLE WITH *WONG-CHU* HIMSELF.

HE'S LOCKED HIMSELF BEHIND THIS *DOOR.*

BUT WHEN A MAN HAS A *MINIATURE BUZZ-SAW* UP HIS INDEX FINGER-- ONE WHICH'LL OUT-PERFORM ANYTHING A DOZEN TIMES ITS *SIZE*--

IT'LL TAKE MORE THAN A SIMPLE LOCK TO STOP HIM!

ZZZZZZZZZZZ

14

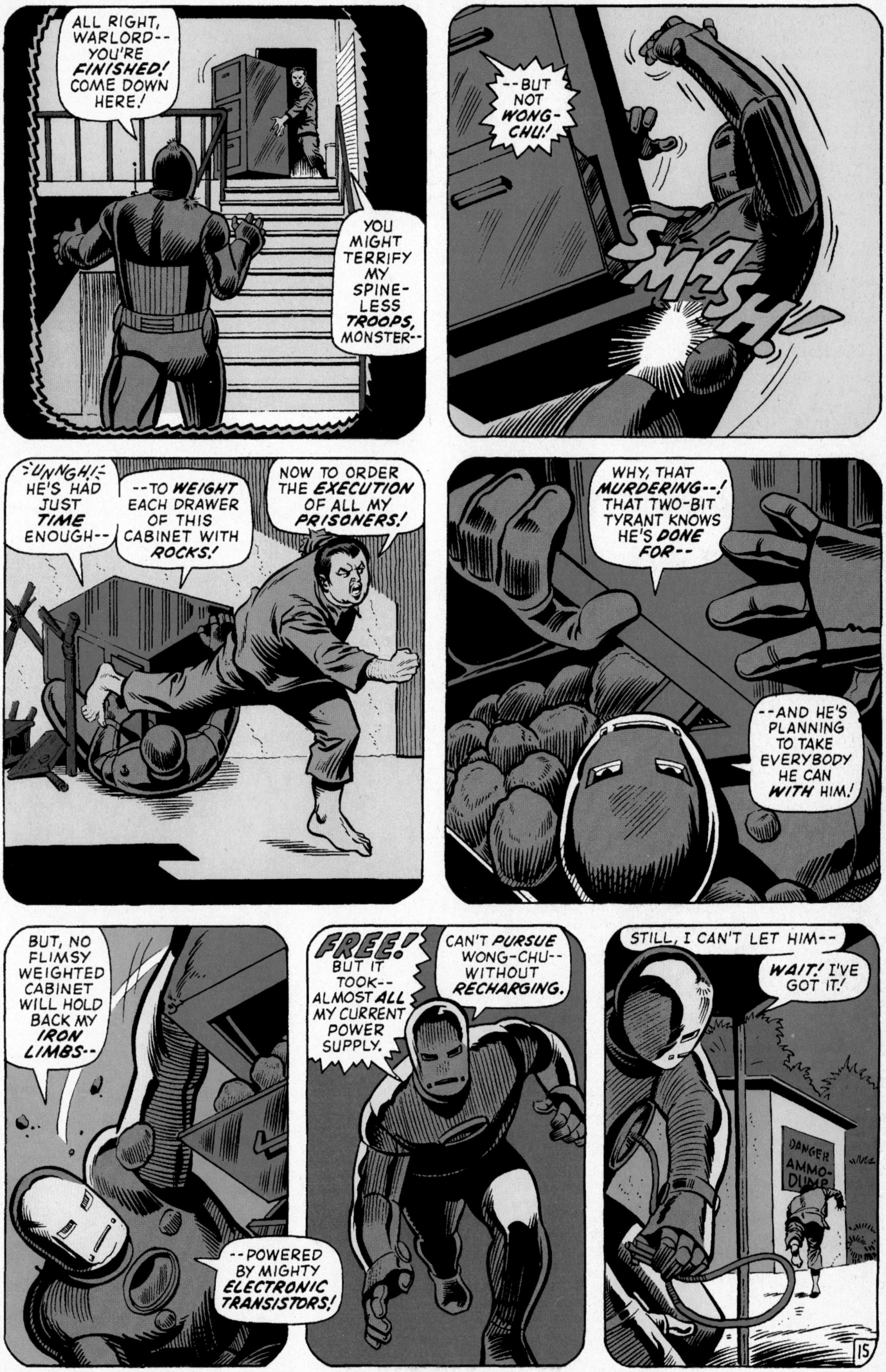
ALL RIGHT, WARLORD-- YOU'RE FINISHED! COME DOWN HERE!
YOU MIGHT TERRIFY MY SPINE-LESS TROOPS, MONSTER--
--BUT NOT WONG-CHU!
SMASH!
UNNGH! HE'S HAD JUST TIME ENOUGH--
--TO WEIGHT EACH DRAWER OF THIS CABINET WITH ROCKS!
NOW TO ORDER THE EXECUTION OF ALL MY PRISONERS!
WHY, THAT MURDERING--! THAT TWO-BIT TYRANT KNOWS HE'S DONE FOR--
--AND HE'S PLANNING TO TAKE EVERYBODY HE CAN WITH HIM!
BUT, NO FLIMSY WEIGHTED CABINET WILL HOLD BACK MY IRON LIMBS--
--POWERED BY MIGHTY ELECTRONIC TRANSISTORS!
FREE! BUT IT TOOK-- ALMOST ALL MY CURRENT POWER SUPPLY.
CAN'T PURSUE WONG-CHU-- WITHOUT RECHARGING.
STILL, I CAN'T LET HIM--
WAIT! I'VE GOT IT!
DANGER AMMO-DUMP
15

YOU'D PLANNED YOUR ARMORED APPARATUS *CAREFULLY*, HADN'T YOU, STARK--?

--*EVEN* DOWN TO THE *LUBRICATING* APPARATUS WHICH NOW JETTED FORTH A THIN, STRONG STREAM OF OIL....!

I ESTIMATED IT *JUST RIGHT!*

THE PRESSURE'S JUST *GREAT* ENOUGH FOR IT TO REACH THAT *AMMO DUMP!*

DANG
AMM
DUM

GUARDS! GUARDS!

SLAY THE PRISONERS --NOW!

BROOM!

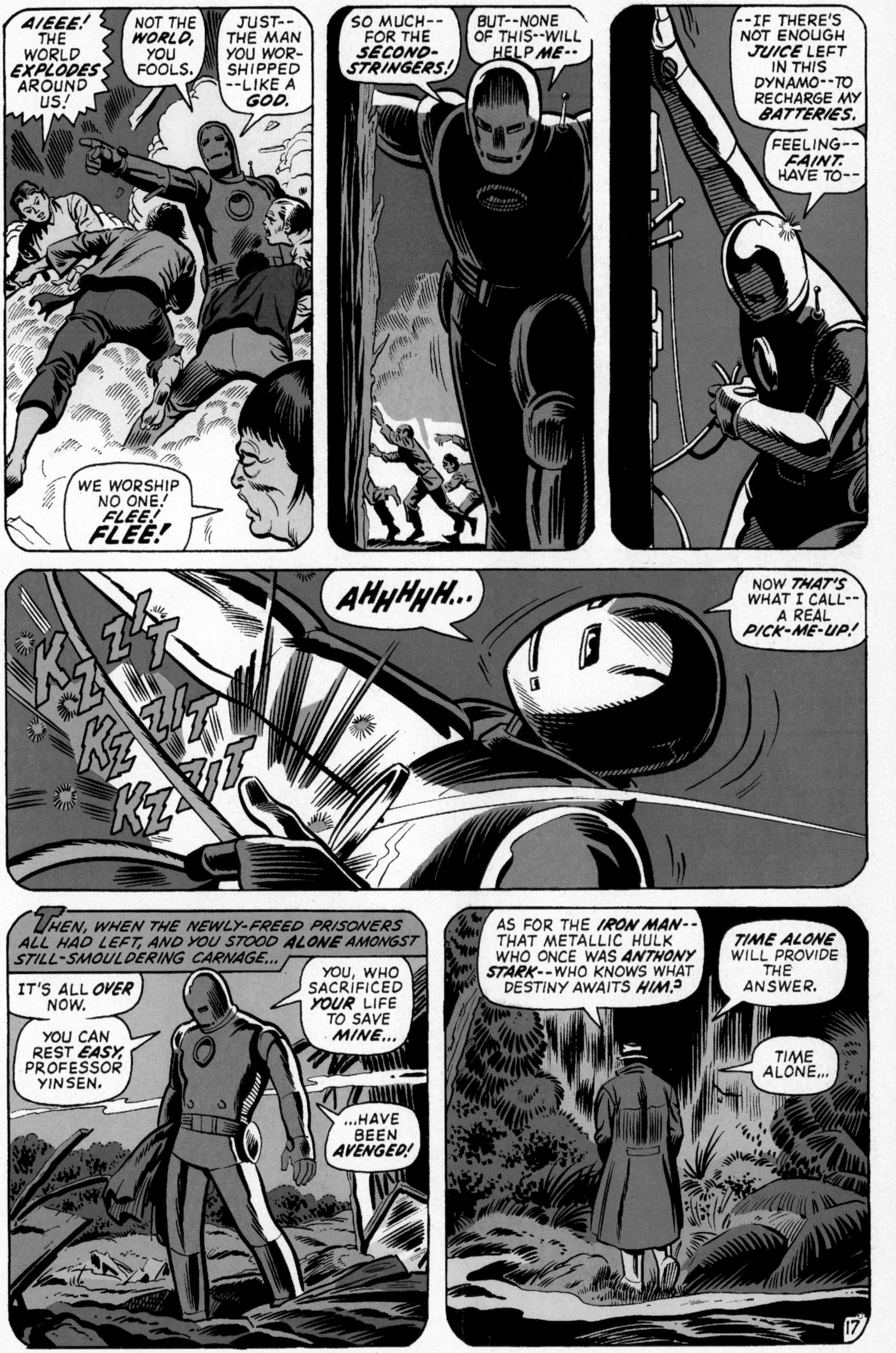

AIEEE! THE WORLD EXPLODES AROUND US!
NOT THE WORLD, YOU FOOLS.
JUST-- THE MAN YOU WORSHIPPED --LIKE A GOD.
WE WORSHIP NO ONE! FLEE! FLEE!
SO MUCH-- FOR THE SECOND-STRINGERS!
BUT--NONE OF THIS--WILL HELP ME--
--IF THERE'S NOT ENOUGH JUICE LEFT IN THIS DYNAMO--TO RECHARGE MY BATTERIES.
FEELING-- FAINT. HAVE TO--
KZZIT KZZIT KZZIT
AHHHHH...
NOW THAT'S WHAT I CALL-- A REAL PICK-ME-UP!
THEN, WHEN THE NEWLY-FREED PRISONERS ALL HAD LEFT, AND YOU STOOD ALONE AMONGST STILL-SMOULDERING CARNAGE...
IT'S ALL OVER NOW.
YOU CAN REST EASY, PROFESSOR YINSEN.
YOU, WHO SACRIFICED YOUR LIFE TO SAVE MINE...
...HAVE BEEN AVENGED!
AS FOR THE IRON MAN-- THAT METALLIC HULK WHO ONCE WAS ANTHONY STARK--WHO KNOWS WHAT DESTINY AWAITS HIM?
TIME ALONE WILL PROVIDE THE ANSWER.
TIME ALONE...
17

AND YOU'RE STILL *WAITING*, AREN'T YOU, SHELLHEAD?

WAITING TO LEARN YOUR *DESTINY*, IF SUCH A THING REALLY *EXISTS*--

--ANYWHERE EXCEPT IN YOUR *MIND*.

IT WOULD BE SO *EASY* TO GIVE IT ALL UP, WOULDN'T IT?

ALL YOU'D HAVE TO DO IS LEAD THE POLICE-- OR THE ARMY--THRU THIS REINFORCED *STEEL* DOOR--

--HAND OVER THESE *BLUE-PRINTS* TO THEM, AND TAKE A *WALK*.

THEY SHOW HOW YOU WORKED, RE-WORKED, *MODIFIED* YOUR ARMOR, AGAIN AND AGAIN...

...TILL IT WAS THE NEARLY-HUMAN *FIGHTING MACHINE* IT IS TODAY,

THERE ARE A LOT OF *LIVES* BOUND UP IN THIS ARMOR... AND THIS ROLLED-UP SCRAP OF PAPER...

ENEMIES WHO TRIED TO *KILL* YOU TO POSSESS ITS POWER...

GIRLS WHOM TONY STARK DARED NOT *EMBRACE*, FOR FEAR THEY'D LEARN HIS SECRET...

EVEN A *FRIEND* OR TWO WHO DONNED THE ARMOR, TO HELP YOU OUT OF A *JAM*...

YES, A *LOT* OF LIVES, TIN MAN...

AND A FEW *DEATHS*, TOO.

18

THE GREAT PLANT IS *CLOSED* NOW...THAT VAST, SPRAWLING ORGANISM WHICH IS THE *HUB* OF THE NETWORK EMPIRE CALLED *STARK INDUSTRIES*...

...*CLOSED* IN MEMORY OF *KEVIN O'BRIEN,* WHO SHALL EVER BE RECALLED AS *FRIEND, NOT FOE...*

AND SOMEHOW, YOU FEEL LIKE A GRIM GOLDEN *GHOST,* WALKING, WALKING...

...*WALKING* SOFTLY, AS THOUGH NOT TO AWAKEN STILL *OTHER GHOSTS...!*

RIGHT HERE. IT HAPPENED *RIGHT HERE...*

IN THIS VERY BUILDING, THE *TEST MODELS* FOR MY FIRST ARMOR WERE CAST AND RE-CAST.

THE *FINISHED PRODUCT* MIGHT HAVE BEEN PIECED TOGETHER HALF A WORLD AWAY--BUT IT ALL *STARTED* HERE.

MY ARMOR-- AND DOZENS OF *OTHER* WEAPONS-- FOR THE ARMY, FOR *SHIELD*--

--WEAPONS I'VE SOME-TIMES BEEN *SORRY* I DESIGNED--

--WEAPONS THAT CAN BE USED TO *KILL* ONE PEOPLE--TO *SAVE* ANOTHER.

SOMETIMES I'M OUT IN A *CROWD,* AND I HEAR SOMEBODY'S SCORNFUL WHISPER:

"MUNITIONS-MAKER!"

AND I FIND MYSELF PONDERING *EVERY* ACTION I EVER *MADE.*

BUT MAYBE THAT'S ALL TO THE *GOOD.*

WHEN A MAN *STOPS* PONDERING HIS ACTIONS --*CEASES* TO WEIGH AND JUDGE HIS EVERY MOTIVE--

MAYBE THAT'S WHEN HE'S *REALLY* IN TROUBLE.

STARK

ALL OF WHICH DOESN'T QUITE ANSWER MY *CURRENT* DILEMMA-- THE QUESTION I KEEP *ASKING* MYSELF--

"MUST THERE BE AN IRON MAN? AND WHY?"

STRANGE I SHOULD WIND UP ASKING IT-- *HERE.*

19

23

HERE, IN FRONT OF THE *BOMBPROOF* CASING WHICH HOUSES MY *FIRST* SUIT OF ARMOR.

GREY. IT USED TO BE GREY.

THEN I MADE IT *GOLD,* SO IT WOULDN'T MAKE ME LOOK SO *SINISTER--* WOULDN'T *FRIGHTEN* PEOPLE I WAS TRYING TO HELP.

BUT... I DON'T KNOW...

MAYBE THOSE PEOPLE WERE *RIGHT* TO BE FRIGHTENED... AND I WAS *WRONG* TO THINK A GOLDEN GALAHAD MADE ANY SENSE IN *1972!*

HOW ABOUT IT, STARK? *HOW ABOUT IT.??*

NO! YOU'VE BEEN *FOOLING* YOURSELF, TONY--TRYING TO TAKE THE *SIMPLE* WAY OUT.

IT'D BE EASY-- *TOO* EASY--TO GIVE IN TO THE *GILBERTS* OF THE WORLD.

BECAUSE FOR EVERY PERSON *KILLED* BECAUSE HE ENCOUNTERED IRON MAN-- A HUNDRED MORE HAVE *LIVED!*

YOU'VE BEEN LOOKING AT IT *ALL WRONG,* STARK!

YOU'RE *NOT* A CIVILIAN. YOU'RE A-- *SOLDIER--* ALBEIT A *RELUCTANT* ONE...

...A SOLDIER IN THE BATTLE FOR HUMAN RIGHTS... *HUMAN DIGNITY!*

THAT'S A WAR THAT'S BEING FOUGHT *EVERY* PLACE, *EVERY* DAY...

...A WAR THAT'S *GOT* TO BE WON, SOME-DAY, SOME-HOW...

AND ONE MAN WHO'S GOT TO *HELP* WIN IT...

20

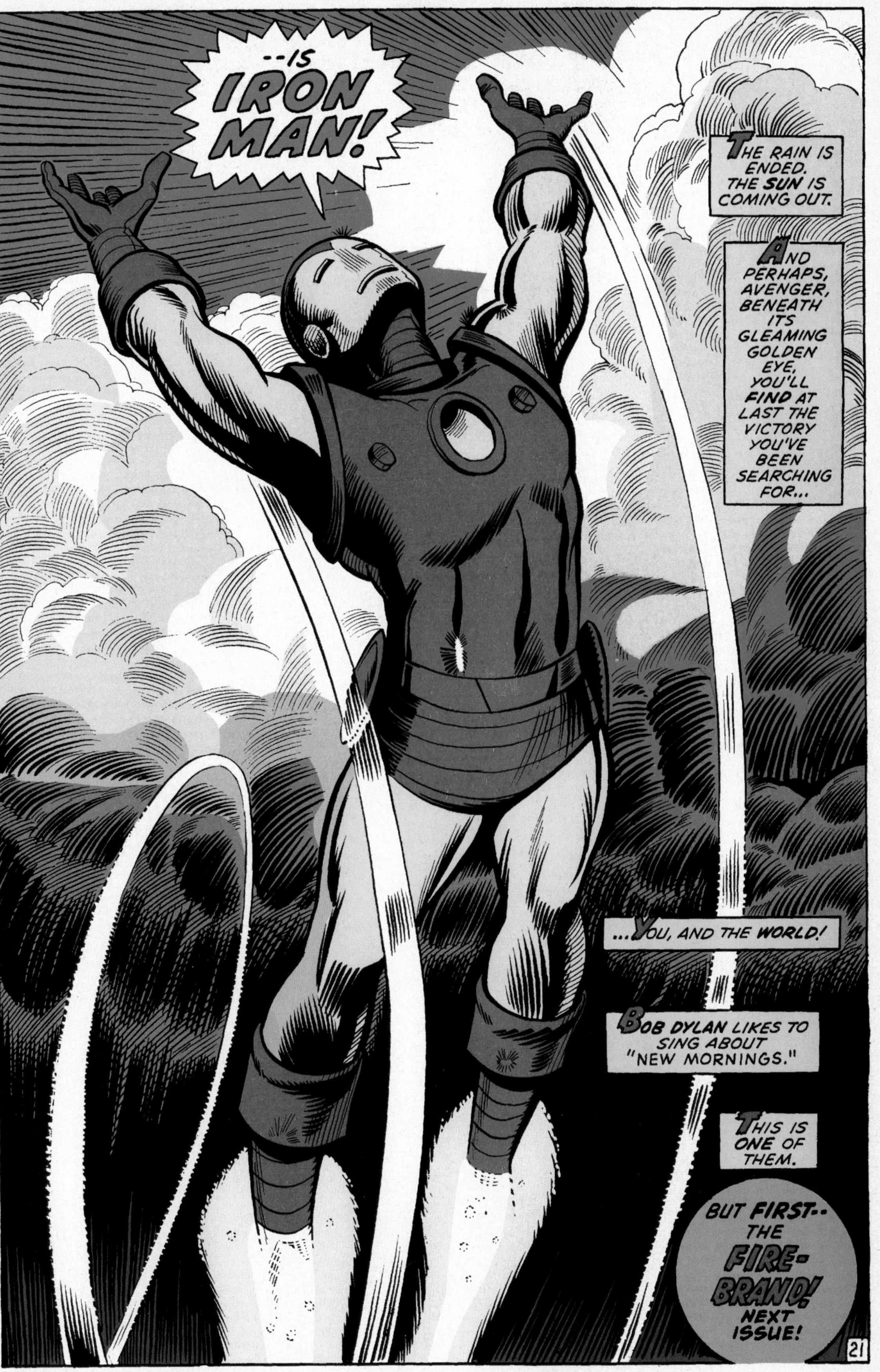
--IS IRON MAN!
THE RAIN IS ENDED. THE SUN IS COMING OUT.
AND PERHAPS, AVENGER, BENEATH ITS GLEAMING GOLDEN EYE, YOU'LL FIND AT LAST THE VICTORY YOU'VE BEEN SEARCHING FOR...
...YOU, AND THE WORLD!
BOB DYLAN LIKES TO SING ABOUT "NEW MORNINGS."
THIS IS ONE OF THEM.
BUT FIRST-- THE FIRE-BRAND! NEXT ISSUE!
21

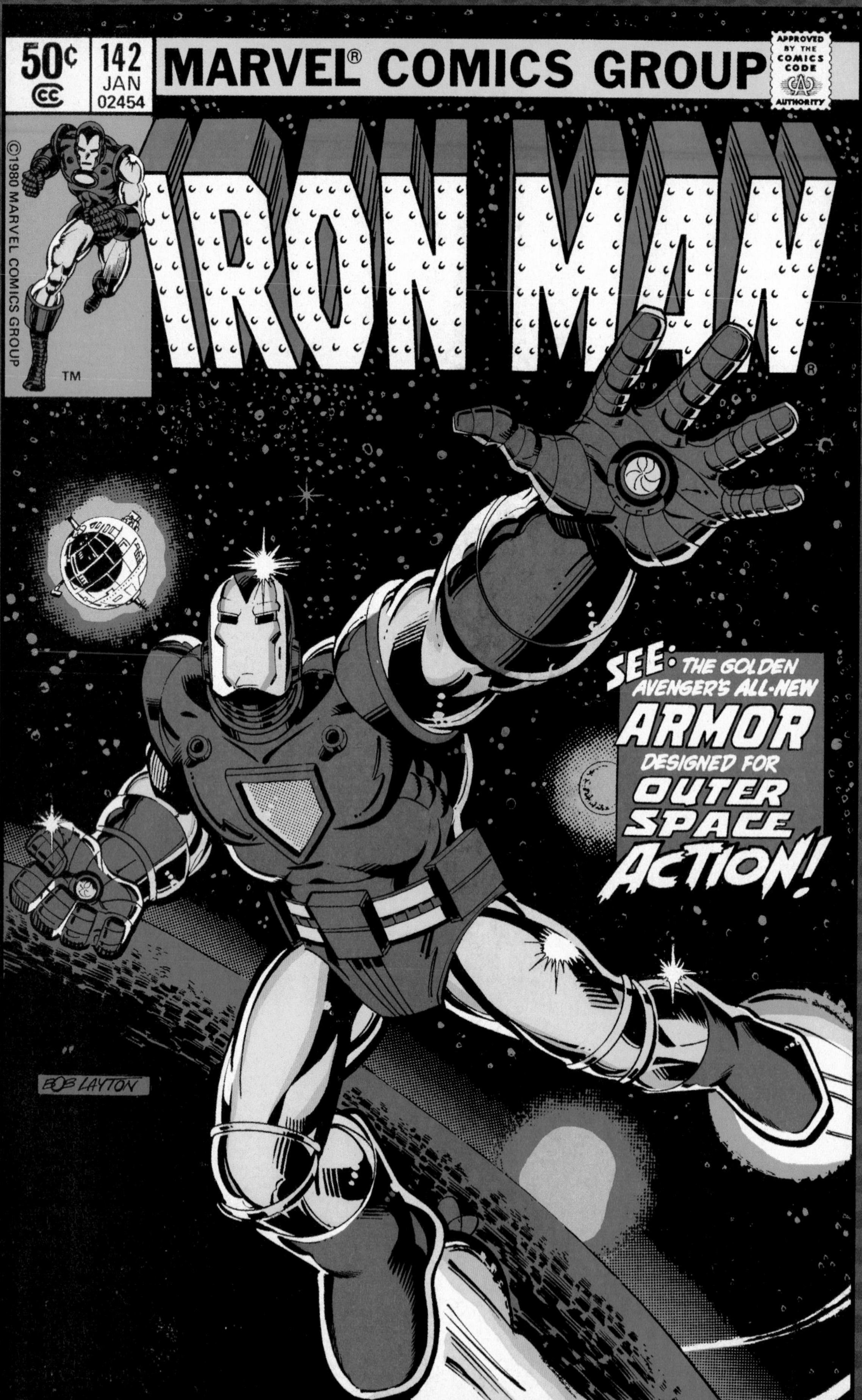
50¢
CC
142
JAN
02454
MARVEL® COMICS GROUP
APPROVED BY THE COMICS CODE AUTHORITY
©1980 MARVEL COMICS GROUP
TM
IRON MAN®
SEE: THE GOLDEN AVENGER'S ALL-NEW
ARMOR
DESIGNED FOR
OUTER SPACE ACTION!
BOB LAYTON

DAVID MICHELINIE — plot/writer · JOHN ROMITA JR. — pencil art · BOB LAYTON — plot/finished art · JOHN COSTANZA — letters · BOB SHAREN — colors · JIM SALICRUP — editor · JIM SHOOTER — editor-in-chief

SKY DIE!

SORRY, FOLKS, BUT I'M PULLING RANK ON YOU. I'M AFRAID WE'VE GOT A SECURITY PROBLEM, MR. STARK.

OKAY, VIC, SPELL IT OUT.

IT'S DOWN THERE, SIR. THOSE *SHIELD* TROOPS MOVED IN LAST NIGHT AND TOOK OVER THE ANALYTICAL LAB COMPLEX, SAID THEY WERE AUTHORIZED BY AN EMERGENCY CONTINGENCY AGREEMENT THEY MADE WITH YOU YEARS AGO. AND THEIR STORY CHECKS, SIR.

BUT WHAT WOULD A SUPER-SPY ORGANIZATION LIKE SHIELD WANT WITH AN S.I. LAB?

IF I MAY SAY, SIR, THAT'S EXACTLY WHAT MY PUBLIC RELATIONS DEPARTMENT IS HAVING A DEVIL OF A TIME EXPLAINING TO THE *PRESS!*

I CAN IMAGINE, MR. PITHINS.

ALL RIGHT, THEN, I'LL GET ON IT IMMEDIATELY. THE REST OF YOU, PLEASE, SUBMIT YOUR REQUESTS IN WRITING -- I'LL TAKE CARE OF THEM AS SOON AS I CAN.

:WHEW: MRS. ARBOGAST, HOW COULD YOU POSSIBLY LET THINGS GET *THIS* CHAOTIC IN JUST ONE WEEK?

HOW COULD... *I?!* MR. STARK, NEED I REMIND YOU THAT I'M AN EXECUTIVE SECRETARY-- A VERY EXCEL-LENT ONE AT THAT. AND AS SUCH, I TRY TO KEEP THIS OFFICE RUNNING AS SMOOTHLY AS POSSIBLE.

BUT IF YOU EXPECT ME TO MAKE *POLICY* DECISIONS WHILE YOU GO GALLIVANTING AROUND THE GLOBE, THEN YOU'LL HAVE TO MAKE ME A VICE PRESIDENT, DOUBLE MY SALARY *AND* GIVE ME A KEY TO THE EXECUTIVE WASHROOM!

SIR!

AH, :HEH: MRS. ARBOGAST...

...YOU'RE RIGHT. ONE HUNDRED PERCENT. AND I APOLOGIZE. I'LL SEE WHAT I CAN DO ABOUT EASING THE SITUATION IN THE FUTURE.

YOU'RE SO CUTE WHEN YOU'RE ANGRY.

MR. STARK, PLEASE!

MAYBE LING AND I SHOULD HEAD BACK TO MANHATTAN TO UNPACK, TONY. IT LOOKS LIKE YOU'RE GOING TO BE RATHER BUSY HERE.

SO IT SEEMS, BETH, THANKS. I'LL CALL YOU LATER.

MRS. ARBOGAST, WOULD YOU PLEASE HAVE A CAR SENT 'ROUND TO TAKE MS. CABE AND HER FRIEND HOME?

OF COURSE, SIR.

I'D BE DELIGHTED.

WELL, AT LEAST SOME THINGS ARE BACK TO NORMAL!

AND MOMENTS LATER, AT THE ANALYTICAL LABS' ENTRANCE...

I'M SORRY, SIR, BUT NO ONE IS ALLOWED BEYOND THIS POINT EXCEPT--

--OH. MR. STARK. GO RIGHT IN, SIR.

3

AND SO HE DOES, SWINGING WIDE THE DOORS OF A FAMILIAR LABORATORY NETWORK HE HAD DESIGNED YEARS BEFORE... AND FINDING THAT FAMILIARITY JARRED BY DOZENS OF UNFAMILIAR FACES--

-- AS CROWDS OF SHIELD SCIENTISTS AND TECHNOS SCURRY ABOUT, RUNNING A VAST ARRAY OF TESTS AND EXPERIMENTS ON SUCH DIVERSE ITEMS AS AUTOMOBILES, LAWN MOWERS... AND HUMAN CORPSES!

COLONEL FURY? I'D LIKE A WORD WITH YOU.

AND THAT WORD IS "WHY"! AS IN WHY HAVE YOU AND YOUR MEN SHUT MY OWN STAFF OUT OF MY OWN LAB--

-- ON THE BASIS OF AN EMERGENCY AGREEMENT I HARDLY EVEN REMEMBER MAKING!

BECAUSE WE'VE GOT AN EMERGENCY, STARK. UNLESS YA CONSIDER A WHOLE FLAMIN' TOWN DYIN' TA BE "NORMAL"!

A WHOLE--? MAYBE YOU'D BETTER EXPLAIN, COLONEL.

THAT'S EXACTLY WHAT I INTEND TA DO, IF YA'LL JUST GIVE ME THE CHANCE!

FER STARTERS, IT APPEARS THAT OVER THE WEEKEND MORE THAN TWO HUNDRED PEOPLE, PETS AN' LIVESTOCK IN A PODUNK BURG CALLED ALLANTOWN, IOWA, DIED. JUST LIKE THAT.

THE WAY WE PIECE IT TOGETHER, THEY MUSTA BEEN EXPOSED TO SOME SORT O' KILLIN' FORCE THAT COVERED A RADIUS OF ALMOST FIVE MILES!

AN' BY RADIUS I MEAN JUST THAT--THE KILL AREA MEASURES AN ALMOST PERFECT CIRCLE! BUT SO FAR, WE DON'T HAVE ANY IDEA AS TO WHAT HAPPENED, OR WHY!

WHICH IS WHY WE CAME HERE. WE HOPED YER SUPER-SOPHISTICATED ANALYSIS GADGETS COULD HELP US FIND A CLUE.

4

AN' IT LOOKS LIKE THEY HAVE, DR. WOLF?

YES, SIR. TO EXPLAIN, WE'VE RECENTLY DETERMINED THAT TRACES OF MICRO-WAVE RADIATION WERE DISPERSED EVENLY THROUGHOUT THE KILL CIRCLE, NO STRONGER AT THE CENTER THAN AT THE EDGES, WHICH INDICATES THAT THE RADIATION MOST PROBABLY CAME FROM ABOVE. POSSIBLY EVEN...

...FROM OUTER SPACE!

I SEE. IN THAT CASE, GENTLEMEN, YOU HAVE MY FULL COOPERATION. THE RESOURCES OF STARK INTERNATIONAL ARE AT YOUR DISPOSAL.

AND PRESENTLY...

CRISIS, CRISIS, CRISIS. NO REST FOR THE WEARY, HUH?

I WOULDN'T KNOW, BABE-- I'M TOO TIRED TO THINK ABOUT IT.

THANKS, STARK. I KNEW WE COULD COUNT ON YA.

WELL, IF YOU WANT TO RELAX, HOW ABOUT COMING OVER TONIGHT? I COULD GIVE LING THE KEYS TO THE CAR--

THANKS, MOM.

-- AND WE COULD DEFROST A COUPLE OF PRIME RIBS I'VE BEEN HOARDING FOR A SPECIAL OCCASION.

MMMM, SOUNDS SCRUMPTIOUS. SHOULD I BRING THE DESERT?

DON'T YOU ALWAYS?

A WRY SMILE LATER, AS A PRIVATE LIMOUSINE TRUNDLES OFF TOWARDS THE LONG ISLAND EXPRESSWAY...

IT'S GETTING TO BE THAT EVERYTIME BETH LEAVES, SHE TAKES A BIGGER PART OF ME WITH HER.

MAYBE IT'S TIME TO START THINKING ABOUT KEEPING HER AROUND ON A MORE PERMANENT BASIS...?

5

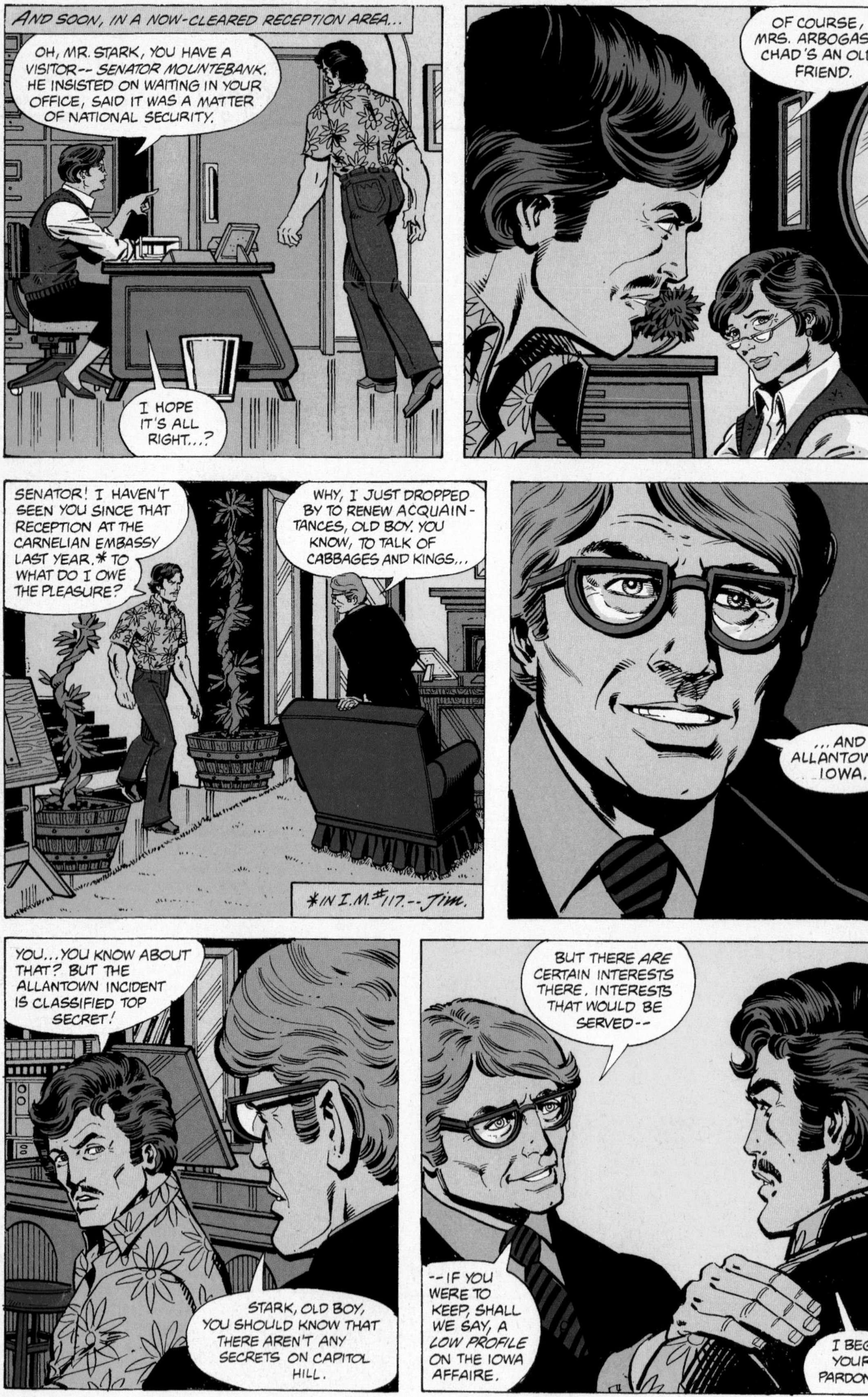
AND SOON, IN A NOW-CLEARED RECEPTION AREA...
OH, MR. STARK, YOU HAVE A VISITOR-- SENATOR MOUNTEBANK. HE INSISTED ON WAITING IN YOUR OFFICE, SAID IT WAS A MATTER OF NATIONAL SECURITY.
I HOPE IT'S ALL RIGHT...?
OF COURSE, MRS. ARBOGAST. CHAD'S AN OLD FRIEND.
SENATOR! I HAVEN'T SEEN YOU SINCE THAT RECEPTION AT THE CARNELIAN EMBASSY LAST YEAR.* TO WHAT DO I OWE THE PLEASURE?
WHY, I JUST DROPPED BY TO RENEW ACQUAINTANCES, OLD BOY. YOU KNOW, TO TALK OF CABBAGES AND KINGS...
*IN I.M. #117.--Jim.
...AND ALLANTOWN, IOWA.
YOU...YOU KNOW ABOUT THAT? BUT THE ALLANTOWN INCIDENT IS CLASSIFIED TOP SECRET!
STARK, OLD BOY, YOU SHOULD KNOW THAT THERE AREN'T ANY SECRETS ON CAPITOL HILL.
BUT THERE ARE CERTAIN INTERESTS THERE, INTERESTS THAT WOULD BE SERVED--
--IF YOU WERE TO KEEP, SHALL WE SAY, A LOW PROFILE ON THE IOWA AFFAIRE.
I BEG YOUR PARDON?
6

TO BE UNCOMMONLY BLUNT, OLD BOY, THERE ARE THOSE WHO WOULD CONSIDER IT A GREAT FAVOR WERE YOU TO DENY SHIELD ACCESS TO YOUR LABORATORIES AND EQUIPMENT.

OH, REALLY? AND IF I DON'T?

WELL, LET'S JUST SAY THAT IT'S COMMON KNOWLEDGE THAT YOUR COMPANY HAS LOW BIDS IN ON SEVERAL VERY LUCRATIVE GOVERNMENT CONTRACTS--

--AND IT WOULD BE SUCH A SHAME IF THOSE BIDS WERE TO BE, AH, LOST IN THE SHUFFLE, DO WE UNDERSTAND EACH OTHER?

PERFECTLY.

GET OUT.

AND, SEVERAL SECONDS LATER...

STRIKE OUT, SENATOR?

HMPH! GOOD WOMAN, YOUR EMPLOYER IS A STUBBORN, DELUDED IDEALIST!

SORRY, SENATOR, I GUESS I SHOULD HAVE WARNED YOU--

--MR. STARK ONLY TAKES BRIBES ON ALTERNATE WEDNESDAYS.

SO MUCH FOR THE "ALIEN INVASION" THEORY. WHATEVER HAPPENED IN ALLANTOWN, ITS ORIGINS WERE VERY DOWN TO EARTH!

AND, APPARENTLY, TOUCHES ON THE SENSIBILITIES OF SOME RATHER POWERFUL PEOPLE!

ANTHONY STARK

7

33

BUT I SUPPOSE THAT'S NICK FURY'S PROBLEM. ME, I'VE GOT A BUSINESS TO RUN -- STARTING WITH MY PROMISE TO MRS. ARBOGAST.

LETTER TO YVETTE AVRIL, EXECUTIVE IN CHARGE, STARK INTERNATIONAL, PARIS BRANCH: *"MA CHER MLLE. AVRIL..."*

ANTHONY STARK

BUT WHILE TONY STARK CONTINUES TO DICTATE HIS CORRESPONDENCE, TWO YOUNG WOMEN ARE RETRIEVING A WEEK'S WORTH OF THEIRS -- AT THE MANHATTAN BROWN-STONE OFFICES OF "BETHANY CABE & LING McPHERSON, SECURITY SPECIALISTS".

THAT'S A LOT OF MAIL FOR JUST ONE WEEK, BETH.

UH-HUH. UNFORTUNATELY, THOUGH, IT LOOKS TO BE MOSTLY *BILLS.*

WELL, AT LEAST THAT BEATS ALL OF THOSE "YOU HAVE ALREADY WON A FREE PRIZE!" HYPES.

I KNOW. "FREE," AS IN $49.95, PLUS TA--

--¡GASP!

BETH? WHAT'S WRONG? YOU LOOK LIKE YOU'VE JUST SEEN A GHOST!

I...I THINK I...

...HAVE!

Mrs. Bethany Van Tilburg
1339 W. 70th St.
New York, New York 10021

NOV 15

8

MORNING MOVES WESTWARD, GIVING WAY TO AFTERNOON AS, ON LONG ISLAND, A WORLD IS BEING SPANNED FROM THIS BUILDING--

--THE S.I. COMMUNICATIONS CENTER--

--WHERE HEAD OF OPERATIONS MICHAEL TRUDEAU KEEPS A TIGHT REIN ON THE VAST BANKS OF RELAYS CONNECTING STARK INTERNATIONAL WITH ITS MYRIAD BRANCHES AROUND THE WORLD...

THAT TOKYO LINE IS STILL BLOCKED, MIKE. WE'RE ROUTING THE SIGNAL THROUGH SINGAPORE IN THE MEANTIME.

OKAY, BILL, JUST KEEP ME INFORMED OF ANY CHANGES AS THEY--EH?

HEY, WHAT'S THAT? A NEW WAY FOR THE BOSS TO KEEP IN TOUCH?

UH, YOU MIGHT SAY THAT. LOOK, BILL, IT'S ALMOST BREAK TIME, SO WHY DON'T YOU HOP DOWN TO THE COMMISSARY AND PICK US UP SOME COFFEE AND PATÉ?

SOUNDS GOOD, MIKE. BE BACK IN A JIFFY.

NO RUSH.

OKAY, TRUDEAU HERE-- WHAT'S UP?

A PROBLEM, MISTER--A BIG ONE!

IT LOOKS LIKE SENATOR MOUNTE-BANK HAS FLUBBED HIS MISSION!

AND THAT MEANS THAT IT'S NOW UP TO YOU TO SEE THAT SHIELD'S INVESTIGATION IS STOPPED!

ME? B-BUT, I'M A SLEEPER, NOT A FIELD AGENT! D-DON'T YOU THINK IT'D BE BETTER IF I STAYED UNDER-COVER UNTIL--

YOU HAVE YOUR ASSIGNMENT, MISTER! NOW DO IT!

Y-YES, SIR, MR. HALE. TRUDEAU OUT.

9

WHILE ELSEWHERE... I'LL BE IN THE PRACTICAL LAB ANNEX IF ANYONE NEEDS ME, MRS. ARBOGAST. IN THE MEANTIME, WOULD YOU PLEASE TRANSCRIBE THIS TAPE--

--AND GET A COPY TO YVETTE AVRIL IN PARIS AS SOON AS POSSIBLE? YOU HAVE THE ADDRESS, DON'T YOU?

OF COURSE, MR. STARK, IT'S IN MY FILES.

NOW IF ONLY I CAN REMEMBER WHETHER "TROLLOP" IS SPELLED WITH ONE "L" OR TWO?

BUT AS THE MOTHERLY MRS. ARBOGAST CONSULTS HER UNIQUE FILING SYSTEM--

-- HER EMPLOYER MAKES HIS WAY TO A NEARBY HANGERLIKE ANNEX, WHERE THE STARK-DESIGNED, N.A.S.A.-COMMISSIONED JUPITER LANDING VEHICLE IS IN THE PROCESS OF BEING RECONSTRUCTED, *

SCOTT! SCOTT LANG! HOW'S IT GOING?

HEY, TONY, ALMOST FINISHED, SHE'LL BE READY FOR THE FINAL TESTS TOMORROW.

* IT WAS DESTROYED BY IRON MAN IN ISSUE #116. -- Salicrup.

Y'KNOW, WORKING ON THIS BABY'S BEEN AN ELECTRONIC TECHNICIAN'S DREAM. THE DESIGN WORK IS BRILLIANT, THE NEW CIRCUITRY IS INGENIOUS, THE WHOLE THING IS A WORK OF ART!

UH, DO I GET MY RAISE NOW?

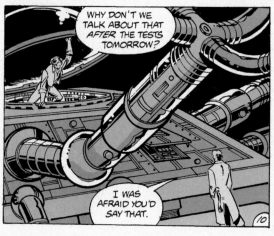

WHY DON'T WE TALK ABOUT THAT AFTER THE TESTS TOMORROW?

I WAS AFRAID YOU'D SAY THAT.

10

BACK BEFORE I TOOK ON MY SECRET IDENTITY AS *IRON MAN*, BEFORE MY COMPANY GOT SO BIG, I USED TO NOT ONLY BUILD THIS STUFF, BUT I'D *TEST* EACH INVENTION PERSONALLY. I GUESS THAT WAS SORT OF RECKLESS, MAYBE EVEN FOOLHARDY... BUT SOMETIMES I MISS IT.

VROOM! VROOM!

SHE LOOKS FINE, SCOTT. YOU AND YOUR MEN HAVE DONE A TERRIFIC JOB.

THANKS.

ONLY THIS TIME, TRY TO KEEP YOUR BODYGUARD FROM PLAYING WITH THE NEW TOYS, HUH? I'D HATE TO HAVE TO PUT THIS SUCKER BACK TOGETHER AGAIN!

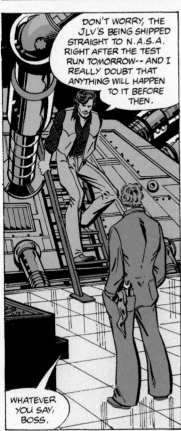

DON'T WORRY, THE JLV'S BEING SHIPPED STRAIGHT TO N.A.S.A. RIGHT AFTER THE TEST RUN TOMORROW-- AND I REALLY DOUBT THAT ANYTHING WILL HAPPEN TO IT BEFORE THEN.

WHATEVER YOU SAY, BOSS.

SEE YOU IN THE MORNING!

EXCUSE ME, MR. LANG?

UH, YES?

HI, I'M MIKE TRUDEAU, HEAD OF THE COMMUNICATIONS DIVISION.

OH, YEAH, WE MET AT THE EMPLOYEE APPRECIATION PARTY A FEW WEEKS BACK.

THAT'S RIGHT, SAY, I HOPE I'M NOT DISTURBING YOU?

NOT AT ALL, MIKE. WITH THE JUPITER LANDING VEHICLE VIRTUALLY COMPLETE, MOST OF MY CREW HAS BEEN ASSIGNED TO OTHER PROJECTS.

SO THE COMPANY IS MORE THAN WELCOME.

GOOD. AS A MATTER OF FACT, THE JLV IS THE REAL REASON I'M HERE. I'VE BEEN HEARING SO MUCH ABOUT IT--

--THAT I JUST THOUGHT I'D DROP BY AND TAKE IT FOR A LITTLE SPIN.

"TAKE IT FOR A--" HA HA HA! HEY, THAT'S A GREAT LINE, MIKE! WHO SAYS YOU COMMUNICATIONS PEOPLE HAVE NO SENSE OF HUMOR?

I DO.

WHOK!

WHILE AT THAT MOMENT, IN A PLUSH PENTHOUSE ATOP THE S.I. ADMINISTRATION BUILDING...

I'M GLAD MOST OF THE MAJOR PROBLEMS OF THE DAY HAVE BEEN IRONED OUT, BUT THAT STILL LEAVES THE MINOR CRISES BE SOLVED, LIKE, FOR INSTANCE--

--WHICH SUIT SHOULD I WEAR TO BETH'S TONIGHT?

AH, YES, DECISIONS, DECISIONS...

12

...AND STILL MORE DECISIONS!

TERRIFIC. I'VE HAD SOME PILOT TRAINING, BUT THIS COCKPIT IS CRAMMED WITH MORE INSTRUMENTS THAN A 747! WHICH ONE DO I ACTIVATE TO GET ME OUT OF HERE?

AHA! THIS LOOKS KIND OF FAMILIAR. IF I JUST PUSH THIS LEVER, THEN PULL BACK ON THE STICK, THAT SHOULD SEND THE JLV HEADING STRAIGHT--

--BACKWARDS?!

SKRACHOOM

REEOOOEEOO!

THE EMERGENCY ALARM!

BLAST! IT ALWAYS RINGS WHEN YOU'RE IN THE SHOWER!

BUT AT LEAST IT'S SOLVED ONE PROBLEM FOR ME!

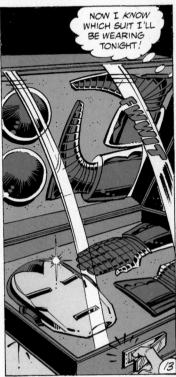

NOW I KNOW WHICH SUIT I'LL BE WEARING TONIGHT!

13

39

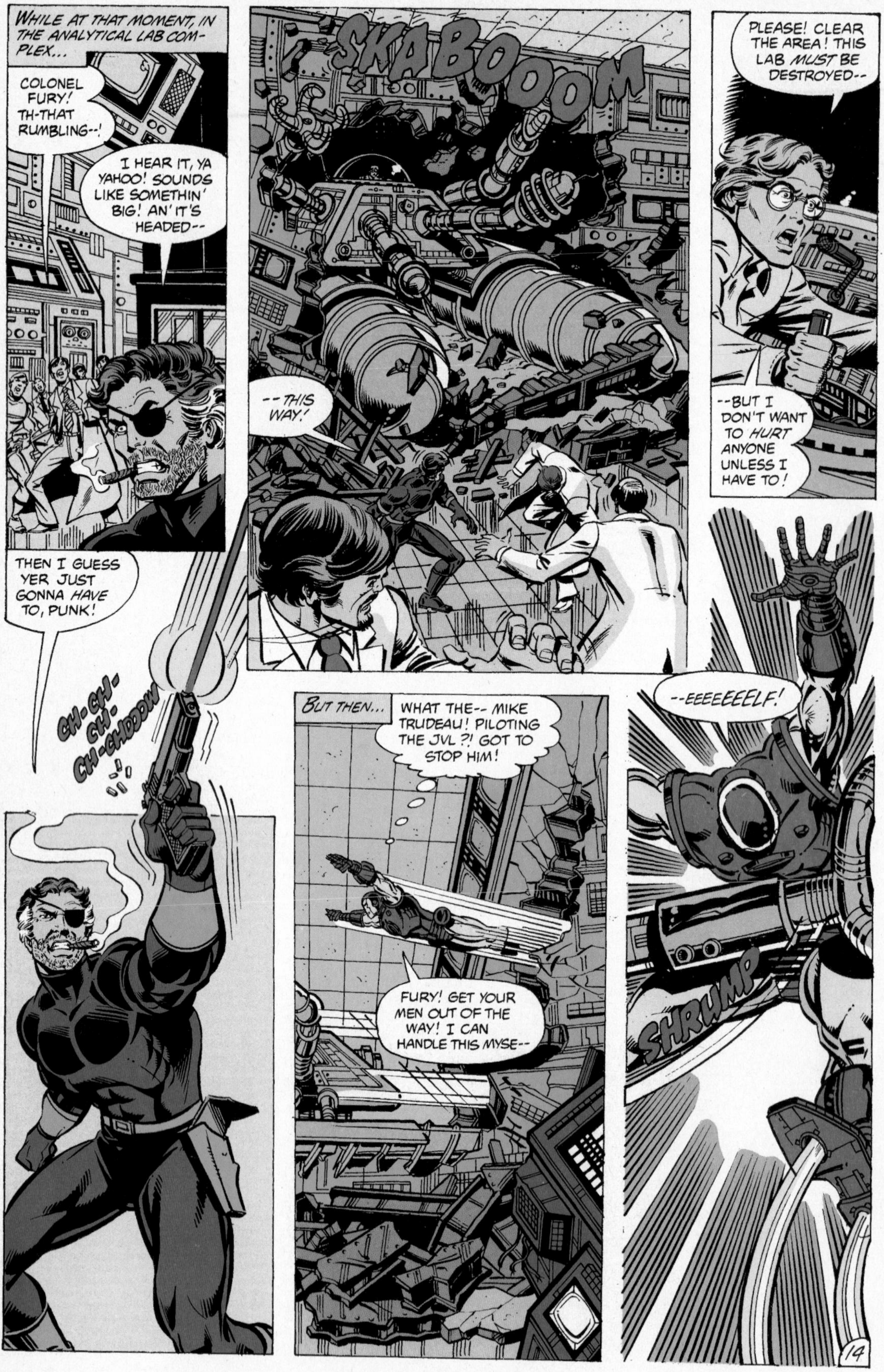
WHILE AT THAT MOMENT, IN THE ANALYTICAL LAB COMPLEX...
COLONEL FURY! TH-THAT RUMBLING--!
I HEAR IT, YA YAHOO! SOUNDS LIKE SOMETHIN' BIG! AN' IT'S HEADED--
SKABOOOM
--THIS WAY!
PLEASE! CLEAR THE AREA! THIS LAB MUST BE DESTROYED--
--BUT I DON'T WANT TO HURT ANYONE UNLESS I HAVE TO!
THEN I GUESS YER JUST GONNA HAVE TO, PUNK!
CH-CH-CH-CH-CHOOOM
BUT THEN...
WHAT THE-- MIKE TRUDEAU! PILOTING THE JVL?! GOT TO STOP HIM!
FURY! GET YOUR MEN OUT OF THE WAY! I CAN HANDLE THIS MYSE--
--EEEEEEEELF!
SHRUMP
14

NICE GOIN', SHELL-HEAD! YA REALLY GOT 'IM ON THE RUN!

≈WHEW≈ I'D FORGOTTEN WHAT A TOUGH OPPONENT THE JLV CAN BE! I'LL HAVE TO TRY SOMETHING LESS DIRECT--

-- LIKE BLASTING A HOLE IN THE FLOOR WITH MY REPULSORS!

SHRA KASH

GREAT! IT WORKED! THE JLV IS FALLING RIGHT INTO THE CRATER!

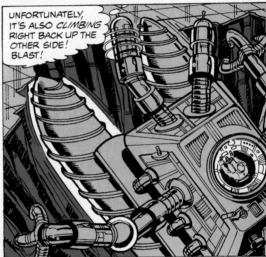

UNFORTUNATELY, IT'S ALSO CLIMBING RIGHT BACK UP THE OTHER SIDE! BLAST!

THIS JUGGERNAUT WAS MADE TO TAKE ON THE HOSTILE SURFACE OF JUPITER, AND THOSE TREADS CAN HANDLE ANYTHING I THROW AT IT!

BUT MAYBE, IF I CAN JUST TURN IT OVER SO THAT ITS TREADS CAN'T GET ANY TRACTION--

-- AGH! FLEW IN TOO CLOSE! TRUDEAU'S GOT ME TRAPPED IN THE LANDER'S MAGNA-GRIPS!

15

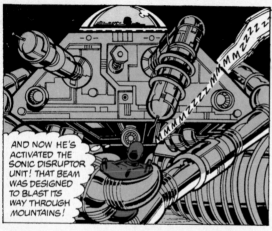

AND NOW HE'S ACTIVATED THE SONIC DISRUPTOR UNIT! THAT BEAM WAS DESIGNED TO BLAST ITS WAY THROUGH MOUNTAINS!

LUCKILY, IT CAN'T DO BEANS AGAINST MY ARMOR'S REFRACTORY COATING!

THOUGH IT HAS CONVINCED ME OF ONE THING:

THIS MECHANICAL MONSTER'S RAMPAGE ISN'T GOING TO BE STOPPED BY PUSSY-FOOTING AROUND! SO--

WHRUNCH

--THE KID GLOVES ARE OFF!

KA-WHAM

BLAST IT.

SHPRING

SPLOD

16

ALL RIGHT, TRUDEAU, JUST WHAT THE BLAZES WERE YOU TRYING TO DO?

N-NO! I'M NOT TELLING YOU ANYTHING! N-N-NOT WITHOUT A LAWYER!

PLEASE DON'T HIT ME!

MARTINELLI, SEE THAT THIS MAGGOT IS TURNED OVER TO THE NASSAU COUNTY POLICE.

MY PLEASURE, IRON MAN.

I DON'T GET IT, SHELL-HEAD. WHY WOULD ONE O' STARK'S EMPLOYEES TRY TO WRECK A PROJECT HE'S NOT EVEN SUPPOSED TO KNOW ABOUT?

I WISH I KNEW, COLONEL FURY. AND I PROMISE YOU--

--I WILL!

TO THAT END, MOMENTS LATER, THE GOLDEN GLADIATOR STEPS FROM A PRIVATE ELEVATOR INTO A SUB-BASEMENT WORK AREA BENEATH THE S.I. ADMINISTRATION BUILDING...

THIS ISN'T JUST SHIELD'S PROBLEM ANY MORE-- IT'S MINE! AND IF I'M GOING TO FIND OUT WHAT'S BEHIND IT ALL--

--IT LOOKS LIKE I'LL HAVE TO GO TO THE PROBLEM'S SOURCE!

I'VE BEEN WORKING ON THESE SUITS OF SPECIAL PURPOSE PROTOTYPE ARMOR IN MY SPARE TIME, AND I THINK #14C IS JUST WHAT THE CURRENT SITUATION CALLS FOR.

IT WAS DESIGNED TO OPERATE FOR EXTENDED PERIODS BEYOND THE EARTH'S ATMOSPHERE.

KLAK

THOUGH IT'S NEVER BEEN FULLY FIELD-TESTED...

"...UNTIL NOW!"

WHRRRRRRRR

17

43

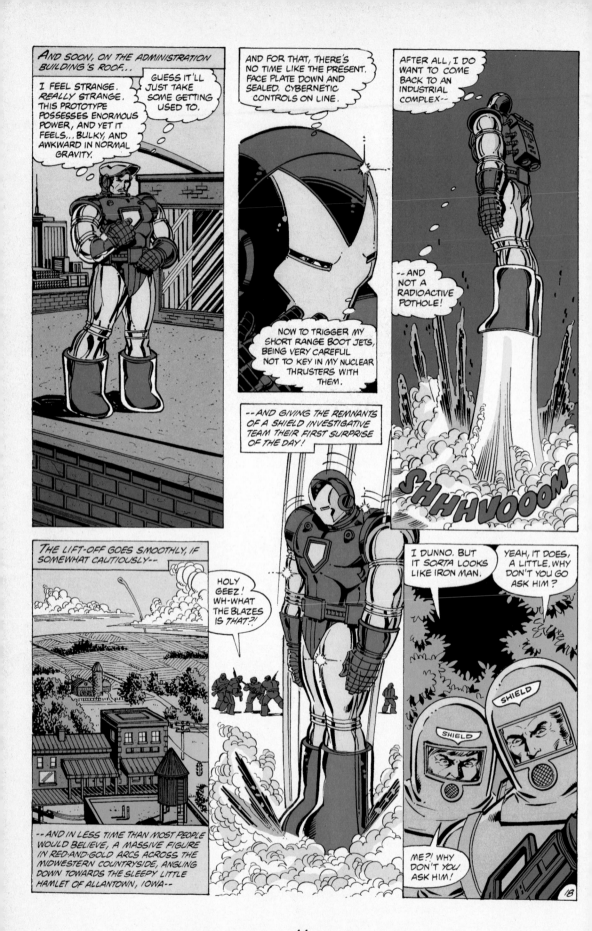

AND SOON, ON THE ADMINISTRATION BUILDING'S ROOF...

I FEEL STRANGE. *REALLY* STRANGE. THIS PROTOTYPE POSSESSES ENORMOUS POWER, AND YET IT FEELS... *BULKY*, AND AWKWARD IN NORMAL GRAVITY.

GUESS IT'LL JUST TAKE SOME GETTING USED TO.

AND FOR THAT, THERE'S NO TIME LIKE THE PRESENT. FACE PLATE DOWN AND SEALED. CYBERNETIC CONTROLS ON LINE.

NOW TO TRIGGER MY SHORT RANGE BOOT JETS, BEING VERY CAREFUL NOT TO KEY IN MY NUCLEAR THRUSTERS WITH THEM.

AFTER ALL, I DO WANT TO COME BACK TO AN INDUSTRIAL COMPLEX--

--AND NOT A RADIOACTIVE POTHOLE!

--AND GIVING THE REMNANTS OF A SHIELD INVESTIGATIVE TEAM THEIR FIRST *SURPRISE* OF *THE DAY*!

SHHHVOOOM

THE LIFT-OFF GOES SMOOTHLY, IF SOMEWHAT CAUTIOUSLY--

HOLY GEEZ! WH-WHAT THE BLAZES IS *THAT*?!

--AND IN LESS TIME THAN MOST PEOPLE WOULD BELIEVE, A MASSIVE FIGURE IN RED-AND-GOLD ARCS ACROSS THE MIDWESTERN COUNTRYSIDE, ANGLING DOWN TOWARDS THE SLEEPY LITTLE HAMLET OF ALLANTOWN, IOWA--

I DUNNO. BUT IT SORTA LOOKS LIKE IRON MAN.

YEAH, IT DOES, A LITTLE. WHY DON'T YOU GO ASK HIM?

ME?! WHY DON'T *YOU* ASK HIM!

SHIELD

SHIELD

18

I GOT A BETTER IDEA--

--LET'S ALL ASK HIM!

BUT THE IRON AVENGER HAS NO TIME FOR ANSWERING QUESTIONS--

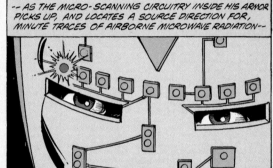

--AS THE MICRO-SCANNING CIRCUITRY INSIDE HIS ARMOR PICKS UP, AND LOCATES A SOURCE DIRECTION FOR, MINUTE TRACES OF AIRBORNE MICROWAVE RADIATION--

--WHICH IN TURN LEADS TO THE SHIELD AGENTS' SECOND SURPRISE OF THE DAY!

SHHKROW

LIKE SOME GRIM, GOLDEN GOLEM, IRON MAN ROCKETS SKY-WARD EVER FASTER...

...UNTIL THE AIR GROWS THIN, AND ALL CLOUDS LIE BELOW...

...AT WHICH POINT HIS JET POWER AUTOMATIC-ALLY SHUTS OFF, AND BOOT-MOUNTED NUCLEAR THRUSTERS TAKE OVER--

-- SENDING HIS BODY SLAMMING AGAINST THE POLARIZED WALLS OF HIS ARMOR WITH THE FORCE OF MULTIPLE GRAVITIES--

--AS HE AT LAST SHATTERS THE OBSTINATE BONDS OF ATMOSPHERE--

--AND HURTLES HEADLONG INTO THE COLD, COMFORTLESS ARMS OF OUTER SPACE!

⑲

I CAN'T HELP IT. NO MATTER HOW MANY TIMES I DO THIS, I STILL GET AN INCREDIBLE FEELING OF AWE. AND I JUST WONDER WHAT PLANET EARTH WOULD BE LIKE IF *EVERYONE* COULD SEE IT FROM THIS PERSPECTIVE.

BUT ENOUGH OF PHILOSOPHY--

-- ACCORDING TO MY SENSORS, THE SOURCE OF THAT TRACE RADIATION IS VERY CLOSE BY. I ONLY HAVE TO MOVE ANOTHER 30 DEGREES SUNWARD AND--

--AW, NO! OF ALL THE PLACES TO STOP AND TAKE IN THE SCENERY--

-- I HAD TO PICK THE PATH OF AN ORBITING *COMMUNICATIONS SATELLITE!*

GOT TO KEY IN MY MANEUVERING ROCKETS AND GET OUT OF THE WAY BEFORE--

-- BLAST! I FORGOT THAT MY COMMAND CIRCUITRY IS MORE SENSITIVE IN THIS ARMOR! I'VE ACTIVATED A DOZEN SYSTEMS WITH ONE THOUGHT!

AND WHAT'S WORSE, THEY'RE CANCELLING EACH OTHER OUT! I'M NOT GOING--

-- ANYWHERE!

PUH-

KUNGG

20

As miles below... NOT SO LOUD, FRED! YOU'LL WAKE RICKY, JR.!

I CAN'T HELP IT, ETHEL! IT'S THAT BUM NEXT DOOR WITH HIS CB RADIO! NOW I CAN'T EVEN GET A TEST PATTERN!

BAM BAM

HEY, YA JERK! STOP WITH THE INTERFER-ENCE!

OR I'M GONNA SHOVE A BIG 10-4 RIGHT UP YER WAZOO!

But the real cause of that disturbed signal is high overhead, in the process of becoming increasingly disturbed himself!

I DON'T UNDERSTAND. MY SENSORS TELL ME THAT THE MICROWAVE'S ORIGIN POINT IS DIRECTLY AHEAD--BUT MY RADAR SCANNER ISN'T SHOWING ANY-THING AT ALL! MAYBE I'M JUST NOT--

--WAIT A MINUTE! THERE *IS* SOMETHING! STARTING TO MOVE OUT OF THE EARTH'S SHADOW! I'M PICKING IT UP VISUALLY! BUT WHAT--?

...Until finally it stands fully exposed, floating silently in the crystal void of space...

In front of Iron Man, a phenomenon grows-- as a glinting length of metal edges slowly into the sunlight...

...Taking definite shape as more and more unfiltered starshine limns its surface, giving it form, and pattern...

...And the golden avenger real-izes for the first time exactly what that phenomenon is:

21

47

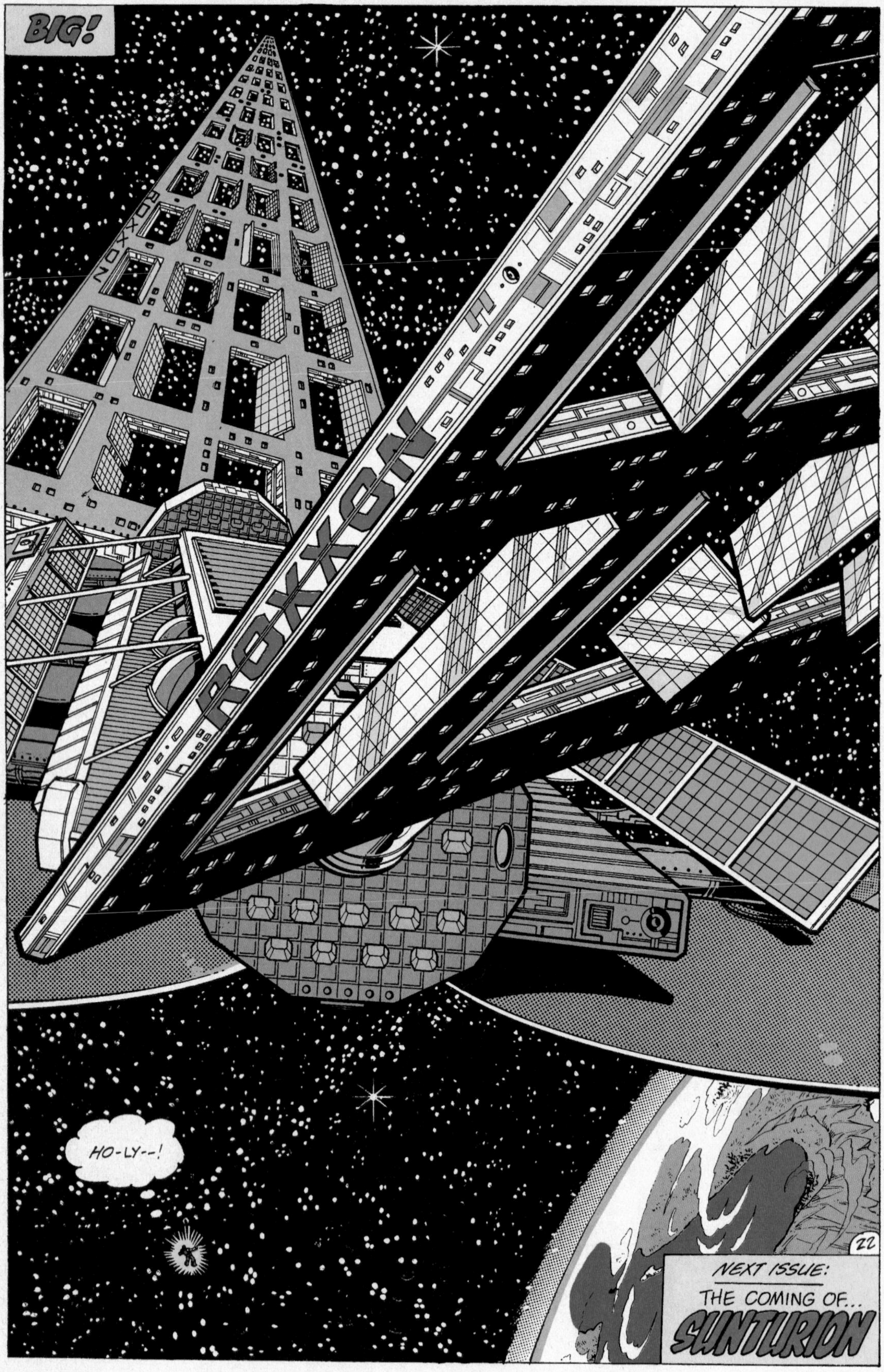
BIG!
ROXXON
ROXXON
HO-LY--!
22
NEXT ISSUE:
THE COMING OF...
SUNTURION

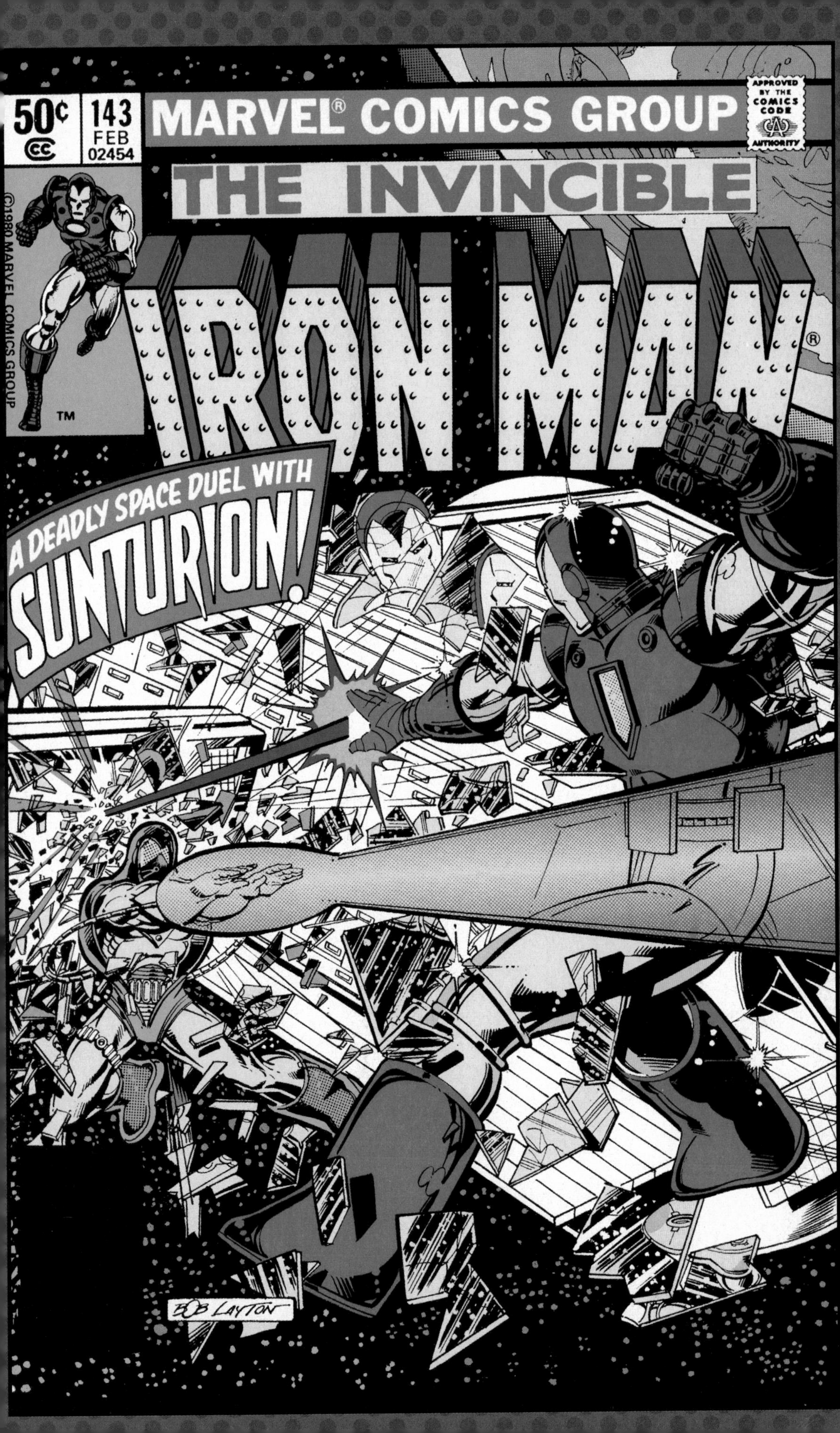
50¢
CC
143
FEB
02454
MARVEL® COMICS GROUP
APPROVED BY THE COMICS CODE CA AUTHORITY
THE INVINCIBLE
IRON MAN®
TM
©1980 MARVEL COMICS GROUP
A DEADLY SPACE DUEL WITH
SUNTURION!
BOB LAYTON

When millionaire industrialist *Tony Stark*, inventor extraordinaire, garbs himself in solar-charged, steel-mesh armor he becomes the world's greatest human fighting machine...

STAN LEE PRESENTS: THE INVINCIBLE IRON MAN

| DAVID MICHELINIE plot/writer | JOHN ROMITA, JR. pencil art | BOB LAYTON plot/finished art | JOHN COSTANZA letters | BOB SHAREN colors | JIM SALICRUP editor | JIM SHOOTER editor-in-chief |

EBONY ON BLACK: THE IMPENETRABLE DARKNESS OF SHADOWS IN SPACE. IT HAD BEEN TO JUST SUCH AN OBSCURING MANTLE THAT TONY STARK, THE INVINCIBLE IRON MAN, HAD COME ONLY MOMENTS AGO, SEARCHING FOR SOLUTIONS. AND IT HAD BEEN THERE THAT HE HAD WITNESSED INSTEAD THE EMERGENCE OF AN IMPOSSIBILITY-- A SILENTLY-ORBITING SPACE STATION FULLY FIVE MILES LONG, SCATTERED WITH ROW AFTER ROW OF MIRRORLIKE REFLECTIVE PANELS.

THE RESULT BEING THAT NOW, AS HE FLOATS WEIGHTLESS IN AN UNTESTED SUIT OF EXPERIMENTAL ARMOR, HE FINDS HIMSELF FACED NOT WITH ANSWERS, BUT, WITH THE BIGGEST QUESTION OF ALL:

WHAT THE BLAZES *IS* THIS THING ?!

ROXON

METER on the SUN!

MY RADAR SCANNER STILL SHOWS A BLANK.

WHIRR

WHATEVER THIS INSTALLATION IS, IT MUST HAVE ONE HECKUVA MASKING SYSTEM!

BUT SINCE I CAN PICK IT UP VISUALLY--

RRRK

RRK

RRK

SNAP

THE AUTO-CAMERA I BUILT INTO THIS PROTOTYPE ARMOR SHOULD BE ABLE TO GET ME ALL THE PHYSICAL PROOF I NEED.

I'LL JUST TAKE A QUICK SWING AROUND THE ENTIRE COMPLEX, MAKE SURE I GET SHOTS FROM ALL ANGLES--

--AND THEN SEE IF I CAN GET INSIDE AND FIND OUT WHAT--

KTUNG

--WHAT?!

METEOR SHOWER! BUT IF IT DAMAGES THE STATION BEFORE I CAN GET ENOUGH EVIDENCE--!

HEY, WHAT AM I WORRYING ABOUT? I'LL JUST TRIGGER MY REPULSOR RAYS AND BLAST THESE ROCKS TO DUST BEFORE THEY--

--HUH?! OH, NO! I FORGOT THIS PROTOTYPE'S STILL GOT SOME BUGS IN IT! MY CYBERNETIC COMMAND TURNED ON MY VARIO-BEAM SPOTLIGHT INSTEAD!

SPATCH

KCHOMP

NUTS

2

BUT AT THAT MOMENT...

WHA--? SOME SORT OF ENERGY BLASTS-- *MELTING* THE METEORS! A-AND NOW I'M PICKING UP A VOICE ON MY ARMOR'S *RADIO CIRCUITS!*

THANK YOU FOR TRYING TO HELP, FRIEND-- BUT I THINK *I* CAN HANDLE THE SITUATION NOW.

I'M *SUNTURION.*

WONDERFUL.

WHAT'S A *"SUNTURION"?*

I AM A *GUARDIAN.* IT IS MY PURPOSE TO PROTECT THIS OUTPOST AGAINST ALL THREATS.

THOSE METEORS, FOR EXAMPLE. I DOUBT THEY WOULD HAVE DAMAGED THE CENTRAL CORE OF THE STATION-- IT'S QUITE WELL-SHIELDED.

BUT THE SOLAR PANELS *ARE* RATHER DELICATE-- TO SAY NOTHING OF BEING A BLOODY NUISANCE TO *REPLACE!*

NOW IF YOU'LL JUST STEP INSIDE, I'M SURE THE STATION'S SUPERVISOR WILL BE DELIGHTED TO EXPLAIN EVERYTHING.

HE'S STARTING TO SPARKLE, TO WAVER! A-AND NOW HE'S... DISAPPEARING!

EVEN *I* CAN'T DO THAT!

3

I'D BETTER BE CAREFUL--THIS COULD BE A TRAP, THOUGH IF I WANT TO FIND OUT WHAT'S GOING ON, I GUESS I DON'T HAVE A WHOLE BUNCH OF CHOICE!

CAUTIOUSLY, IRON MAN MAKES HIS WAY TO AN AIRLOCK SET IN AN OUTER WALL OF THE IMMENSE STRUCTURE--

--AND, ONCE INSIDE...

A FEW DAYS AGO, SEVERAL HUNDRED PEOPLE IN ALLANTOWN, IOWA WERE *KILLED* BY A MYSTERIOUS BARRAGE OF MICROWAVE RADIATION. *

* *IN IM #140.
-- Salicrup.*

AND SINCE I'VE TRACED THE SOURCE OF THAT BARRAGE TO THIS STATION, I'VE GOT TO BE READY FOR ANYTHING, ANYTHING AT--

HOW DO YOU DO?

--ALL?

THE PARTICULARS OF YOUR METALLIC SHELL DIFFERS A BIT FROM THE PHOTOGRAPHS I'VE SEEN, BUT FROM THE GENERAL CONFIGURATION I ASSUME THAT I'M ADDRESSING... IRON MAN?

THAT'S RIGHT, MISTER, AND JUST WHO THE BLAZES ARE YOU?

DO FORGIVE ME, I'M ARTHUR DEARBORN, DESIGNER AND ADMINISTRATOR OF THIS STATION.

IN FACT, YOU'RE MORE THAN WELCOME, IT'S BEEN SOME TIME SINCE I'VE BEEN ABLE TO DISCUSS MY BRAIN-CHILD WITH SOMEONE WHO COULD APPRECIATE HER.

PLEASE, LET ME SHOW YOU AROUND...

AND I WELCOME YOU TO STAR WELL I.

AND, AFTER A SHORT TOUR THAT IMPRESSES EVEN THE BRILLIANT MIND OF ANTHONY STARK...

WHILE THESE ARE MY LIVING QUARTERS. A BIT OPULENT, GRANTED, BUT SINCE STAR WELL IS ALMOST TOTALLY AUTOMATED, I WANTED THE AREA WHERE I WOULD BE SPENDING MOST OF MY TIME TO BE COMFORTABLE.

4

BY "ALMOST" AUTOMATED, I ASSUME THAT YOU'RE REFERING TO SUNTURION?

SUNTURION IS, WELL, A SPECIAL CASE. WOULD YOU CARE TO JOIN ME FOR LUNCH? THE ARTICHOKE PASTE IS REALLY QUITE GOOD.

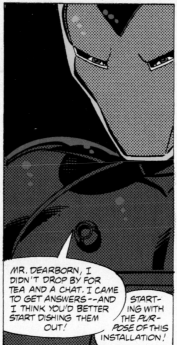

MR. DEARBORN, I DIDN'T DROP BY FOR TEA AND A CHAT. I CAME TO GET ANSWERS--AND I THINK YOU'D BETTER START DISHING THEM OUT!

STARTING WITH THE PURPOSE OF THIS INSTALLATION!

THE PURPOSE, MY GOOD MAN, IS TO SAVE THE HUMAN RACE.

OH, REALLY?

REALLY. BUT PERHAPS I'D BEST START FROM THE BEGINNING...

"...IN RECENT YEARS, IT'S BECOME PAINFULLY OBVIOUS THAT THE GREATEST THREAT TO GLOBAL PEACE AND SECURITY IS THE DEPLETION OF FOSSIL FUELS. IF WORLD WAR III IS EVER FOUGHT, IT WILL BE FOUGHT OVER ENERGY.

"WHICH IS WHY I DESIGNED STAR WELL-- THE ULTIMATE RECEPTION AND STORAGE UNIT FOR SOLAR RADIATION.

"AFTER A SLIGHT DELAY WHILE MY EMPLOYERS, THE ROXXON OIL CORPORATION, SOUGHT ENOUGH RARE VIBRANIUM WITH WHICH TO CONSTRUCT THE SPACECRAFT NEEDED TO LAUNCH STAR WELL'S COMPONENTS INTO ORBIT-- *

"--THE STATION WAS BUILT, COMPLETE WITH ULTRA-SOPHISTI-CATED SHIELD DEVICES TO PREVENT RADAR DETECTION, IN ORDER TO SIDESTEP UNWANTED GOVERNMENT INTERVENTION-- AND INCIDENTALLY, TO KEEP THE PROJECT A SECRET FROM ROXXON'S COMPETITORS.

* SEE IRON MAN #'s 120-121. --J.S.

"IN THE WEEKS SINCE STAR WELL'S COMPLETION, EXTENSIVE TESTS HAVE BEEN CARRIED OUT-- MAINLY CENTERING ON THE FOCUSING OF SOLAR ENERGY INTO TIGHT BEAM MICROWAVES WHICH ARE THEN TRANSMITTED TO RECEPTION ANTENNAE ON EARTH, WHERE THEY ARE THEN CONVERTED INTO HEAT AND ELECTRICITY, THUS ASSURING THE WORLD OF AN UNINTERRUPTED SUPPLY OF HIGH GRADE ENERGY. AT A FAIR PRICE, OF COURSE." 5

I DON'T SUPPOSE, DEARBORN, THAT ONE OF THOSE "*EXPERIMENTS*" COULD HAVE CAUSED THE DEATHS OF OVER TWO HUNDRED PEOPLE IN A SMALL TOWN IN IOWA A COUPLE OF DAYS AGO?

UH, WELL, I-I DO ADMIT THAT THERE WAS A *SLIGHT* MALFUNCTION IN THE TRANSMISSION LOCKUP AT APPROXIMATELY THAT TIME...

...BUT IS THAT *REALLY* IMPORTANT?

I MEAN, WHAT ARE THE LIVES OF A FEW HUNDRED, WHEN WE'RE DEVELOPING A TECHNOLOGY THAT COULD SAVE *MILLIONS!*

MR. DEARBORN, I CAN SEE THE GOOD, EVEN THE *NECESSITY,* OF WHAT YOU'RE DOING--

--BUT I CAN'T RECONCILE IT WITH THE MURDER OF INNOCENT PEOPLE, SO I'M AFRAID THAT I'LL HAVE TO--

BRREEEERREEERREEE

--EH? WHAT'S THAT?

IT'S THE EXTERIOR DETECTION ALARM, WHICH SEEMS TO SUGGEST, IRON MAN--

--THAT YOU'VE BEEN FOLLOWED!

BENEATH THE EXPRESSIONLESS METAL OF HIS MASK, A FURROW OF CONCERN GROWS ON TONY STARK'S BROW-- WHILE ON PLANET EARTH, BEFORE THE WEST GERMAN EMBASSY, A SIMILAR SEAM CREASES THE FOREHEAD OF THAT GENTLEMAN'S FREQUENT COMPANION, MS. BETHANY CABE...

YOU SURE YOU DON'T WANT ME TO GO WITH YOU, BETH?

BUS STOP

6

THANKS, LING, BUT AMBASSADOR SCHMIDT'S COMMUNIQUE SAID THAT THE MEETING WAS CONFIDENTIAL. YOU GO ON AND SHOP; I'LL MEET YOU FOR LUNCH.

THE YOUNG ORIENTAL LEAVES, TURNING BACK ONCE TO WATCH AS HER BUSINESS PARTNER AND BEST FRIEND REACHES, HESITANTLY, TO KNOCK UPON AN OMINOUS DARK-WOOD DOOR.

THOK THOK

AND PRESENTLY, IN AN INTERIOR OFFICE...

HERR AMBASSADOR, MS. CABE TO SEE YOU.

DANKE, FRAU BUCHER. HOW DO YOU DO, MS. CABE? I AM LUDWIG SCHMIDT.

UND THIS IS WOLFGANG KÜHN, ONE OF OUR AGENTS WHO WAS RECENTLY RELEASED FROM DETENTION IN THE EASTERN BLOCK AS PART OF A PRISONER EXCHANGE.

GUTTENMARGEN, FRAULEIN.

I BELIEVE, MS. CABE, THAT IT WOULD BE GOOD IF YOU WERE TO SIT DOWN NOW, BECAUSE I MUST TELL YOU THAT WOLFGANG HAS BROUGHT US SOME RATHER STARTLING NEWS, NEWS ABOUT--

-- YOUR HUSBAND!

7

56

AND, SPEAKING OF SHOCKS...

A RUSSIAN DEFENSE SATELLITE! IT MUST HAVE BEEN REROUTED FROM A PARALLEL ORBIT!

BUT I THOUGHT YOU SAID THIS STATION WAS RADAR-SHIELDED!

IT IS-- BUT *YOU'RE* NOT! THE RUSSIANS PROBABLY FOLLOWED YOUR SIGNAL AND THEN DIVERTED ONE OF THEIR ORBITING VEHICLES FOR A VISUAL CHECK! THEY--

"-- OH, BLAST! IT LOOKS LIKE THE KREMLIN'S DECIDED THAT WE'RE A THREAT TO THEIR NATIONAL SECURITY! THE SATELLITE IS LAUNCHING A SQUADRON OF ATTACK DRONES--

"--ARMED WITH LASERS!"

DEARBORN, I DON'T LIKE WHAT YOU'VE DONE WITH THIS STATION-- BUT I LIKE REACTIONARY AGGRESSION EVEN LESS! SO IF YOU'LL HELP ME WITH THE AIRLOCK, I'LL TRY TO STOP THOSE--

--HNH?!

AGAIN, IRON MAN, YOUR CONCERN IS APPRECIATED-- BUT I THINK I CAN HANDLE THE SITUATION. AFTER ALL--

8

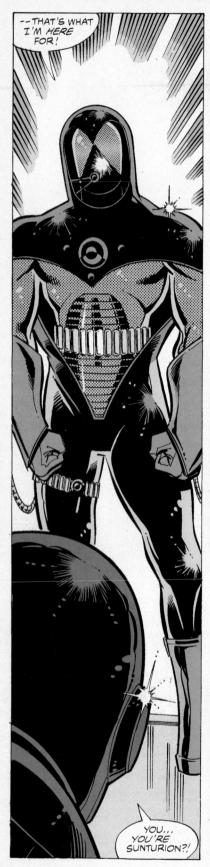

--THAT'S WHAT I'M *HERE* FOR!

YOU... YOU'RE SUNTURION?!

BUT HOW--? I-I MEAN, WHAT--?

I'LL EXPLAIN LATER. AT THE MOMENT, I HAVE SOME RATHER FRAGILE COLLECTOR PANELS TO PROTECT.

WITH A SELF-CONFIDENT SPARKLE, THE SOLAR GUARDIAN WINKS OUT--

-- AND, A SINGLE MICRO-SECOND LATER, WINKS BACK IN A *FULL QUARTER-MILE* AWAY!

I'VE HEARD THAT ONE OF THE MUTANTS THEY CALL THE *X-MEN* CAN PULL A STUNT LIKE THAT.

BUT SEEING IT WITH MY OWN EYES IS SOMETHING ELSE!

NEVERTHELESS, EVEN WITH A NIFTY BAG OF TRICKS, SUNTURION MIGHT NEED HELP!

HURRIEDLY--OR AT LEAST AS MUCH SO AS HIS BULKY, PROTOTYPE ARMOR WILL ALLOW AT NORMAL GRAVITY-- IRON MAN MAKES HIS WAY TO A NEARBY AIRLOCK...

... AND MOMENTS LATER ROCKETS ONTO THE SCENE OF AWESOME COMBAT!

SUNTURION, LOOK OUT! COMING IN FROM YOUR LEFT!

NO PROBLEM, IRON MAN. I CAN ABSORB QUITE A BIT OF LASER ENERGY.

IN FACT, I CAN EVEN LOCK ON TO THE ACTIVE BEAM--

-- AND SEND SOME OF MY OWN ENERGY BACK ALONG THE LINE OF TRANSMISSION, CAUSING THE DRONE TO OVERLOAD!

SHKRUMP

NICE. BUT MAYBE IT'S TIME I SHOWED SUNTURION THAT HE'S NOT THE ONLY ONE WHO CAN TAKE CARE OF HIMSELF. I'LL JUST AIM MY REPULSORS AT THOSE TWO INCOMING DRONES AND--

-- BLAST! I KEEP FORGETTING THE ROUGH EDGES IN MY COMMAND CIRCUITRY! THIS TIME I ACCIDENTALLY TRIGGERED MY BOOT THRUSTERS!

OF COURSE, THERE'S NO NEED TO TELL SUNTURION THAT HAVING THE DRONES CRASH INTO EACH OTHER WAS A MISTAKE! ⸝AHEM⸝

SHPOOM

10

GOOD WORK, AVENGER. BUT NOW THAT THE DRONES ARE CONCENTRATING ON *US*, I SUGGEST WE TRY LEADING THEM AWAY FROM STAR WELL!

SOUNDS LIKE GOOD STRATEGY TO ME, SUNTURION.

LET'S DO IT!

THREE MORE DRONES, COMING IN FAST! BUT MAYBE THIS TIME I CAN *USE* THE MAL-FUNCTIONS I'VE BEEN RUNNING INTO!

SINCE I NOW KNOW WHICH CIRCUIT ACTIVATES MY SPOTLIGHT BEAM, I CAN USE IT TO BATHE THE DRONES IN HIGH INTENSITY LIGHT, BLINDING THEIR VISUAL SENSORS--

CHUSH!

--AND CAUSING ONE OF THEM TO FLY SMACK DAB INTO AN OLD FASHIONED ROUNDHOUSE RIGHT!

11

AS FOR THE OTHER TWO, THEY CAN HELP ME TEST SOME OF THIS ARMOR'S MORE *UNIQUE* CAPABILITIES.

--I JUST TAKE AIM, THEN DISENGAGE MY GAUNTLETS' EXO-UNITS!

P-TOK

P-TOK

TO WIT: AFTER MAKING SURE THAT MY MENTAL COMMAND IS LOCKED INTO THE PROPER CIRCUIT LINE--

"THOSE UNITS WERE DESIGNED AS LONG-RANGE GRAPPLES, AND ONCE THEY'VE GOT A SOLID GRIP ON THE ATTACK DRONES--"

--ALL I HAVE TO DO IS GIVE THEM A GOOD YANK, BRING THEM TOGETHER ON A COLLISION COURSE--

KRAPASH

--AND THOSE DRONES WILL BE SMASHED INTO MORE PIECES THAN TED KENNEDY'S PRESIDENTIAL DREAMS!

PLEASED THAT AT LEAST ONE ASPECT OF HIS PROTOTYPE ARMOR HAS FUNCTIONED CORRECTLY, IRON MAN QUICKLY REELS IN THE EXO-GAUNTLET GRAPPLES...

12

61

...WHILE NEARBY, THE TRANS-MUTED ADMINISTRATOR OF STAR WELL STATION TAKES ON A TRIO OF ENEMY CRAFT IN HIS OWN DISTINCTIVE MANNER.

THEY'RE CLOSING TO ASSAULT RANGE!

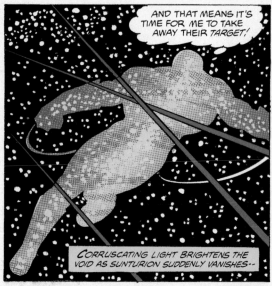

AND THAT MEANS IT'S TIME FOR ME TO TAKE AWAY THEIR *TARGET!*

CORRUSCATING LIGHT BRIGHTENS THE VOID AS SUNTURION SUDDENLY VANISHES--

--LEAVING THREE COMPUTERIZED DRONES TO HOVER SILENTLY IN ELECTRONIC CONFUSION--

--UNTIL A SECOND CORRUSCATION FROM BEHIND *TAKES THEIR ATTENTION--*

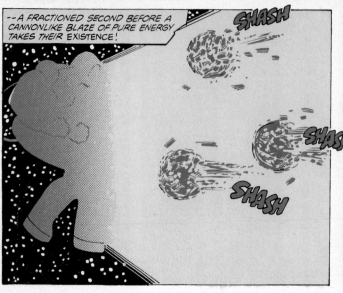

--A FRACTIONED SECOND BEFORE A CANNONLIKE BLAZE OF PURE ENERGY TAKES THEIR EXISTENCE!

SHASH

SHASH

SHASH

THIS HAS GONE ON LONG ENOUGH. IT'S TIME TO CUT THESE DRONES OFF AT THE SOURCE!

WHICH, IF I'VE IDENTIFIED AND TRACED THEIR COMMAND SIGNAL WAVELENGTH CORRECTLY, APPEARS TO BE--

13

"--JUST SOUTH OF MOSCOW!"

IT GOES WELL, ANATOLY.

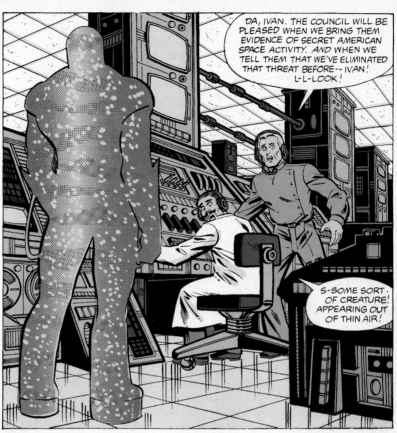

DA, IVAN. THE COUNCIL WILL BE PLEASED WHEN WE BRING THEM EVIDENCE OF SECRET AMERICAN SPACE ACTIVITY. AND WHEN WE TELL THEM THAT WE'VE ELIMINATED THAT THREAT BEFORE-- IVAN! L-L-LOOK!

S-SOME SORT OF CREATURE! APPEARING OUT OF THIN AIR!

ZASH

H-HE'S DESTROYED THE DRONE CONTROLS, AND OUR RECORDING BANKS! A-AND NOW HE'S DISAPPEARING! BUT WHAT WILL THE COUNCIL THINK?

I...I'VE ALWAYS WANTED TO VISIT SIBERIA, ANATOLY, ;SNIFF; REALLY I HAVE.

WHILE AT THAT MOMENT, IN THE BATTLEGROUND OF SPACE...

THE DRONES--

14

63

--THEY'VE STOPPED DEAD!

AND SUNTURION'S NOWHERE IN SIGHT!

IT LOOKS LIKE DEARBORN'S *"DISAPPEARING ACT"* IS MORE POWERFUL THAN I THOUGHT-- HE MUST HAVE TAKEN THE FIGHT ALL THE WAY TO THE RUSSIAN CONTROL CENTER!

WHICH MEANS THAT I'D BETTER GET BACK THROUGH THE AIRLOCK--

HE DOES.

--AND START LOOKING AROUND STAR WELL. BECAUSE THERE'S SOMETHING HERE THAT I *HAVE* TO FIND--

"-- BEFORE SUNTURION RETURNS!"

I'M GLAD I WASN'T FORCED TO HURT ANY OF THOSE RUSSIAN TECHNICIANS.

I KNOW THAT LIVES ARE ALWAYS LOST WHEN THE UNKNOWN IS CHALLENGED, BUT THAT STILL DOESN'T MAKE THE BURDEN ANY EASIER TO--

PIPELINE TO STAR WELL. COME IN, STAR WELL.

-- EH?

OH, UH STAR WELL HERE.

YOUR PROGRESS REPORT IS OVERDUE, DEARBORN. WHY THE DELAY?

15

I'M SORRY, MR. HALE,* BUT I'VE HAD SOME PROBLEMS.

PROBLEMS? WHAT SORT OF PROBLEMS?

*JONAS HALE COMMAND-ED THE ROXXON VIBRANIUM SCHEME IN *I.M.* #120-121--J.S.

THIS, KIND, "CAPTAIN".

WHA--? BUT YOU'RE SUPPOSED TO BE ALONE, DEARBORN! WHO'S THAT COMING UP BEHIND YOU? IT... IT ALMOST LOOKS LIKE...

...IRON MAN?! WH-WHAT THE BLAZES ARE YOU DOING THERE?

THE SAME THING I DID IN THE ATLANTIC, HALE-- I'M SHUTTING YOUR OPERATIONS DOWN!

M-MR. HALE, I CAN EXPLAIN--!

SAVE YOUR BREATH, DEARBORN, POLICY IS QUITE CLEAR IN SITUATIONS LIKE THIS. YOU AND STAR WELL ARE BOTH VALUABLE ASSETS-- BUT ROXXON'S SECUR-ITY IS EVEN *MORE* VALUABLE.

I'M AFRAID I HAVE NO CHOICE.

IRON MAN! H-HE'S ACTIVATING THE SELF-DESTRUCT CYCLE!

I WOULDN'T WORRY ABOUT THAT, MR. DEARBORN. YOU SEE, I'VE HAD EX-PERIENCE WITH ROXXON'S MANIA FOR DESTROYING EVIDENCE.

SO WHILE YOU WERE GONE, I SEARCHED THIS STATION, FOUND THE INEVITABLE DESTRUCT MECHANISM-- AND DISCON-NECTED IT!

16

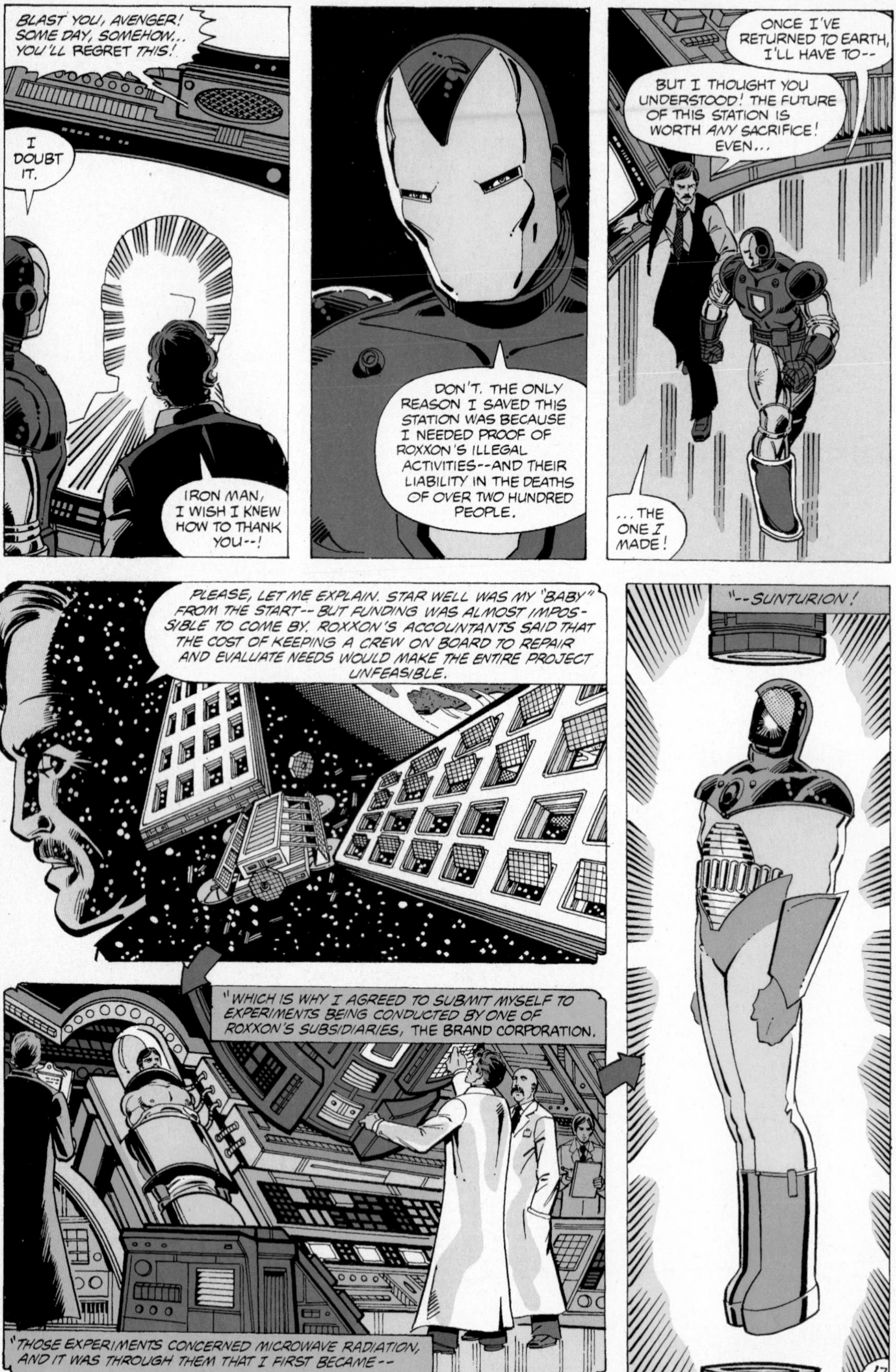

BLAST YOU, AVENGER! SOME DAY, SOMEHOW... YOU'LL REGRET THIS!
I DOUBT IT.
IRON MAN, I WISH I KNEW HOW TO THANK YOU--!
DON'T. THE ONLY REASON I SAVED THIS STATION WAS BECAUSE I NEEDED PROOF OF ROXXON'S ILLEGAL ACTIVITIES--AND THEIR LIABILITY IN THE DEATHS OF OVER TWO HUNDRED PEOPLE.
ONCE I'VE RETURNED TO EARTH, I'LL HAVE TO--
BUT I THOUGHT YOU UNDERSTOOD! THE FUTURE OF THIS STATION IS WORTH ANY SACRIFICE! EVEN...
...THE ONE I MADE!
PLEASE, LET ME EXPLAIN. STAR WELL WAS MY "BABY" FROM THE START-- BUT FUNDING WAS ALMOST IMPOSSIBLE TO COME BY. ROXXON'S ACCOUNTANTS SAID THAT THE COST OF KEEPING A CREW ON BOARD TO REPAIR AND EVALUATE NEEDS WOULD MAKE THE ENTIRE PROJECT UNFEASIBLE.
"WHICH IS WHY I AGREED TO SUBMIT MYSELF TO EXPERIMENTS BEING CONDUCTED BY ONE OF ROXXON'S SUBSIDIARIES, THE BRAND CORPORATION.
"THOSE EXPERIMENTS CONCERNED MICROWAVE RADIATION, AND IT WAS THROUGH THEM THAT I FIRST BECAME--
"--SUNTURION!
17

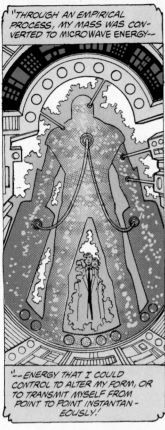

"THROUGH AN EMPIRICAL PROCESS, MY MASS WAS CONVERTED TO MICROWAVE ENERGY--

"--ENERGY THAT I COULD CONTROL TO ALTER MY FORM, OR TO TRANSMIT MYSELF FROM POINT TO POINT INSTANTANEOUSLY!"

"I THEN VOLUNTEERED AS THE ENTIRE CREW OF STAR WELL, FOR SINCE I COULD BE COMPLETELY REPLENISHED BY RADIATION FROM THE SUN, ONLY MINIMAL FOOD, OXYGEN AND LIVING SPACE WOULD NEED TO BE ALLOTED FOR THE SAKE OF OCCASIONAL VISITORS.

"A NEW BUDGET WAS DRAWN, THE PROJECT COMMITTEE ACCEPTED IT, AND STAR WELL WAS COMPLETED. I HAD WON. OF COURSE, I KNEW I COULD NEVER WALK THE EARTH AGAIN AS A NORMAL HUMAN BEING, BUT THEN...

"...I DID SAY ANY SACRIFICE, DIDN'T I?"

MR. DEARBORN, I THINK I HONESTLY ADMIRE YOU, BUT I'M AFRAID THAT DOESN'T MATTER.

I STILL HAVE MY OWN STANDARDS, MY OWN BELIEFS, AND I HAVE TO LIVE BY THEM. I HOPE YOU UNDERSTAND.

I DO, IRON MAN. BELIEVE ME...

I DO.

AND SOON, OUTSIDE... BY TEARING THE BANKS OF SOLAR PANELS AWAY FROM STAR WELL'S CENTRAL CORE, I SHOULD BE ABLE TO CRIPPLE THE STATION'S FUNCTIONAL CAPACITY--

--WHILE STILL LEAVING ENOUGH PHYSICAL EVIDENCE FOR A GOVERNMENT INVESTIGATION TO DETERMINE THE FULL EXTENT OF--

NOOOOOOO!

WHAT--?

FAZZZHHAK

I DON'T WANT TO KILL YOU, IRON MAN-- BUT I WON'T LET THIS STATION BE DESTROYED!

UHHN. MY ARMOR'S REFRACTORY COATING... WAS BARELY ABLE TO WITHSTAND SUNTURION'S MICROWAVE BLAST!

19

SO I'D BETTER TAKE THE OFFENSIVE WHILE I STILL CAN! AND SINCE MY REPULSORS HAVEN'T BEEN TERRIBLY RELIABLE TODAY, THE CONCUSSION BURSTS I BUILT INTO THIS PROTOTYPE'S EPAULETS WILL HAVE TO DO!

CHOOM

GIVE UP, IRON MAN! I KNOW YOU'RE HURT-- OR YOUR POWER BLAST WOULDN'T MISS ME BY SO WIDE A MARGIN!

I WASN'T AIMING AT YOU, SUNTURION! I WAS AIMING FOR THE REFLECTIVE PANEL BEHIND YOU!

UNG!

WAMM

CHOONG

HAVE TO WORK FAST, WHILE SUNTURION'S STUNNED! GOT TO BREAK ONE OF THESE MIRRORED PANELS LOOSE, ANGLE IT TO REFLECT IN THE RIGHT DIRECTION--

-- AND HOPE THAT I CAN HIT MY RATHER FORMIDABLE ADVERSARY WITH MORE UNFILTERED SUNLIGHT THAN HE CAN TAKE!

YOU'RE QUITE RESOURCEFUL, IRON MAN! BUT IF YOU'RE THINKING TO OVER-LOAD MY CIRCUITS, YOU MUST HAVE FORGOTTEN--

20

--THAT I HAVE NONE! MY BODY IS PURE MICROWAVE ENERGY--

BIWHOK

--WHICH YOU'VE JUST HELPED TO REPLENISH!

KRAKALEEESH

THE SPACESCAPE SPARKLES WITH A SHOWER OF REFLECTIVE SHARDS, AS SUNTURION CLOSES FOR THE COUP DE GRÂCE...

...ONLY TO FIND HIS OPPONENT SOMEWHAT UNWILLING TO SUCCUMB! THE TWO STRUGGLE, BLASTS OF MICROWAVE ENERGY STABBING WILDLY, MISSING THEIR TARGET...

...AND STRIKING INSTEAD STAR WELL'S SHIELDED CORE-- ALONG WITH THE UNSHIELDED COUPLING UNIT THAT HOLDS IT TO A FINAL BANK OF SOLAR COLLECTORS!

AND ONCE FREE, THE MASSIVE CORE BEGINS TO MOVE, BUILDING MOMENTUM FROM THE IMPACT OF THE UN-GOVERNED BLASTS, FLOATING SILENTLY AWAY.

21

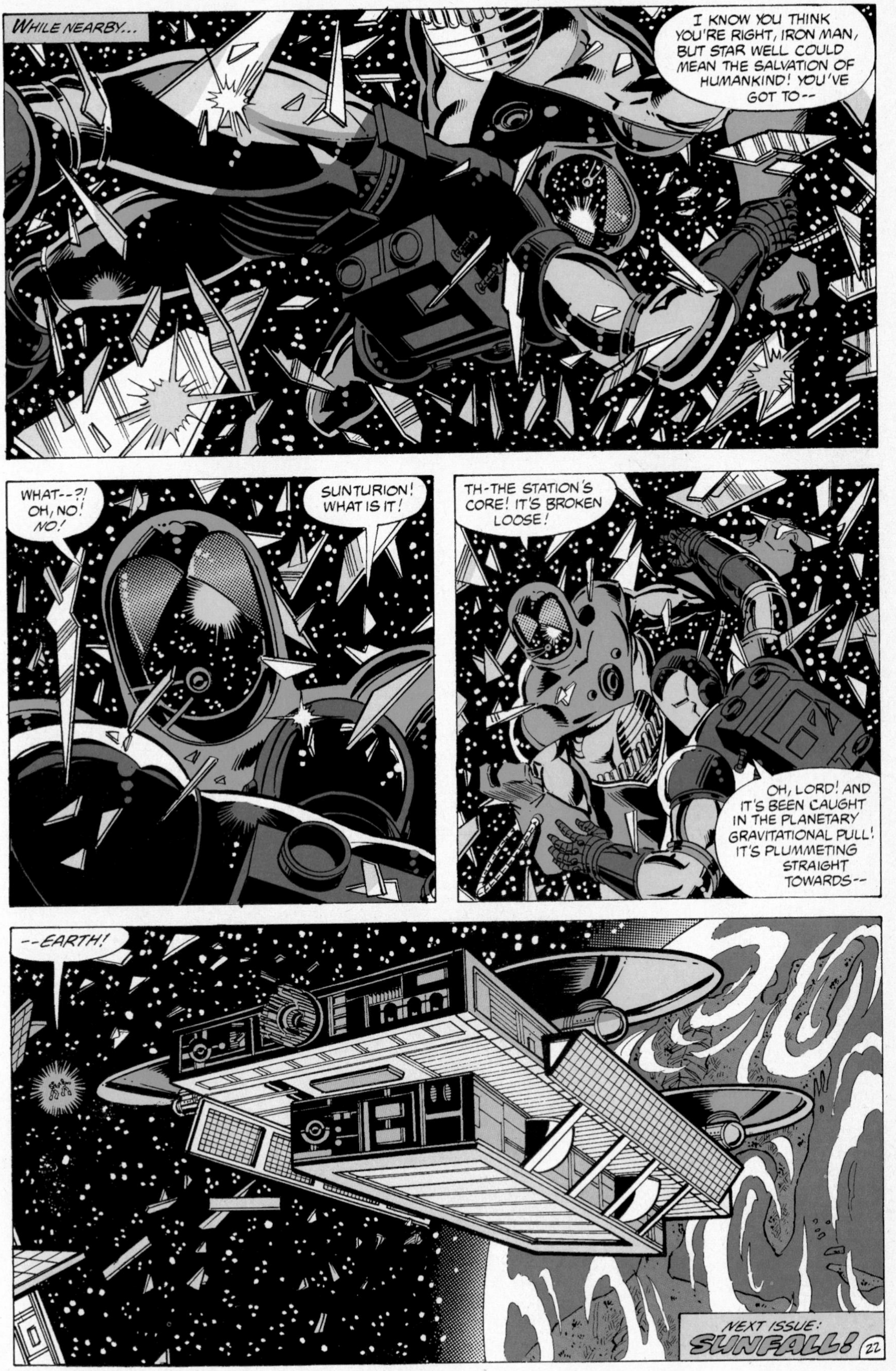
WHILE NEARBY...
I KNOW YOU THINK YOU'RE RIGHT, IRON MAN, BUT STAR WELL COULD MEAN THE SALVATION OF HUMANKIND! YOU'VE GOT TO--
WHAT--?! OH, NO! NO!
SUNTURION! WHAT IS IT!
TH-THE STATION'S CORE! IT'S BROKEN LOOSE!
OH, LORD! AND IT'S BEEN CAUGHT IN THE PLANETARY GRAVITATIONAL PULL! IT'S PLUMMETING STRAIGHT TOWARDS--
--EARTH!
NEXT ISSUE: SUNFALL!
22

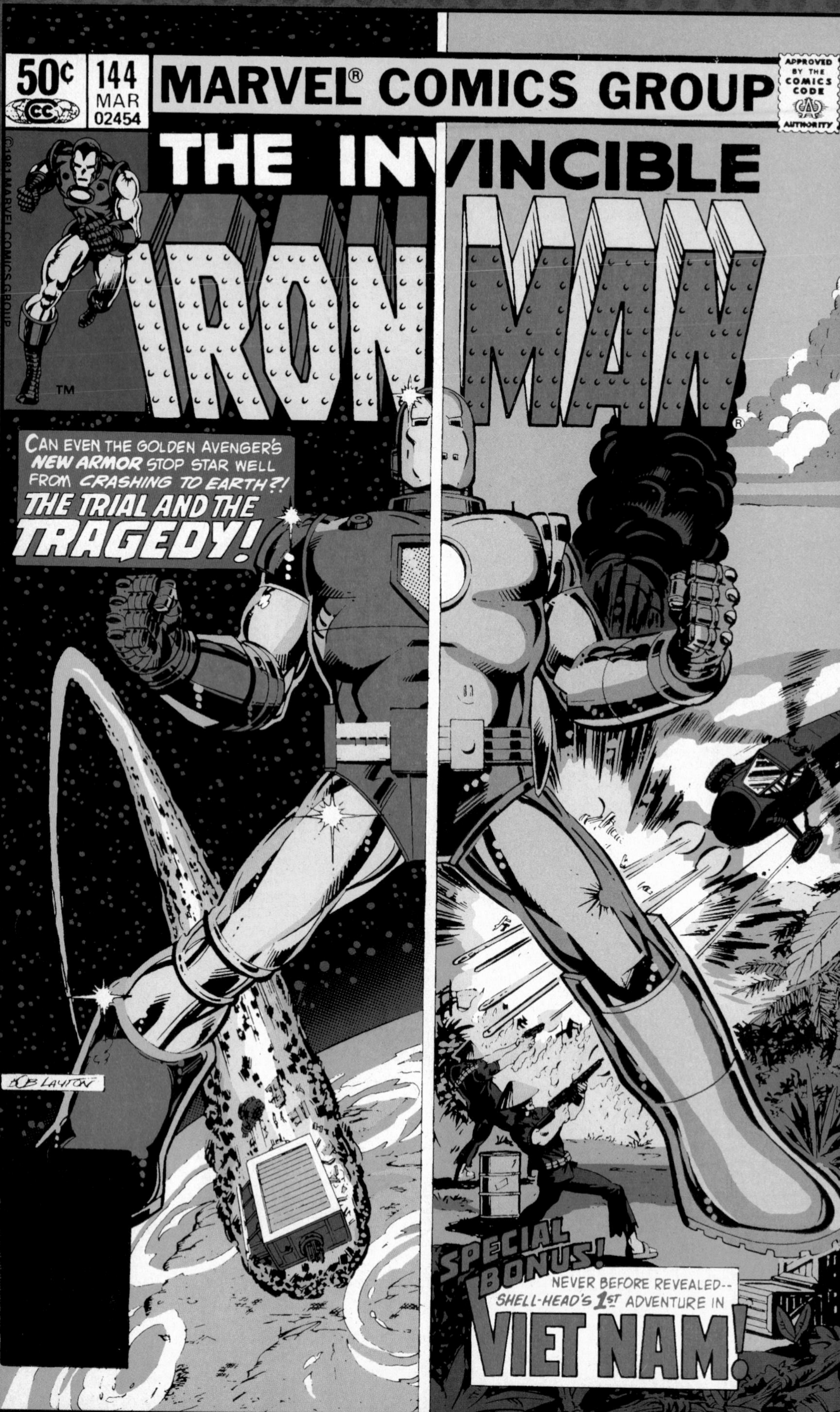
50¢
144
MAR
02454
MARVEL® COMICS GROUP
APPROVED BY THE COMICS CODE AUTHORITY
©1981 MARVEL COMICS GROUP
THE INVINCIBLE
IRON MAN®
CAN EVEN THE GOLDEN AVENGER'S NEW ARMOR STOP STAR WELL FROM CRASHING TO EARTH?!
THE TRIAL AND THE TRAGEDY!
BOB LAYTON
SPECIAL BONUS!
NEVER BEFORE REVEALED-- SHELL-HEAD'S 1ST ADVENTURE IN
VIET NAM!

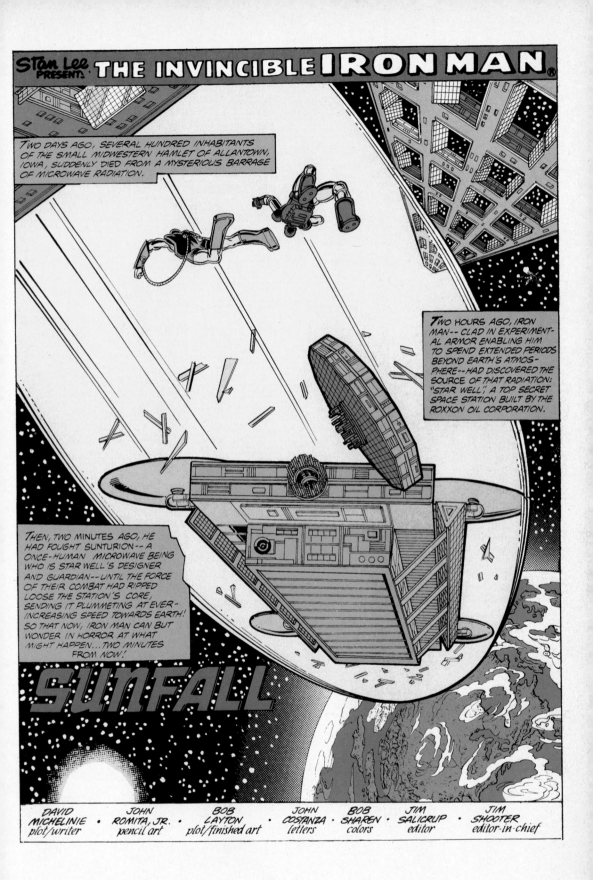

STAN LEE PRESENTS: THE INVINCIBLE IRON MAN.

Two days ago, several hundred inhabitants of the small midwestern hamlet of Allantown, Iowa, suddenly died from a mysterious barrage of microwave radiation.

Two hours ago, Iron Man--clad in experimental armor enabling him to spend extended periods beyond Earth's atmosphere--had discovered the source of that radiation: "Star Well," a top secret space station built by the Roxxon Oil Corporation.

Then, two minutes ago, he had fought Sunturion--a once-human microwave being who is Star Well's designer and guardian--until the force of their combat had ripped loose the station's core, sending it plummeting at ever-increasing speed towards Earth! So that now, Iron Man can but wonder in horror at what might happen...two minutes from now!

SUNFALL

DAVID MICHELINIE
plot/writer
• JOHN ROMITA, JR. •
pencil art
BOB LAYTON
plot/finished art
• JOHN COSTANZA •
letters
BOB SHAREN
colors
• JIM SALICRUP •
editor
JIM SHOOTER
editor-in-chief

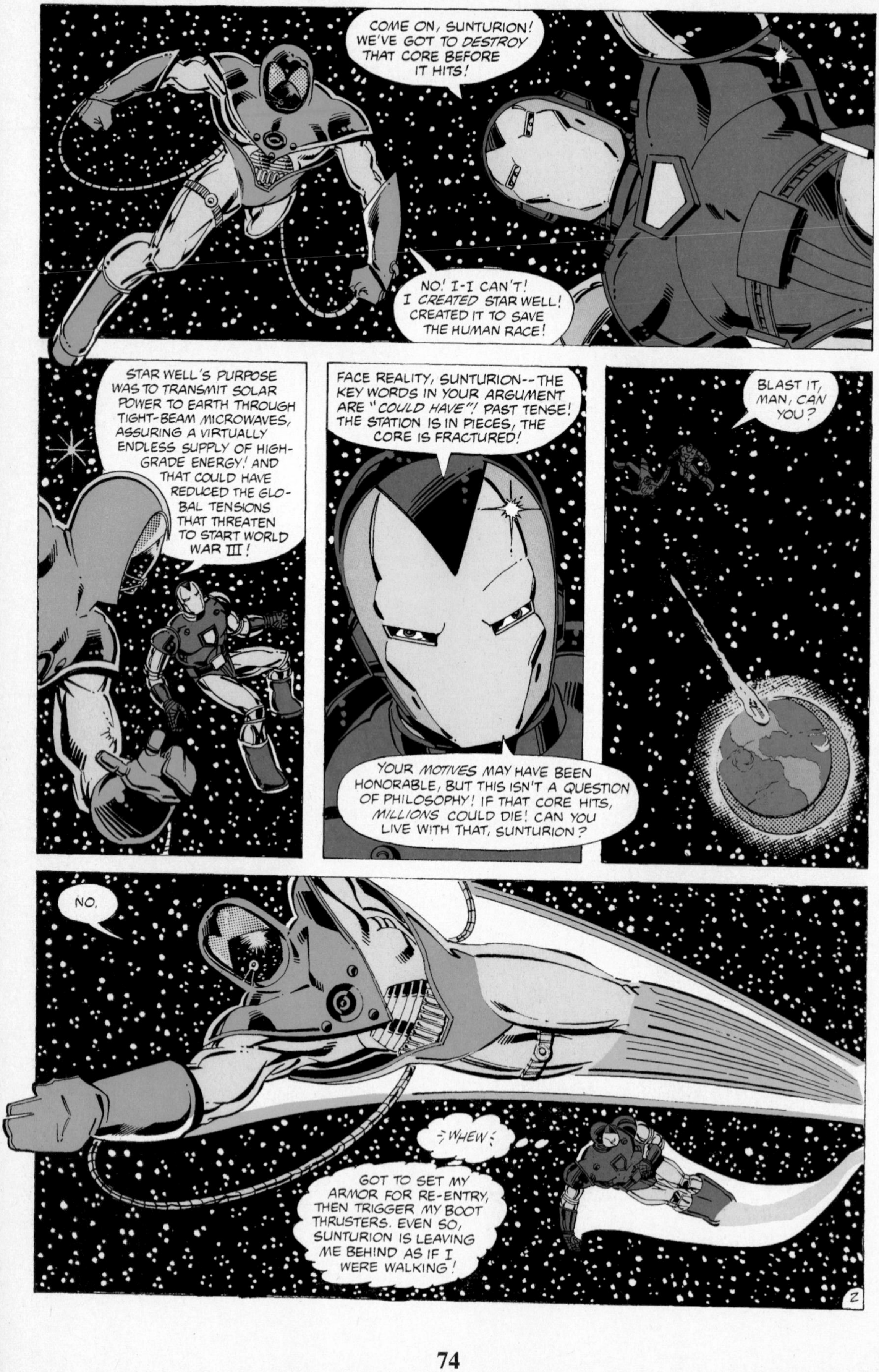
COME ON, SUNTURION! WE'VE GOT TO DESTROY THAT CORE BEFORE IT HITS!
NO! I-I CAN'T! I CREATED STAR WELL! CREATED IT TO SAVE THE HUMAN RACE!
STAR WELL'S PURPOSE WAS TO TRANSMIT SOLAR POWER TO EARTH THROUGH TIGHT-BEAM MICROWAVES, ASSURING A VIRTUALLY ENDLESS SUPPLY OF HIGH-GRADE ENERGY! AND THAT COULD HAVE REDUCED THE GLOBAL TENSIONS THAT THREATEN TO START WORLD WAR III!
FACE REALITY, SUNTURION--THE KEY WORDS IN YOUR ARGUMENT ARE "COULD HAVE"! PAST TENSE! THE STATION IS IN PIECES, THE CORE IS FRACTURED!
YOUR MOTIVES MAY HAVE BEEN HONORABLE, BUT THIS ISN'T A QUESTION OF PHILOSOPHY! IF THAT CORE HITS, MILLIONS COULD DIE! CAN YOU LIVE WITH THAT, SUNTURION?
BLAST IT, MAN, CAN YOU?
NO.
WHEW
GOT TO SET MY ARMOR FOR RE-ENTRY, THEN TRIGGER MY BOOT THRUSTERS. EVEN SO, SUNTURION IS LEAVING ME BEHIND AS IF I WERE WALKING!
2

I'LL HAVE TO CHECK INTO MICROWAVES AS A POWER MODE WHEN I GET BACK TO EARTH,

THAT IS, IF I GET BACK!

LIKE DESPERATE STEEDS IN A ONE-SIDED RACE, MEN AND MACHINE ROCKET TOWARDS AN UNSUSPECTING EARTH--

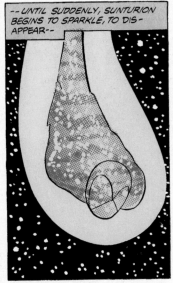

-- UNTIL SUDDENLY, SUNTURION BEGINS TO SPARKLE, TO DISAPPEAR--

-- AND THEN TO REAPPEAR A HEARTBEAT LATER IN THE CONTROL ROOM OF THE DISABLED STAR WELL!

IT'S TOO BAD IRON MAN DISCONNECTED STAR WELL'S SELF-DESTRUCT SYSTEM*-- IT COULD HAVE COME IN HANDY ABOUT NOW.

*LAST ISSUE. --Jim

AS IT IS, I'LL HAVE TO TRY USING THE STATION'S MANEUVERING ROCKETS AS RETROS!

AND JUST HOPE THEY SLOW THE CORE DOWN LONG ENOUGH TO--

SCHROOMMM

-- OH, BLAST! IT--

-- DIDN'T WORK, IRON MAN!

WHA--?! GEEZ, I WISH YOU'D STOP POPPING IN AND OUT LIKE THAT!

NEVERTHELESS, I'M AFRAID YOURS ISN'T THE ONLY BAD NEWS!

3

I'VE JUST CALCULATED THAT, GIVEN ITS CURRENT SPEED AND ANGLE OF DESCENT, STAR WELL IS GOING TO SMASH INTO THE EARTH RIGHT ON TOP OF SARASOTA, FLORIDA!

OUR ONLY HOPE IS TO ALTER THE STATION'S COURSE, SEND IT INTO AN UNINHABITED AREA!

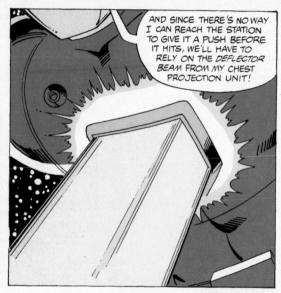

AND SINCE THERE'S NO WAY I CAN REACH THE STATION TO GIVE IT A PUSH BEFORE IT HITS, WE'LL HAVE TO RELY ON THE *DEFLECTOR BEAM* FROM MY CHEST PROJECTION UNIT!

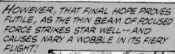

HOWEVER, THAT FINAL HOPE PROVES FUTILE, AS THE THIN BEAM OF FOCUSED FORCE STRIKES STAR WELL -- AND CAUSES NARY A WOBBLE IN ITS FIERY FLIGHT!

NO GOOD, I'M TOO WEAK. OUR BATTLE DEPLETED MY POWER RESERVES. AND WITHOUT A MASSIVE ENERGY SOURCE TO RECHARGE THEM...

...THERE'S NOTHING I CAN DO.

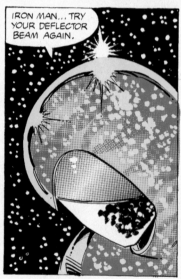

IRON MAN... TRY YOUR DEFLECTOR BEAM AGAIN.

BUT I JUST TOLD YOU, I'M TOO WEAK TO--

PLEASE! JUST TRY!

WELL, OKAY, BUT I DON'T SEE WHAT GOOD IT WILL--

--HNH?! I-I FEEL POWER! AN INCREDIBLE SURGE OF POWER! A-AND MY DEFLECTOR BEAM--IT'S GETTING STRONGER!

4

IT'S SUNTURION! IT'S GOT TO BE! HIS BODY IS COMPOSED OF PURE MICROWAVE ENERGY-- AND HE'S *USING* THAT ENERGY TO POWER MY DEFLECTOR CIRCUITS!

YES, BUT HAS THAT POWER BOOST COME IN TIME? *IRON MAN CAN BUT PRAY AS HE CONCENTRATES--

--WHILE MILES BELOW, STAR WELL STATION CLEAVES THE EARTH'S ATMOSPHERE LIKE A TORCH THROUGH BUTTER--

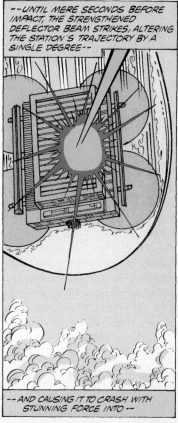

--UNTIL MERE SECONDS BEFORE IMPACT, THE STRENGTHENED DEFLECTOR BEAM STRIKES, ALTERING THE STATION'S TRAJECTORY BY A SINGLE DEGREE--

-- AND CAUSING IT TO CRASH WITH STUNNING FORCE INTO --

--THE GULF OF MEXICO!

SPLABOOOM

NOW THERE'S SOMETHING YOU DON'T SEE EVERY DAY, EDGAR.

WHAT'S THAT, CHAUNCEY?

A SUPER HERO KNOCKING A SATELLITE INTO THE GULF.

MY, MY, MY.

5

SUNTURION! WE DID IT! WE--

--SUNTURION?

SUNTURION!

BUT THE ONLY ANSWER THE GOLDEN AVENGER HEARS IS THE REVERBERATING RUMBLE OF DYING THUNDER.

AND AS HE HOVERS QUIETLY OVER THE SLOWLY SETTLING WATERS, IRON MAN KNOWS THAT THAT IS THE ONLY ANSWER HE'LL HAVE.

FOR THE ENERGY HE HAD USED TO SAVE SARASOTA HAD BEEN THE VERY ESSENCE OF A MAN.

A MAN WILLING, FOR THE SAKE OF OTHERS, TO ABANDON NOT ONLY HIS LIFE, BUT HIS LIFE'S DREAM AS WELL.

AND THAT, IN THE END, IS THE NOBLEST SACRIFICE OF ALL...

EPILOGUE: THE NEXT DAY, AFTER RETURNING PROTOTYPE ARMOR TO A PRIVATE LAB FOR FURTHER IMPROVEMENTS--

--THAT ARMOR'S BUILDER RETURNS TO HIS OFFICES AT STARK INTERNATIONAL--

--WHERE...

ONLY ONE MESSAGE, MR. STARK. FROM ROXXON OIL. THEY'RE SPONSORING A CELEBRITY GOLF TOURNAMENT--

--WITH THE PROCEEDS GOING TO FAMILIES OF THE VICTIMS OF THAT ANTHRAX EPIDEMIC IN ALLANTOWN, IOWA.

"ANTHRAX"? IS THAT WHAT THEY'RE CALLING IT?

YES, SIR. SHALL I TELL THEM YOU'LL ATTEND?

Roxxon

Dear Mr. Stark,

You are cordi... participate in our celeb... Golf Tournament with... to the families of All...

Sir... Jon...

WHAT YOU CAN TELL THEM, MRS. ARBOGAST--

--IS THAT THEY MAY KINDLY STICK THEIR INVITATION UP THEIR CORPORATE ASSETS! IN THE MEANTIME, PLEASE HOLD MY CALLS, WILL YOU?

I THINK I'D LIKE TO BE ALONE FOR AWHILE...

6

When millionaire industrialist *Tony Stark*, inventor extraordinaire, garbs himself in solar-charged, steel-mesh armor he becomes the world's greatest human fighting machine..:.

STAN LEE PRESENTS: THE INVINCIBLE IRON MAN ®

DAVID MICHELINIE writer/plot • JOE BROZOWSKI pencil art • BOB LAYTON finished art/plot • JOHN COSTANZA letters • BOB SHAREN colors • JIM SALICRUP editor • JIM SHOOTER editor-in-chief

THERE COMES A TIME IN THE LIFE OF EVERYONE FAMOUS WHEN HE MUST FACE A GATHERING OF HIS ADMIRERS AND DETRACTORS. SUCH MEETINGS ARE CALLED "CONVENTIONS".

HOWEVER, AS A SLEEK, PRIVATE LEAR JET LEAVES THE RUNWAY AT STARK INTERNATIONAL AIRPORT, TONY STARK FINDS HIS PLANS SUDDENLY ALTERED BY A RATHER FRIGHTENING DETOUR!

AND IT IS FOR ONE SUCH ASSEMBLAGE THAT MILLIONAIRE INDUSTRIALIST ANTHONY STARK *IS* CURRENTLY BOUND-- TO BE SPECIFIC: THE 14TH ANNUAL CONCLAVE OF ELECTRONICS ENGINEERS AND INNOVATORS, BEING HELD AT THE PARK SHERATON HOTEL IN DALLAS, TEXAS.

LOOK OUT! THAT TRANSPORT'S HEADING STRAIGHT AT US! WE'RE GOING TO *CRASH!*

BUY epic

GAS

Apocalypse Then

1

NOT IF *I* CAN HELP IT, CHIEF! BUT YOU'D BETTER START HANDIN' OUT THE AIRSICK BAGS, 'CAUSE THIS IS GONNA BE--

--TIGHT!

¿G...G... GULP!¿

TOWER TO S.I.-1. SORRY ABOUT THAT LITTLE MIX-UP, WE HAD A TEMPORARY PROBLEM WITH OUR GROUND CONTROL READOUT. GLAD NO ONE WAS HURT.

YOU'LL PROBABLY HAVE TO MAKE A STATEMENT TO AN *F.A.A.* HEARING WHEN YOU GET BACK, THOUGH.

I GOT A STATEMENT I'D LIKE TO MAKE RIGHT NOW, DUDE, 'CEPT IT'D PROBABLY MELT YOUR EARPHONES!

UH, RIGHT. TOWER OUT!

RHODE

RHODEY, HAVE I EVER TOLD YOU THAT YOUR FLYING SKILLS MAKE WALDO PEPPER LOOK LIKE A KID WITH A KITE?

Y'MEAN THIS WEEK?

SERIOUSLY, JIM, I SOMETIMES THINK YOU COULD FLY THE PANTS OFF OF IRON MAN HIMSELF. AND AS FOR HAVING JUST SAVED MY LIFE--

2

SAY, BOSS, FORGET IT. I WAS JUST DOIN' MY JOB.

BUT, SETTLING BACK INTO THE CRUSHED VELOUR OF THE SEAT CUSHION, TONY STARK KNOWS THAT LIFE-SAVING IS NOT A PART OF HIS PILOT'S SALARIED DUTIES. FOR IF IT HAD BEEN--

--HE WOULD NOT BE ALIVE TO THINK ABOUT IT TODAY!

THE GLEAMING-NEW LEAR JET SHOOTS SOUTH-WARDS THROUGH THE AFTERNOON SKY, AND THE RELAXING INVENTOR FINDS HIS MIND FILING BACKWARDS, SIFTING THROUGH MEMORIES--

--ARRIVING FINALLY AT SOUTHEAST ASIA DURING THE VIETNAMESE WAR, WHERE HE HAD COME TO TEST HIS THEORIES OF REVERSE MAGNETISM WITH NEW AMERICAN ORDNANCE...

...AND HAD INSTEAD FALLEN VICTIM TO ONE OF THE VIET CONG'S OLDEST WEAPONS, THE BOOBY-TRAPPED MINE...

WHRAAAMMMM

...ONE THAT HAD LEFT A PIECE OF SHRAPNEL LODGED DANGEROUSLY CLOSE TO HIS HEART.

3

CAPTURED, HE HAD PRE-
TENDED TO AID FELLOW
PRISONER, PROFESSOR
YINSEN, *IN BUILDING A
SUPER-WEAPON FOR A
VIETNAMESE DESPOT
NAMED WONG-CHU--*

--WHEN IN REALITY, THEY
HAD CONSTRUCTED A
SUIT OF IRON ARMOR
WITH WHICH TO HELP KEEP
STARK'S RAPIDLY
WEAKENING HEART
BEATING.

THEN, THREATENED
WITH DISCOVERY
MERE MOMENTS
BEFORE THAT ARMOR
COULD BE ACTIVATED,
YINSEN HAD BOUGHT
THEM TIME--

BOOM
DOW DOW

--AT THE COST
OF HIS LIFE.

THAT DEBT HAD
BEEN REPAID BY
TONY STARK AS
IRON MAN, WHEN
HE HAD FOUGHT
WONG-CHU, AND
HAD BESTED HIM...

DANGER
AMMO
DUMP

...ULTIMATELY!

BLAAAAM

HE HAD THOUGHT
THAT TO BE THE END.
BUT WITH HUNDREDS
OF MILES OF UN-
FAMILIAR, ENEMY-
HELD JUNGLE
BETWEEN HIM AND
SAFETY, IT HAD
PROVEN MERELY TO
BE--

--THE BEGINNING!

AND THUS, A SHORT HALF-HOUR AFTER THAT
REALIZATION, IN A CLEARING THICK WITH THE
HEAT OF A MIDDAY SUN AND A NEAR-
FRAZZLED TEMPER...

BLAST! THIS BIRD
AIN'T NEVER GONNA
FLY AGAIN!

4

MAYBE IF I'D SEEN WHERE THOSE ROCKETS COME FROM, I'D'VE BEEN ABLE TO DODGE 'EM. BUT INTELLIGENCE SAID THERE WEREN'T ANY VC LAUNCHERS WITHIN MILES!

SHOOT, GUESS IT MUSTA BEEN "SWAMP GAS" THAT TURNED MY CHOPPER INTO--

CLANK!

--EH? SOUNDS LIKE HEAVY MACHINERY! MAYBE A TANK SNEAKIN' UP BEHIND!

AWRIGHT, YA SKUNKY LITTLE PIGS, YOU AIN'T TAKIN' JIM RHODES BY...SUR...PRISE...?

WHAT THE BLOODY--?

PLEASE! DON'T BE AFRAID! I'M AN AMERICAN!

I JUST NEED TO USE YOUR HELICOPTER'S BATTERIES, MY ELECTRICAL SYSTEM IS NEARLY DEPLETED, AND IF I DON'T RECHARGE SOON-- --I'LL DIE!

YOU GONNA DIE ANY-WAY, YOU TAKE ONE MORE STEP! I'M WARNIN' YA!

STAY BACK!

RATATATATAT

PHWEENG PTANG SPEOW!

OH, MAMA. LOOKS LIKE I'VE STEPPED IN THE BAAAD STUFF THIS TIME!

LOOK, I TOLD YOU, I'M NOT GOING TO HURT YOU! ALL I WANT IS--

5

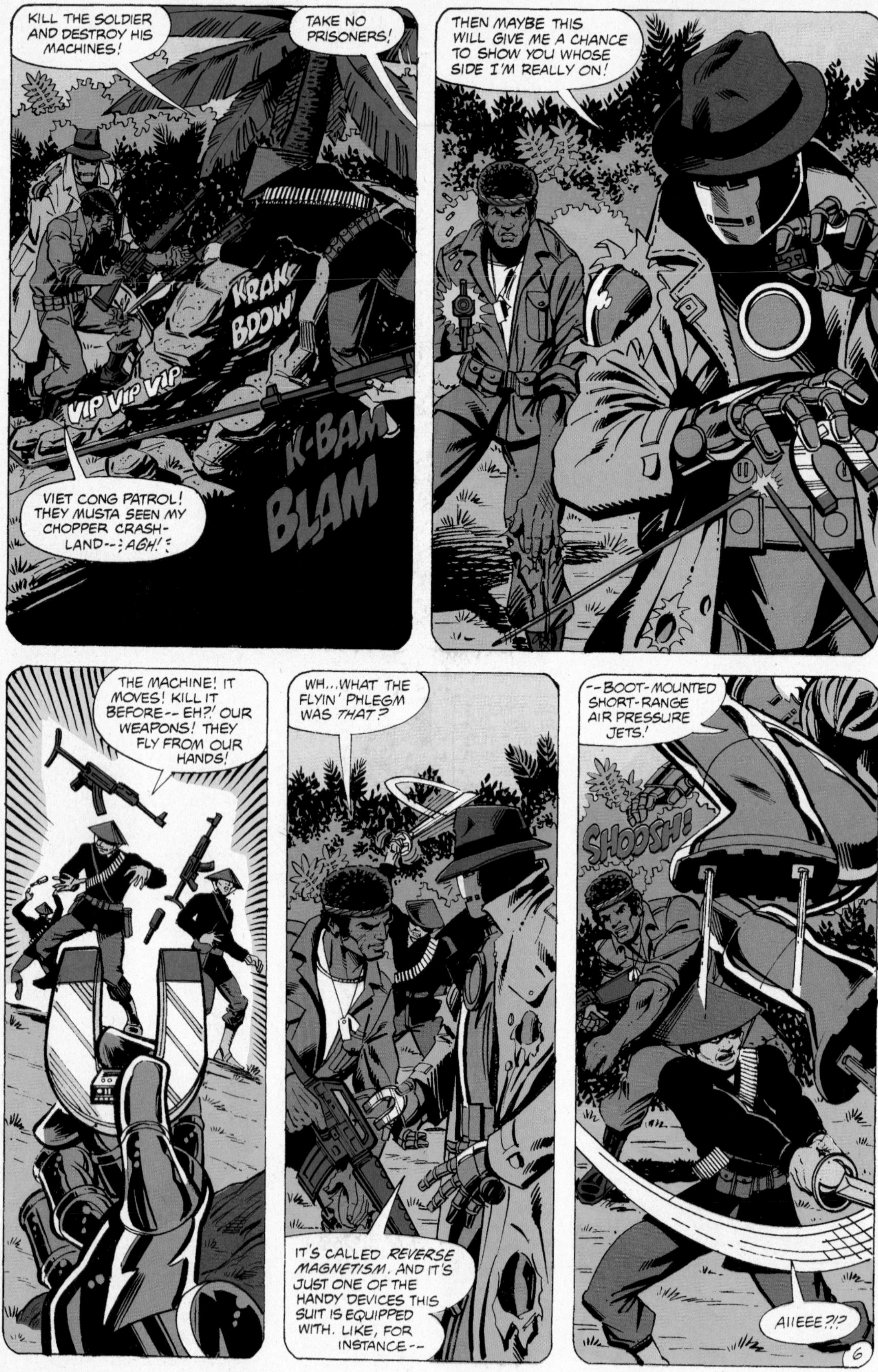
KILL THE SOLDIER AND DESTROY HIS MACHINES!
TAKE NO PRISONERS!
KRAK BDOW
VIP VIP VIP
VIET CONG PATROL! THEY MUSTA SEEN MY CHOPPER CRASH-LAND-- AGH!
K-BAM BLAM
THEN MAYBE THIS WILL GIVE ME A CHANCE TO SHOW YOU WHOSE SIDE I'M REALLY ON!
THE MACHINE! IT MOVES! KILL IT BEFORE-- EH?! OUR WEAPONS! THEY FLY FROM OUR HANDS!
WH...WHAT THE FLYIN' PHLEGM WAS THAT?
IT'S CALLED REVERSE MAGNETISM. AND IT'S JUST ONE OF THE HANDY DEVICES THIS SUIT IS EQUIPPED WITH. LIKE, FOR INSTANCE--
--BOOT-MOUNTED SHORT-RANGE AIR PRESSURE JETS!
SHOOSH!
AIIEEE?!?
6

FAR OUT!

BUT THE VC AIN'T EXACTLY PIKERS! THEY'RE SETTIN' UP AN *RGV7*-- A *BAZOOKA!* THINK YOUR REVERSE FRAMASAN CAN HANDLE THAT?

WELL, IT HASN'T BEEN WIDELY FIELD TESTED YET--

-- BUT ACCORDING TO THEORY--

CHOOM

--YEP!

BLAM

WHOOEE! JUST LOOK AT THEM PAJAMA-BOYS RUN! I STILL DON'T KNOW WHO YOU ARE, METAL MAN, BUT ANYONE WHO CAN ROUT THE VC LIKE THAT IS OKAY IN MY BOOK!

WAP

I APPRECIATE... THE CONFIDENCE, SOLDIER. BUT NOW... ABOUT THOSE BATTERIES...?

POWER... ALMOST DRAINED! CHEST FEELS LIKE ...IT'S ON FIRE!

7

HOWEVER, THE RECHARGING CONNECTIONS HAD BEEN JURY-RIGGED IN TIME, AND AS THE LAST WATTS OF ELECTRICITY HAD BEEN DRAINED FROM THE HELICOPTER'S BATTERIES...

THANKS, LIEUTENANT, I NEEDED THAT.

WE STILL GOT PROBLEMS, THOUGH. I KNOW THE WAY TO THE AMERICAN DEFENSE PERIMETER, BUT WE'LL HAVE TO WALK IT.

NO PROBLEM, LIEUTENANT, JUST HOP ON UP. WITH THIS SUIT ON, I CAN'T EVEN FEEL THE WEIGHT.

UH. DON'T MENTION IT.

AND WHILE MY LEG WOUND AIN'T BAD, IT IS GONNA SLOW US UP, ESPECIALLY IF THOSE VC COME BACK FOR--

WELL, OKAY. BUT IF WE'RE GONNA BE THIS INTIMATE, YOU'D BETTER START CALLIN' ME "RHODEY." MY FRIENDS DO.

ALL RIGHT, RHODEY. AND YOU CAN CALL ME IRON MAN.

"IRON MAN," HUH? I'D NEVER'VE GUESSED...

TIME HAD PASSED SLOWLY, AND AFTER AN HOUR'S TRUDGE THROUGH THE SWELTERING MAZE OF JUNGLE...

SAY, IRON MAN, YOU THINK WE COULD REST A SPELL? I MEAN, IT'S NOT LIKE I DON'T APPRECIATE THE RIDE--

--BUT AN EASY CHAIR YOU'RE NOT!

SURE, RHODEY, HERE YOU GO. I'LL JUST STAND IF YOU DON'T MIND.

I'VE GOT TO DO SOMETHING ABOUT THE FLEXIBILITY OF THIS ARMOR WHEN I GET BACK TO MY LAB!

8

SO TELL ME, TALL, DARK AN' BURNISHED, WHAT BRINGS YOU TO THE 'NAM?

WHAT-- OH, WELL, UM, I WAS HELPING A MAN NAMED TONY STARK WITH SOME EXPERIMENTS. YES, THAT'S IT.

MR. STARK WAS CAPTURED BY THE VIET CONG AND I, ER, HELPED HIM ESCAPE.

ONLY I SORT OF GOT LOST TRYING TO ESCAPE, MYSELF.

IT HAPPENS.

WANT A PUFF?

WELL, ACTUALLY, I'M TRYING TO CUT DOWN. BUT UNDER THE CIRCUMSTANCES, I DON'T SEE WHY NO--

-- OOPS! S-SORRY ABOUT THAT. I GUESS I HAVEN'T GOT AS MUCH CONTROL OVER THESE GLOVES AS I'D LIKE.

SAY WHAT?!

AW, MAN, THAT WAS MY LAST ONE! NOW I'LL HAVE TO GET BACK TO SAIGON!

PFFT

SPWEEEE

HUH?

SNIPER! WITH A SILENCER! TAKE COVER!

WHY?

9

WH-WH-WHADYOU MEAN, "WHY", FOOL! BECAUSE--

PFFT PFFT PFFT PFFT

SPLAK SPLINS

PKANK

-- CAUSE...

SKRRRUMP

KUHWOOMP

WELL, NOW, WHY DON'T YOU JUST FORGET I EVEN ASKED. : SHEESH :

SHALL WE GO?

THE JOURNEY HAD CONTINUED, DELIBERATELY, CAUTIOUSLY. AND WHEN ANOTHER HOUR HAD PASSED...

I'LL TRY TO RIG SOME OF THESE REEDS SO YOU CAN GET A DRINK, IRON MAN, AND THEN I THINK WE'D BETTER GET OUT OF HERE.

THESE BOMBED-OUT VILLAGES AREN'T ALWAYS DEAD.

AS A MATTER OF FACT, IT WAS SOMEWHERE AROUND HERE THAT THOSE ROCKETS CLIPPED MY CHOPPER'S TAIL, STRANGE...

AND THAT'S NOT THE ONLY ODD THING, RHODEY, UNLESS VIETNAMESE GEOGRAPHY BREAKS A LOT OF RULES.

10

BECAUSE IT LOOKS TO ME LIKE THIS STREAM IS COMING RIGHT OUT OF THAT TREE TRUNK!

THAT AIN'T NO TREE -- LOOK AT THE LINE ALONG THE GROUND!

YEP, IT'S JUST LIKE I THOUGHT-- CANVAS! THIS WHOLE BACK-DROP IS PART OF A FANCY CAMOUFLAGE!

BUT IF THE VIET CONG WOULD GO TO THIS MUCH TROUBLE, THEY MUST BE HIDING SOMETHING--

-- BIG!

NO FOOLIN'! THIS MUST BE THE ROCKET BASE THAT ZAPPED MY CHOPPER!

WE GOTTA GET BACK TO THE AMERICAN LINES AND CALL AN AIR STRIKE ON THIS PLACE BEFORE--

-- BLAST! WHAT'D I TELL YOU 'BOUT THESE "DEAD" VILLAGES? WE BEEN SUCKERED!

YES, THAT DOES SEEM TO RATHER LIMIT OUR OPTIONS!

BRRRRP BRRRP
KPOW
POW POW

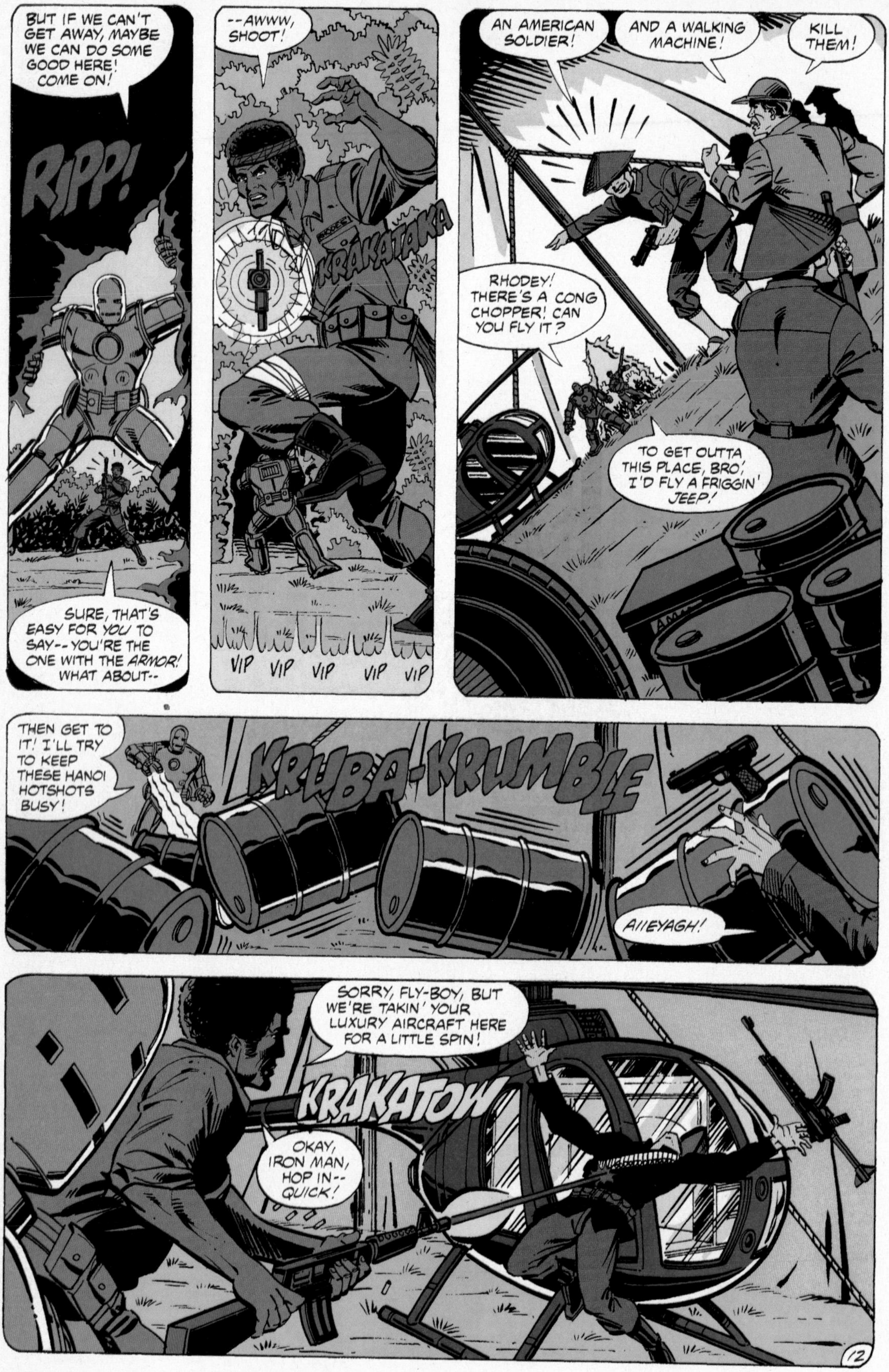
BUT IF WE CAN'T GET AWAY, MAYBE WE CAN DO SOME GOOD HERE! COME ON!
RIPP!
SURE, THAT'S EASY FOR YOU TO SAY-- YOU'RE THE ONE WITH THE ARMOR! WHAT ABOUT--
--AWWW, SHOOT!
KRAKATAKA
VIP VIP VIP VIP VIP
AN AMERICAN SOLDIER!
AND A WALKING MACHINE!
KILL THEM!
RHODEY! THERE'S A CONG CHOPPER! CAN YOU FLY IT?
TO GET OUTTA THIS PLACE, BRO', I'D FLY A FRIGGIN' JEEP!
THEN GET TO IT! I'LL TRY TO KEEP THESE HANOI HOTSHOTS BUSY!
KRUBA-KRUMBLE
AIIEYAGH!
SORRY, FLY-BOY, BUT WE'RE TAKIN' YOUR LUXURY AIRCRAFT HERE FOR A LITTLE SPIN!
KRAKATOW
OKAY, IRON MAN, HOP IN-- QUICK!
12

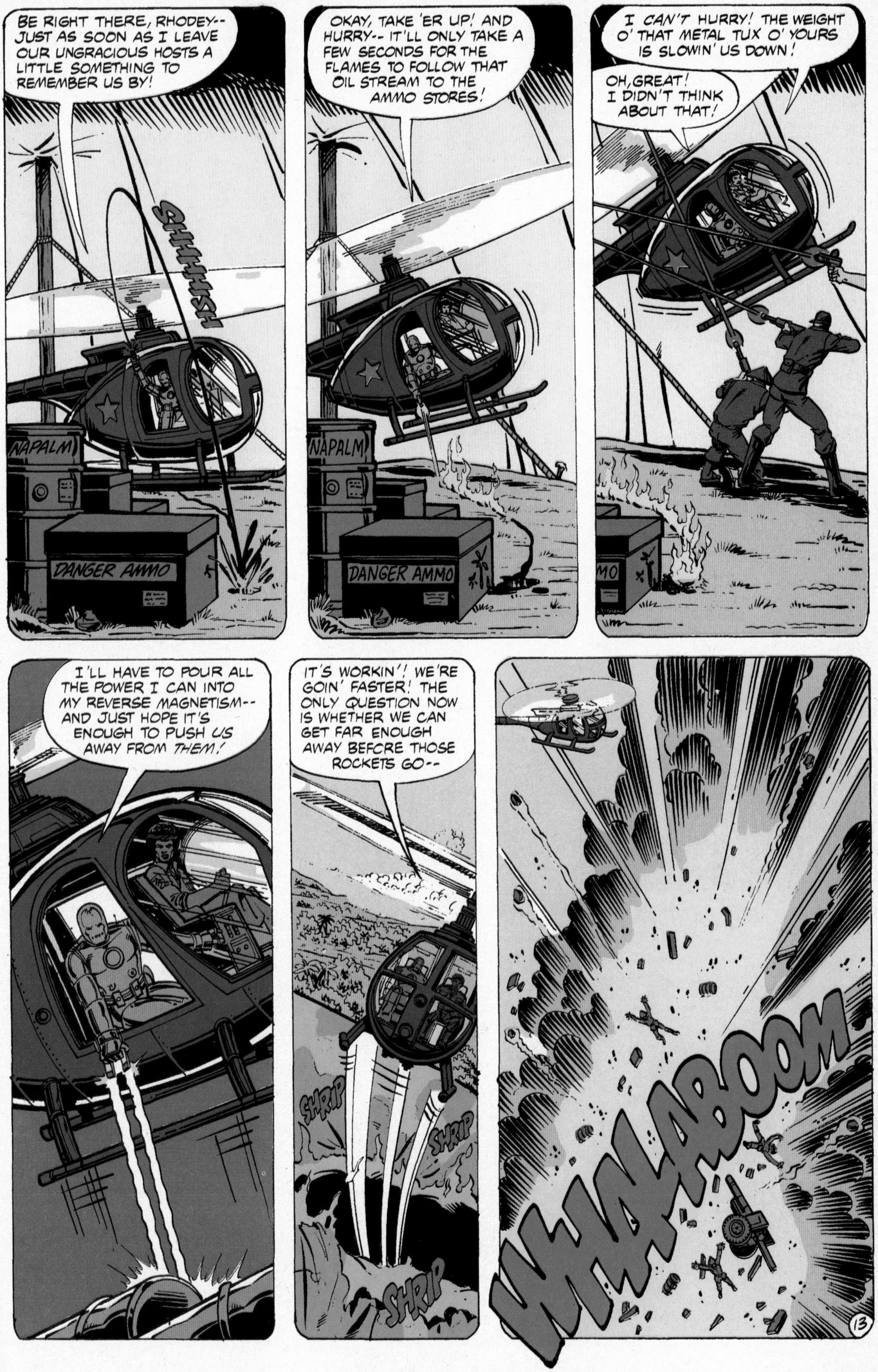
BE RIGHT THERE, RHODEY-- JUST AS SOON AS I LEAVE OUR UNGRACIOUS HOSTS A LITTLE SOMETHING TO REMEMBER US BY!
SHHHHSH!
NAPALM
DANGER AMMO
OKAY, TAKE 'ER UP! AND HURRY-- IT'LL ONLY TAKE A FEW SECONDS FOR THE FLAMES TO FOLLOW THAT OIL STREAM TO THE AMMO STORES!
NAPALM
DANGER AMMO
I CAN'T HURRY! THE WEIGHT O' THAT METAL TUX O' YOURS IS SLOWIN' US DOWN!
OH, GREAT! I DIDN'T THINK ABOUT THAT!
I'LL HAVE TO POUR ALL THE POWER I CAN INTO MY REVERSE MAGNETISM-- AND JUST HOPE IT'S ENOUGH TO PUSH US AWAY FROM THEM!
IT'S WORKIN'! WE'RE GOIN' FASTER! THE ONLY QUESTION NOW IS WHETHER WE CAN GET FAR ENOUGH AWAY BEFORE THOSE ROCKETS GO--
SHRIP
SHRIP
SHRIP
WHHABOOM
13

THE DEBRIS! LOOK OUT!

"LOOK OUT"?! WHADYA THINK I'M DOIN', TIN PANTS-- DRIVIN' THIS THING WITH MY EYES CLOSED?

BUT, WITHIN SECONDS...

IT...IT'S OVER! WE MADE IT!

YEAH. I JUST WISH WE HAD TIME TO GO BACK AN' PICK UP MY STOMACH.

AND THUS, A HALF-HOUR LATER, AT A RADAR INSTAL-LATION ALONG THE AMERICAN FORCES' NORTHERN DEFENSE PERIMETER...

BOGEY, CAPTAIN! COMIN' IN FROM THE COMMUNIST SECTOR!

THIS IS CAPTAIN HAYS! ALL UNITS TO FULL ALERT! LOOKS LIKE WE GOT US A VC CHOPPER COMIN' TO CALL!

AMERICAN LINES DEAD AHEAD, IRON MAN. WE'RE ALMOST HOME.

HOWEVER...

SHEEOOF

SOME HOMECOMING! THEY THINK WE'RE VIET CONG! THOSE ARE GROUND-TO-AIR ROCKETS!

OH, NO! NOT TWICE IN ONE DAY!

HEY, YOU COMBAT-HAPPY JOES, I'M AMERICAN! LIEUTENANT JAMES R. RHODES, U.S. MARINES!

SORRY, MISTER, YOU'LL HAVE TO DO BETTER THAN THAT, YOU'VE GOT FIVE SECONDS--THEN WE LOOSE ANOTHER VOLLEY!

UH...UH... WILSON PICKET! BIG MACS! UM... ER... MINI-SKIRTS!

14

NOT GOOD ENOUGH, CHARLIE. AND YOUR FIVE SECONDS ARE UP!

METS?

PENNANT?

AW, CRUD! THE METS'LL WIN A *PENNANT* BEFORE I CAN CONVINCE THESE JOKERS!

THEY'RE AMERICAN!

THE PASSAGE HAD BEEN EASY THEN, WITH A CODED SECURITY NUMBER ALLOWING THE PURLOINED HELICOPTER TO STOP BRIEFLY ON THE ROOF OF AN EXPERIMENTAL LAB STATION--

--AND TO DEPOSIT A MOST UNUSUAL PASSENGER THERE BEFORE HEADING SOUTHWARD TO SAIGON.

AFTERWHICH, AS THAT PASSENGER HAD RETURNED TO QUARTERS THAT NOW SEEMED SOMEHOW ALIEN...

MY TOP SECRET SECURITY STATUS HELPED ME AVOID EMBARRASSING QUESTIONS THIS TIME, BUT I THINK I'D BETTER STOCK UP ON EXCUSES.

MEANWHILE, THOUGH, IT SEEMS THIS CHEST PLATE IS ALL I NEED TO KEEP MY HEART BEATING-- I WON'T HAVE TO WEAR THE WHOLE SUIT OF ARMOR ALL THE TIME.

BUT WHATEVER I END UP DOING, I'VE A FEELING THAT, FROM THIS DAY ON...

I'LL PROBABLY BE NEEDING THEM IN THE FUTURE.

THOUGH I HAD BETTER TRIM THE PLATE DOWN A BIT, UNLESS I WANT TO BUY A WHOLE NEW WARDROBE JUST TO COVER IT!

...MY LIFE IS NEVER GOING TO BE THE SAME

15

THE NEXT FEW DAYS HAD PASSED IN SECLUSION FOR TONY STARK, AND IN RECUPERATION FOR JIM RHODES. UNTIL AT LAST...

I'M STILL KINDA WOBBLY, NURSE. MAYBE YOU BETTER HOLD ME A LITTLE TIGHTER, HMM?

BASE HOSPITAL SAIGON

NCY

LT. RHODES?

HOW DO YOU DO? I'M TONY STARK.

"STARK"? YOU THE GUY THAT IRON DUDE WAS TALKIN' ABOUT?

THAT'S RIGHT. HE TOLD ME ALL ABOUT HOW YOU HELPED HIM GET TO SAFETY, AND I WANTED TO THANK YOU.

I WOULD HAVE LOST A VERY CLOSE FRIEND IF IRON MAN HADN'T MADE IT.

MR. STARK, I THINK WE BOTH DID OUR SHARE O' SAVIN'.

NEVERTHELESS, YOU'RE A GOOD MAN. IF I EVER REQUIRE THE SERVICES OF A PILOT WHILE I'M HERE, I HOPE YOU'LL BE AVAILABLE.

AND IF YOU NEED A JOB WHEN THESE HOSTILITIES ARE OVER, PLEASE DON'T HESITATE TO GIVE ME A CALL.

THANKS FOR THE OFFER, MR. STARK. ONCE I FINISH CLEANIN' UP THESE JUNGLES FOR UNCLE SAM, I'LL SURE KEEP THAT IN MIND.

16

IN TIME, THE WAR FINALLY ENDED, AND TONY STARK HAD GONE ON TO HEAD THE GLOBE-SPANNING INDUSTRIAL CONGLOMERATE KNOWN AS STARK INTERNATIONAL-- ALL THE WHILE DEVELOPING AND REFINING THE ARMOR AND THE IDENTITY OF THE SUPER HERO CALLED IRON MAN.

ROXXON

WHILE JIM RHODES HAD PURSUED SEVERAL RATHER COLORFUL CAREERS BEFORE TAKING STARK UP ON HIS OFFER AND BECOMING HIS PRIVATE PILOT, HIS CHIEF AVIATION ENGINEER AND, ULTIMATELY--

-- HIS FRIEND...

HEY, TONY, BOSS!

WHA--OH. SORRY. GUESS I WAS DAYDREAMING.

WE'RE ALMOST TO DALLAS, YOU WANT TO TAKE US IN?

NO, THANKS. I'M A GOOD PILOT-- BUT I PREFER BEING FLOWN BY THE BEST.

AW, SHUCKS, CHIEF, YOU KEEP THAT UP YOU'RE GONNA TURN MY HEAD, AND UNTIL WE GET BACK ON THE GROUND--

--THAT COULD BE DOWNRIGHT DANGEROUS!

CUTE, RHODEY, REAL CUTE...

17

THE INVINCIBLE

IRON MAN®

DON'T MISS SHELL-HEAD'S **NEW STEALTH ARMOR!**

THE NOW-EBON AVENGER MUST RISK CAUSING AN **INTERNATIONAL CRISIS** BY SLIPPING INTO BERLIN TO SAVE THE WOMAN HE LOVES!

When millionaire industrialist *Tony Stark*, inventor extraordinaire, garbs himself in solar-charged, steel-mesh armor he becomes the world's greatest human fighting machine...

Stan Lee PRESENTS: THE INVINCIBLE IRON MAN ®

HIGH ABOVE THE MIDNIGHT MOUNTAINS OF EAST GERMANY FLIES A MAN.

AN IRON MAN.

CLAD IN POLARIZED, METAL-MESH ARMOR OF HIS OWN DESIGN, HE SOARS ALMOST SILENTLY, HIS POWERFUL BOOT JETS DAMPENED BY ADVANCED MICROBAFFLES--

-- EVEN AS AN INGENIOUS WAVE MODIFIER BENDS RADAR RAYS AROUND HIM, RENDERING HIM ELECTRONICALLY INVISIBLE, FOR HE KNOWS THAT DETECTION BY LOCAL AUTHORITIES WOULD ALMOST CERTAINLY END HIS DESPERATE MISSION HERE, AT THE COST OF TWO VERY SPECIAL LIVES: HIS OWN...

...AND THAT OF THE WOMAN HE LOVES!

ESCAPE FROM HEAVEN'S HAND!

DAVID MICHELINIE   JOHN ROMITA, JR.   BOB LAYTON   JOE ROSEN   GLYNIS WEIN   JIM SALICRUP   JIM SHOOTER
PLOT / WRITER   PENCIL ART   PLOT / FINISHED ART   LETTERS   COLORS   EDITOR   EDITOR-IN-CHIEF

THERE IT IS-- *DER HAND VON HIMMEL,* EAST GERMANY'S TOP SECRET RESEARCH COMPLEX!

AND SO FAR, MY PROTOTYPE "STEALTH" ARMOR IS PERFORMING PERFECTLY!

I REALIZED A NEED FOR SPECIALIZED ARMOR TO BE USED IN CLANDESTINE SITUATIONS AFTER RADAR TRACKED ME TO THE *STAR WELL* SPACE STATION.*

*BACK IN IRON MAN #143. --SALICRUP.

WHRRR

BUT I NEVER THOUGHT I'D BE TESTING MY BRAINCHILD LIKE THIS!

SNK SNK

SNK

OKAY, PRELIMINARY PHOTOGRAPHIC SURVEY IS COMPLETE, THOUGH IF YOU ASK ME, THOSE BUILDINGS LOOK AS PHONY AS A TWO DEUTSCHE-MARK BILL!

SO, IF I WANT TO FIND OUT WHETHER THERE'S MORE TO THIS PLACE THAN MEETS THE EYE, I GUESS IT'S INTO THE PROVERBIAL *LION'S DEN* FOR ME!

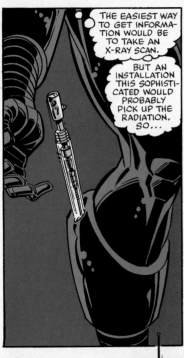

THE EASIEST WAY TO GET INFORMATION WOULD BE TO TAKE AN X-RAY SCAN.

BUT AN INSTALLATION THIS SOPHISTICATED WOULD PROBABLY PICK UP THE RADIATION, SO...

"...I'LL TRY SOMETHING A LITTLE DIFFERENT: A SONIC SCAN!"

FRRRING

THIS PROBE EMITS ULTRA-FREQUENCY SOUND WAVES, CREATING A PATTERN THAT SHOULD SEND BACK DETAILED PICTURES OF ANYTHING INSIDE THAT MOUNTAIN-- DOWN TO THE LAST PEBBLE!

AND THE PROCESS IS SO NEW THAT THE EAST GERMANS WOULD HAVE TO BE REALLY GOOD TO EVEN NOTICE IT!

THUS, AS IRON MAN ACTIVATES A SCAN RECEIVER IN HIS LEFT EPAULET, HE SMILES CONFIDENTLY.

PERHAPS...

HNH?!

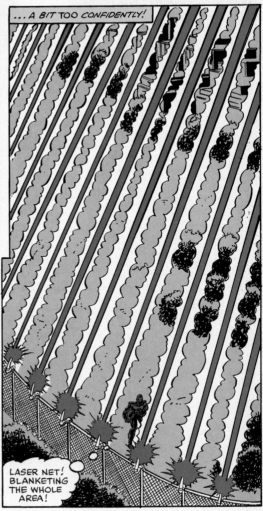

...A BIT TOO CONFIDENTLY!

LASER NET! BLANKETING THE WHOLE AREA!

"BLAST! THEY *ARE* GOOD!"

I'D BETTER GET THE PROBE BACK AND--

--EH? THAT SOUND!

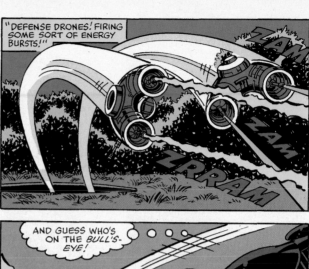

"DEFENSE DRONES! FIRING SOME SORT OF ENERGY BURSTS!'"

ZAM

ZRRAM

AND GUESS WHO'S ON THE *BULL'S-EYE!*

VRRAP

VDOW

THIS "STEALTH" ARMOR WAS DESIGNED TO UTILIZE EVERY BIT OF SPACE FOR DETECTION AND EVASION COMPONENTS! AND THAT MEANT GOING WITHOUT MY *REPULSOR RAYS*--

--OR ANY OTHER ACTIVE WEAPONRY! WHICH MEANS THAT IF I WANT TO STAY ALIVE, I'LL HAVE TO--

--IMPROVISE!

SHROFF

BOOT JETS ROAR--

--AS THEIR FULL RE-ACTIVE FORCE IS FOCUSED ON ONE OF THE ATTACKING DRONES--

WHOOOMP

--TO SEND IT SPINNING DIRECTLY INTO THE PATH OF THE SECOND!

I'VE RETRIEVED THE SONIC PROBE! NOW TO GET OUT OF HERE BEFORE ANY GUARDS SHOW UP--

--AND RECOGNIZE ME AS A POTENTIAL INTERNATIONAL INCIDEN--

--EYYAAAGGH!

SHRRAZZASH

THE LIMITED LASER RESISTANCE...OF MY REFRACTORY COATING...

...SHOULD'VE GOTTEN ME THROUGH THAT NET... WITH BARELY A SCRATCH!

BUT THOSE LASERS... TOO POWERFUL...

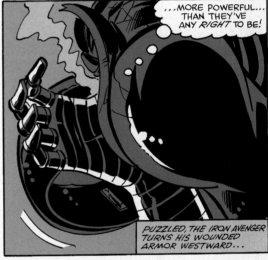

...MORE POWERFUL... THAN THEY'VE ANY RIGHT TO BE!

PUZZLED, THE IRON AVENGER TURNS HIS WOUNDED ARMOR WESTWARD...

...AND SOME TIME LATER HE ANGLES OVER THE OUTSKIRTS OF WEST BERLIN, BEGINNING A SHAKY DESCENT--

--TOWARDS THE SPRAWLING INDUSTRIAL PARK KNOWN AS STARK INTERNATIONAL, GERMAN DIVISION.

PURPOSEFULLY, HE PASSES ULTRA-MODERN OUTER BUILDINGS, MOVING INSTEAD TO THE ORIGINAL CORE OF THE COMPLEX--

--A BRICK-WALLED MUNITIONS FACTORY CONSTRUCTED DURING WORLD WAR II.

THAT MANUFACTORY HAS BEEN IDLE FOR MORE THAN A DECADE, AND THUS NO ONE IS THERE TO NOTICE AS IRON MAN SWOOPS DOWN TOWARDS A DORMANT SMOKE-STACK...

...AND THEN PLUNGES INTO IT!

THE 'STACK LEADS DIRECTLY TO A SERIES OF SECRET UNDERGROUND BUNKERS BUILT BY THE NAZIS--

--BUNKERS WHICH NOW SERVE AS PRIVATE LABORATORIES FOR THE MAN INSIDE THE IRON MAN ARMOR--

--TONY STARK.

UNG GUESS THOSE LASERS MESSED UP MY RETRACTION CIRCUITS.

NORMALLY, I WOULDN'T HAVE TO DO THIS BY HAND. BUT THEN, "NORMALLY"--

--I WOULDN'T EVEN *BE* HERE!

AS HE STRUGGLES TO REMOVE HIS DAMAGED ARMOR, TONY CONSIDERS CIRCUMSTANCE, AND CHANGE.

FOR SOME TIME, HE'D BEEN HAPPY, THE ROUGH SPOTS IN HIS LIFE SMOOTHED OVER BY THE LOVE HE SHARED WITH BETHANY CABE.

BUT WITH JARRING SUDDENNESS, THAT RELATIONSHIP HAD ALTERED, BETH HAD BECOME DISTANT, SECRETIVE. SHE'D GONE HER OWN WAY--

--PURSUING SOME MYSTERIOUS QUEST TO EUROPE.

AND IT HAD BEEN JUST DAYS BEFORE WHEN THE RESULTS OF THAT QUEST HAD BECOME KNOWN--

DAILY BUGLE

PRISONER IN E. GERMANY

--AS BETH HAD BEEN ARRESTED BEHIND THE IRON CURTAIN ON CHARGES OF ESPIONAGE!

THROUGH SOCIAL AND POLITICAL CONTACTS, TONY HAD SOUGHT INFORMATION. BUT THE ONLY DETAIL HE COULD FERRET OUT WAS THAT BETH HAD BEEN TAKEN TO AN EAST GERMAN SECURITY COMPLEX--

--ONE THAT HAD EUPHEMISTICALLY BEEN DUBBED "HEAVEN'S HAND."

HE HAD PULLED EVERY MARKER THEN, DRAWN ON EVERY BIT OF CONTROL HE HAD OVER THE INTERNATIONAL COMMUNITY--

--UP TO AND INCLUDING ATTEMPTS TO "RENT" INFLUENCE FROM CERTAIN AMBASSADORIAL CIRCLES, ALL TO BUILD ENOUGH PRESSURE TO FORCE BETH'S RELEASE.

HIS DIPLOMATIC ASSAULT HAD BEEN MIGHTY.

BUT HEAVEN'S HAND HAD BEEN MIGHTIER.

IF ANYTHING'S GOING TO GET BETH OUT OF THERE ALIVE, IT'S ME--ALONE!

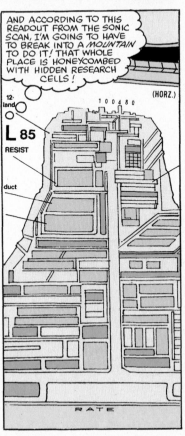

AND ACCORDING TO THIS READOUT FROM THE SONIC SCAN, I'M GOING TO HAVE TO BREAK INTO A MOUNTAIN TO DO IT! THAT WHOLE PLACE IS HONEYCOMBED WITH HIDDEN RESEARCH CELLS!

I GUESS I'D BETTER GET STARTED. EVERY MINUTE BETH STAYS IN THAT CAGE PUTS HER FARTHER AWAY FROM FREEDOM--

--AND TAKES ANOTHER BIG CHUNK OUT OF MY SOUL!

AN UNOFFICIAL ELEVATOR HUMS--

--AND MOMENTS LATER, SEVERAL LEVELS ABOVE, A DISGUISED DOORWAY SLIDES UPWARD--

--OPENING ONTO THE OCCASIONALLY USED OFFICE OF S.1'S AMERICAN-BASED OWNER AND PRESIDENT.

QUICKLY, THAT SELFSAME INDUSTRIALIST CROSSES THE ROOM, DEACTIVATES A POWERFUL ELECTRONIC LOCK MECHANISM--

--AND ENTERS A SHADOWED RECEPTION CUBICLE BEYOND, AN AREA DESERTED BUT FOR THE MAN HE HAD LEFT THERE SOME HOURS BEFORE: JIM RHODES, TONY STARK'S PRIVATE PILOT...

...AND HIS FRIEND.

RHODEY?

AW, C'MON, CHARLENE. ÷YAWN÷

MAN'S GOTTA SLEEP SOMETIME.

RHOOOODEY?

OH, AWRIGHT, JUST ONE MORE KISS AN' THEN-- HUH?

I THINK YOU'RE CUTE TOO.

OH. UH, H-HI, CHIEF!

I-I MUSTA DOZED OFF, JOCKEYIN' YOUR LEAR JET ACROSS THE ATLANTIC THIS MORNIN' KINDA POOPED ME OUT.

THAT'S UNDERSTANDABLE.

BUT RIGHT NOW I NEED YOU ALERT. IRON MAN JUST GOT BACK WITH SOME TECHNICAL DATA AND WE HAVE TO WORK IT INTO OUR PLANS.

WE MOVE TOMORROW NIGHT.

BUT BEFORE TOMORROW NIGHT COMES TOMORROW, AND AS THE SUN RISES OVER HEAVEN'S HAND, THAT DAY PROMISES TO BE AN EVENTFUL ONE INDEED...

MOVE ALONG, FRÄULEIN CABE--

--THE INTERROGATION ROOM IS JUST A LITTLE FURTHER.

IS THIS IT? IS THIS WHAT I'VE TRAVELED HALF A WORLD TO FIND? OR HAVE I BEEN TRICKED?

MAYBE... MAYBE I'VE FOOLED MYSELF...?

NO! SNAP OUT OF IT, LADY! YOU'VE COME THIS FAR, YOU MIGHT AS WELL SEE IT THROU--

--¡GASP!-

IT....IT'S TRUE! IT'S HIM! MY HUSBAND, ALEX--

--HE'S ALIVE!

B...BETH? I-IS THAT YOU?

BETHANY?!

LIEBLING! I-I'D GIVEN UP HOPE! OH, HOW I'VE MISSED YOU!

I'VE MISSED YOU, TOO, DARLING.

AND I HAVE! BUT WHY DO I FEEL SO STRANGE? ALEX IS MY HUSBAND, AND I LOVE HIM!

DON'T I...?

PLEASE, MAKE YOUR-SELF COMFORTABLE, MS. CABE. I AM *ANATOL DUBROV*, AN OFFICER OF THE RUSSIAN KGB. MAY I COUNT ON YOUR COOPERATION?

SIT ON IT.

I SEE.

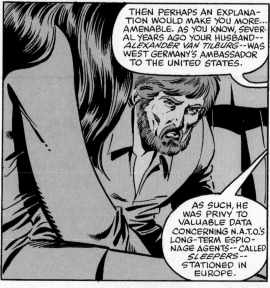

THEN PERHAPS AN EXPLANA-TION WOULD MAKE YOU MORE... AMENABLE. AS YOU KNOW, SEVER-AL YEARS AGO YOUR HUSBAND-- *ALEXANDER VAN TILBURG*--WAS WEST GERMANY'S AMBASSADOR TO THE UNITED STATES.

AS SUCH, HE WAS PRIVY TO VALUABLE DATA CONCERNING N.A.T.O.'S LONG-TERM ESPIO-NAGE AGENTS-- CALLED *SLEEPERS*-- STATIONED IN EUROPE.

TO GAIN THAT INFORMATION, WE ARRANGED FOR HERR VAN TILBURG'S "DEATH,"* AND THEN BROUGHT HIM TO THIS INSTALLATION.

WE HAD HOPED TO USE HIS KNOWN DEPENDENCE ON DRUGS TO PRY THE DATA FROM HIM.

*SEE IRON MAN #/28.-- J.S.

BUT OUR DOCTORS MISCALCULATED-- THE MAN'S MIND WAS MORE DELICATE THAN WE THOUGHT-- AND THE CHEMICALS THEY USED SENT HIM INTO A STATE RESEMBLING CATATONIA.

IT IS ONLY RECENTLY THAT HIS SENSIBILITIES HAVE RETURNED.

NATURALLY, WE DISCARDED THE PLAN TO USE DRUGS, AND SET ABOUT FINDING ANOTHER LEVER. YOU, MS. CABE, ARE THAT LEVER.

WE LEAKED INFORMA-TION THAT YOUR HUS-BAND WAS STILL ALIVE, AND COUNTED ON YOUR SENSE OF LOYALTY TO BRING YOU TO HIM.

"AND NOW THAT IT HAS, HERR VAN TILBURG WILL TELL US EVERYTHING WE WISH TO KNOW.

"OR HE WILL WATCH YOU SUFFER A FATE THAT EVEN *HIS* DRUG-ROTTED BRAIN COULD NEVER IMAGINE!"

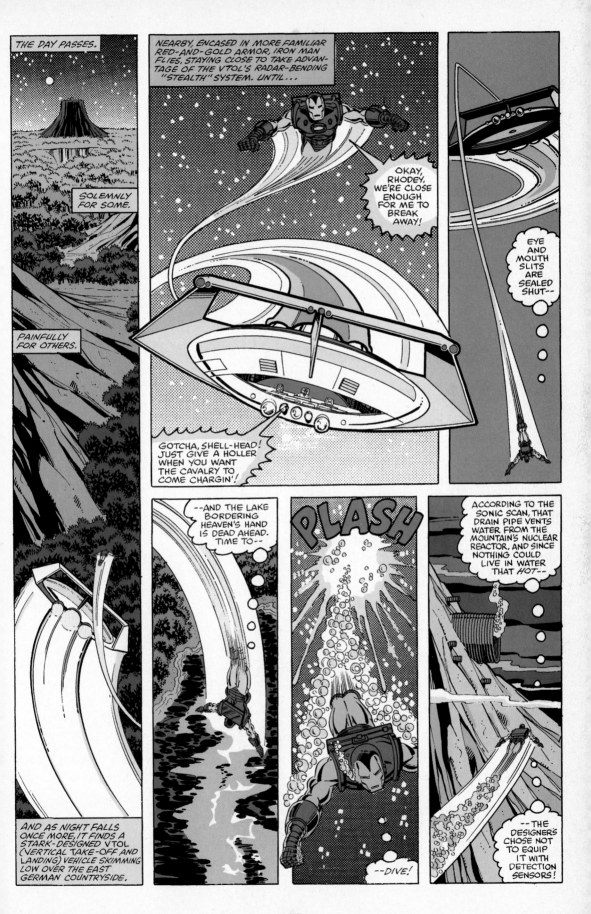

THE DAY PASSES.

SOLEMNLY FOR SOME.

PAINFULLY FOR OTHERS.

NEARBY, ENCASED IN MORE FAMILIAR RED-AND-GOLD ARMOR, IRON MAN FLIES, STAYING CLOSE TO TAKE ADVANTAGE OF THE VTOL'S RADAR-BENDING "STEALTH" SYSTEM. UNTIL...

OKAY, RHODEY, WE'RE CLOSE ENOUGH FOR ME TO BREAK AWAY!

GOTCHA, SHELL-HEAD! JUST GIVE A HOLLER WHEN YOU WANT THE CAVALRY TO COME CHARGIN'!

EYE AND MOUTH SLITS ARE SEALED SHUT--

AND AS NIGHT FALLS ONCE MORE, IT FINDS A STARK-DESIGNED VTOL (VERTICAL TAKE-OFF AND LANDING) VEHICLE SKIMMING LOW OVER THE EAST GERMAN COUNTRYSIDE.

--AND THE LAKE BORDERING HEAVEN'S HAND IS DEAD AHEAD. TIME TO--

PLASH

--DIVE!

ACCORDING TO THE SONIC SCAN, THAT DRAIN PIPE VENTS WATER FROM THE MOUNTAIN'S NUCLEAR REACTOR, AND SINCE NOTHING COULD LIVE IN WATER THAT HOT--

--THE DESIGNERS CHOSE NOT TO EQUIP IT WITH DETECTION SENSORS!

GUESS THEY NEVER EXPECTED A VISIT FROM SOMEONE WHO CARRIES HIS OWN TEMPERATURE-CONTROLLED ENVIRONMENT *WITH* HIM!

DEEP WITHIN THE HEART OF HEAVEN'S HAND IS A REACTOR ROOM. AND WITHIN THAT ROOM THERE RUNS A PIPELINE USED TO CARRY STEAM FROM WATER HEATED BY THE ATOMIC REACTOR. SAID STRUCTURE IS SO FAMILIAR THAT IT IS USUALLY IGNORED.

USUALLY.

SKRRRRRIP

LIEBER GOTT! THE PIPE-- IT HAS RUPTURED!

EVACUATE THE ROOM! SOUND AN ALARM!

GENERALLY, I'D PREFER TO KEEP A LOWER PROFILE WHEN SNEAKING INTO AN ENEMY STRONGHOLD!

BUT ALL THIS STEAM, COMBINED WITH THE RAMPANT PANIC, SHOULD COVER MY ENTRANCE JUST FINE!

THOUGH IT DOES MAKE FINDING THE DECONTAMI-NATION FACILITIES A BIT DIFFICULT.

AH! THERE THEY ARE!

NOW TO COOL DOWN MY ARMOR ENOUGH SO THAT IT WON'T FRY ME WHEN I TAKE IT OFF--

--AND THEN I CAN GET READY FOR THE DANGEROUS PART OF THIS MISSION!

METAL-MESH ARMOR IS QUICKLY DEPOLARIZED, THEN REMOVED. AND IN MOMENTS, A GOLDEN AVENGER IS REPLACED BY--

--MAJOR ANTON SHTARK, EAST GERMAN ARMY!

GUT ABEND, HERR MAJOR.

GUT ABEND, YA.

WELL, LOOKS LIKE MY DISGUISE PASSES MUSTER. NOW TO SEE IF I CAN USE IT TO FIND--

--THE AMERIKANISH FRÄULEIN, KORPORAL. WHERE IS SHE KEPT?

IN DETENTION BLOCK ZWÖLF, HERR MAJOR. TWO CORRIDORS OVER.

DANKE.

AND PRESENTLY, IN DETENTION BLOCK ZWÖLF...

--AM SORRY, MAJOR SHTARK. I CAN'T SEEM TO LOCATE THE AUTHORIZATION PAPERS YOU MENTION.

THEN PERHAPS, KAMERAD, YOUR EYESIGHT COULD BE IMPROVED--

--BY A MONTH'S DUTY LOOKING FOR DIRT IN THE OFFICERS' LATRINE!

I WILL SEE THAT THE PRISONER IS BROUGHT AROUND AT ONCE, MEIN HERR.

REMEMBER, YOU WILL TREAT YOUR INTERROGATOR WITH CIVILITY AND RESPECT AT ALL TIMES.

RIGHT. IN A PIG'S--

--EYE?

HI, BABE.

COME ALONG, FRÄULEIN. SCHNELL!

AND SOON, IN A DESERTED STOREROOM...

TONY! WHAT THE BLAZES ARE *YOU* DOING HERE?!

WHAT AM I *DOING*? WELL, YOUNG LADY, I WAS JUST IN THE NEIGHBORHOOD AND THOUGHT I'D DROP BY TO RESCUE YOU!

BLAST IT, TONY, I THOUGHT YOU *KNEW* ME BETTER!

DO YOU THINK I'D EVER BE CAPTURED IF I DIDN'T *WANT* TO BE? THIS WHOLE THING WAS A SET-UP! I ARRANGED IT ALL TO RESCUE ALEX!

ALEX?

THAT'S RIGHT--MY HUSBAND! HE'S STILL ALIVE!

WHEN I FOUND OUT, I *LET* MYSELF BE TAKEN, KNOWING THAT THE EAST GERMANS WOULD PROBABLY BRING ME HERE! I EVEN HIRED A BAND OF MERCENARIES TO ATTACK THIS INSTALLATION TO CREATE A DIVERSION SO I COULD BREAK ALEX *OUT*!

THEIR ATTACK IS SCHEDULED FOR TONIGHT! BUT WITH YOU HERE, THAT COMPLICATES MATTERS CONSIDERABLY!

YOUR... HUSBAND?

LOOK, WE DON'T HAVE TIME FOR THAT! JUST--

BDAM BLAM KRAK

GUNSHOTS!

IT'S THE MERCS! THEY'VE STARTED! AND THE EXPLOSIVES I HAD SMUGGLED IN FOR THE BREAKOUT--

--ARE BACK IN MY *CELL*!

THERE'S ONLY ONE CHANCE FOR ANY OF US TO GET OUT ALIVE NOW! YOU'VE GOT TO CHANGE, TONY!

CHANGE?

INTO IRON MAN!

GOOD LORD. YOU...YOU KNOW?

I'VE KNOWN FOR SOME TIME, TONY. EVEN BEFORE MADAME MASQUE CONFIRMED MY SUSPICIONS BACK IN CONNECTICUT.* WHEN YOU'RE SO CLOSE TO A PERSON, YOU CAN SENSE...WELL...

PLEASE, TONY. CHANGE?

*IN IM #139.--J.S.

I...I-I DON'T KNOW, BETH. THIS IS A LOT TO TAKE IN.

I'M...A LITTLE CONFUSED.

BUT NO. YOU'RE RIGHT, OF COURSE. FOR BETTER OR WORSE...

...YOU'RE RIGHT.

AND SO IT BEGINS.

A PROCESS MADE FAMILIAR BY DUPLICATION A THOUSAND TIMES, OVER MANY YEARS.

ONLY NOW, THE MOVEMENTS SEEM AWKWARD, SELF-CONSCIOUS, FOR NEW ELEMENTS HAVE ENTERED THE EQUATION:

TWO EYES, NOT MERELY WATCHING... BUT KNOWING.

THOUGH AS THE FINAL PIECES OF A COMPLICATED MAN ARE PUT IN PLACE, THAT TENSION IS EASED SOMEWHAT BY THE EQUATION'S APPARENT SOLUTION:

TWO HEARTS...

...ACCEPTING.

MOMENTS LATER, OUTSIDE OF A TOP-SECURITY INTERROGATION CHAMBER--

--TWO GUARDS WHO THOUGHT THEY HAD PULLED AN EASY ASSIGNMENT--

--FIND THEY WERE WRONG!

WAS DER TEUFFEL--?!

EIN FLIEGEN--

CHAKOOOM

THANKS, TONY-- BUT I'LL TAKE OVER FROM HERE.

I'VE GOT A SCORE TO SETTLE!

OKAY, DUBROV, NOW IT'S YOUR TURN TO COOPERATE! FALL DOWN--

P-DOW

P-DOW

--OR THE NEXT ONE GOES THROUGH YOUR HEAD!

COME ON, ALEX, WE'RE BREAKING OUT! CAN YOU WALK?

I... I'M NOT CERTAIN...

BLAST! I NEED SOME HELP, IRON MAN!

IRON MAN? I SAID I NEED HELP!

TONY STARK STANDS STILL, TORN BETWEEN LOYALTY AND JEALOUSY, NAILED BY A DEEP SENSE OF HATRED THAT SHOCKS HIM AS MUCH AS DISGUSTS HIM.

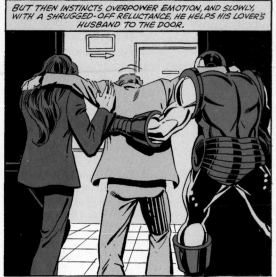

BUT THEN INSTINCTS OVERPOWER EMOTION, AND SLOWLY, WITH A SHRUGGED-OFF RELUCTANCE, HE HELPS HIS LOVER'S HUSBAND TO THE DOOR.

HOWEVER, IN THE ADJOINING CORRIDOR...

YOU'LL HAVE TO GET HIM OUT AS BEST YOU CAN, BETH! WE'VE GOT COMPANY!

AND IT'S UP TO ME TO "ENTERTAIN" THEM--

--WITH A FEW THOUSAND VOLTS OF ELECTRIC IRON MAN!

SHRRAZZH

THAT JOLT WASN'T ENOUGH TO DO PERMANENT DAMAGE, BUT IT SHOULD KEEP THESE COMRADES SNOOZING FOR A FEW HOURS!

NOW TO CYBERNETICALLY TRIGGER MY RADIO CIRCUITS, AND...

SNEAK THIEF TO HOVERBIRD! SNEAK THIEF TO HOVERBIRD! ALL RIGHT, RHODEY--

--BRING 'ER IN!

WHILE ELSEWHERE, EMERGING FROM A HOLE BLASTED BY HER MERCENARY TEAM...

LET'S GET OUT OF HERE!

I'M AFRAID THAT WON'T BE EASY, FRÄULEIN. THE SOLDIERS HAVE ANTCIPATED OUR ESCAPE ROUTE--

"--AND THEY'VE BLOCKED IT WITH TANKS!"

"NOT TO WORRY, HEINRICH--

"--WE'VE GOT A SECRET WEAPON OF OUR OWN!"

KRA-KA

PASH

"WE EVEN HAVE AN AIRLIFT COMING IN TO TAKE US HOME!"

AND, AS THE VTOL LANDS...

TERRIFIC. THE BOSS DIDN'T TELL ME I'D BE TAKIN' A WHOLE ARMY BACK!

OKAY, IRON MAN, THEY'RE ALL ABOARD!

BUT WITH THIS MUCH EXTRA WEIGHT, WE'RE GONNA BE MOVIN' A LITTLE SLOW!

JUST TAKE OFF, RHODEY--

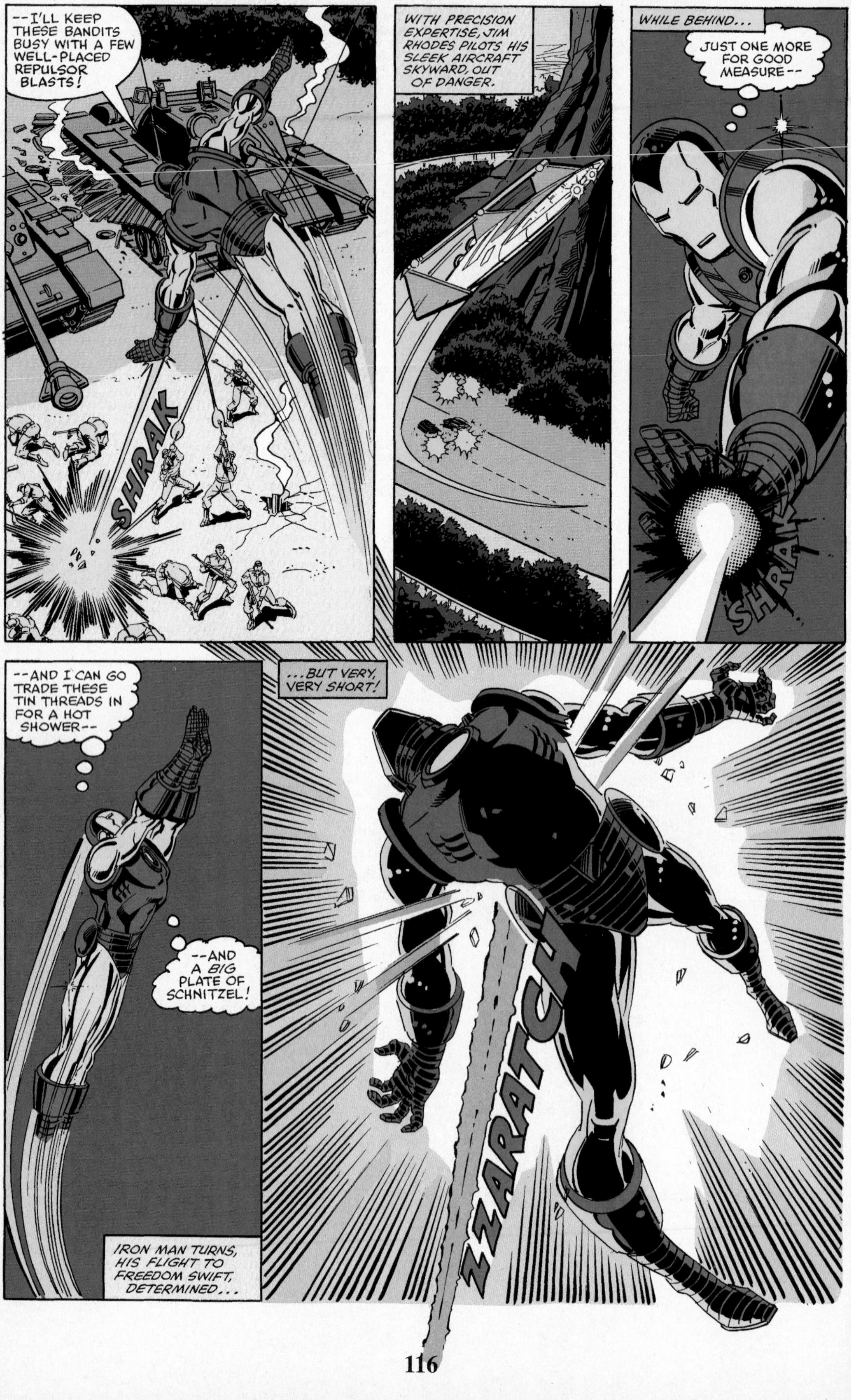

--I'LL KEEP THESE BANDITS BUSY WITH A FEW WELL-PLACED REPULSOR BLASTS!
SHRAK
WITH PRECISION EXPERTISE, JIM RHODES PILOTS HIS SLEEK AIRCRAFT SKYWARD, OUT OF DANGER.
WHILE BEHIND...
JUST ONE MORE FOR GOOD MEASURE--
SHRAK
--AND I CAN GO TRADE THESE TIN THREADS IN FOR A HOT SHOWER--
--AND A BIG PLATE OF SCHNITZEL!
IRON MAN TURNS, HIS FLIGHT TO FREEDOM SWIFT, DETERMINED...
...BUT VERY, VERY SHORT!
ZZARATCH

NUMBED AND UNCONSCIOUS, HE PLUMMETS, NOT KNOWING WHAT HIT HIM...

...OR SOME 600 METERS LATER, WHAT HE HITS!

CHAWHOMB

IT'S IRON MAN! H-HE'S BEEN SHOT! WE'VE GOT TO TURN AROUND!

SORRY, BETH, MY ORDERS ARE TO GET US BACK--AND THOSE ORDERS COME STRAIGHT FROM THE BOSS!

BUT IRON MAN IS--

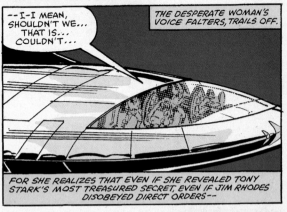

--I-I MEAN, SHOULDN'T WE... THAT IS... COULDN'T...

THE DESPERATE WOMAN'S VOICE FALTERS, TRAILS OFF.

FOR SHE REALIZES THAT EVEN IF SHE REVEALED TONY STARK'S MOST TREASURED SECRET, EVEN IF JIM RHODES DISOBEYED DIRECT ORDERS--

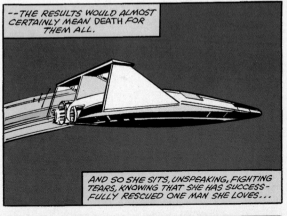

--THE RESULTS WOULD ALMOST CERTAINLY MEAN DEATH FOR THEM ALL.

AND SO SHE SITS, UNSPEAKING, FIGHTING TEARS, KNOWING THAT SHE HAS SUCCESSFULLY RESCUED ONE MAN SHE LOVES...

...ONLY TO HELPLESSLY LOSE ANOTHER.

117

AND BELOW...

LOOK AT HIM. ONE OF THE MIGHTIEST OF THE MIGHTY. AN AVENGER--

--DROPPED BY A SINGLE BLAST FROM *MY* HAND!

--THE LIVING LASER!

:HEH: HE CAME LOOKING FOR A WOMAN, HIS EMPLOYER'S GIRLFRIEND--

--LITTLE REALIZING THAT HE'D FIND *ME* AS WELL!

BUT HE'LL LEARN SOON ENOUGH. FOR HE'LL AWAKEN...

...ONLY TO *DIE!* TO FALL WITH BURNING FINALITY BEFORE THE UNPARALLELED POWER OF--

NEXT ISSUE:
UH, WOULDJA BELIEVE...
THE LIVING LASER?

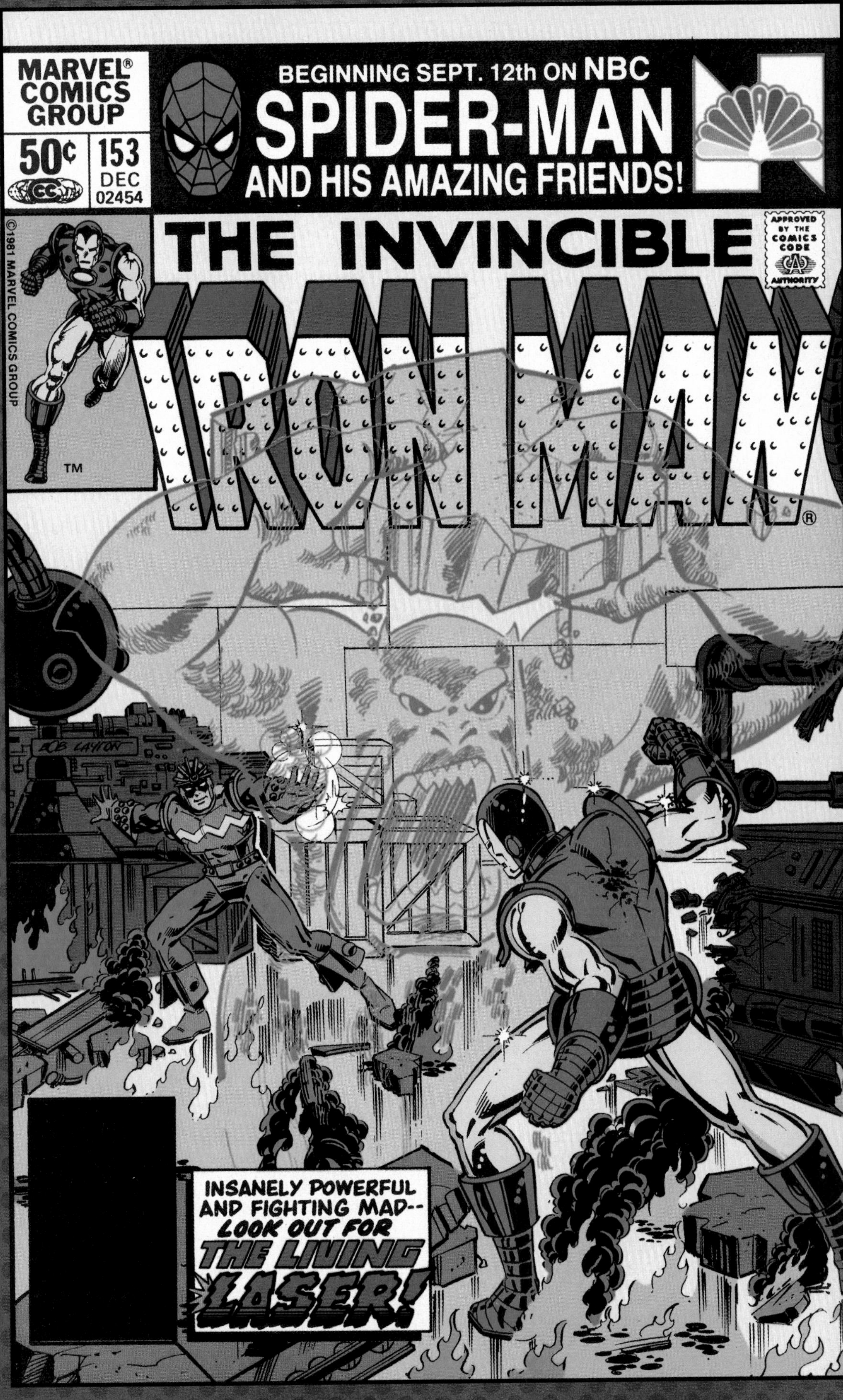

MARVEL® COMICS GROUP
50¢
153
DEC
02454
BEGINNING SEPT. 12th ON NBC
SPIDER-MAN
AND HIS AMAZING FRIENDS!
THE INVINCIBLE
IRON MAN®
APPROVED BY THE COMICS CODE AUTHORITY
©1981 MARVEL COMICS GROUP
TM
INSANELY POWERFUL AND FIGHTING MAD-- LOOK OUT FOR THE LIVING LASER!

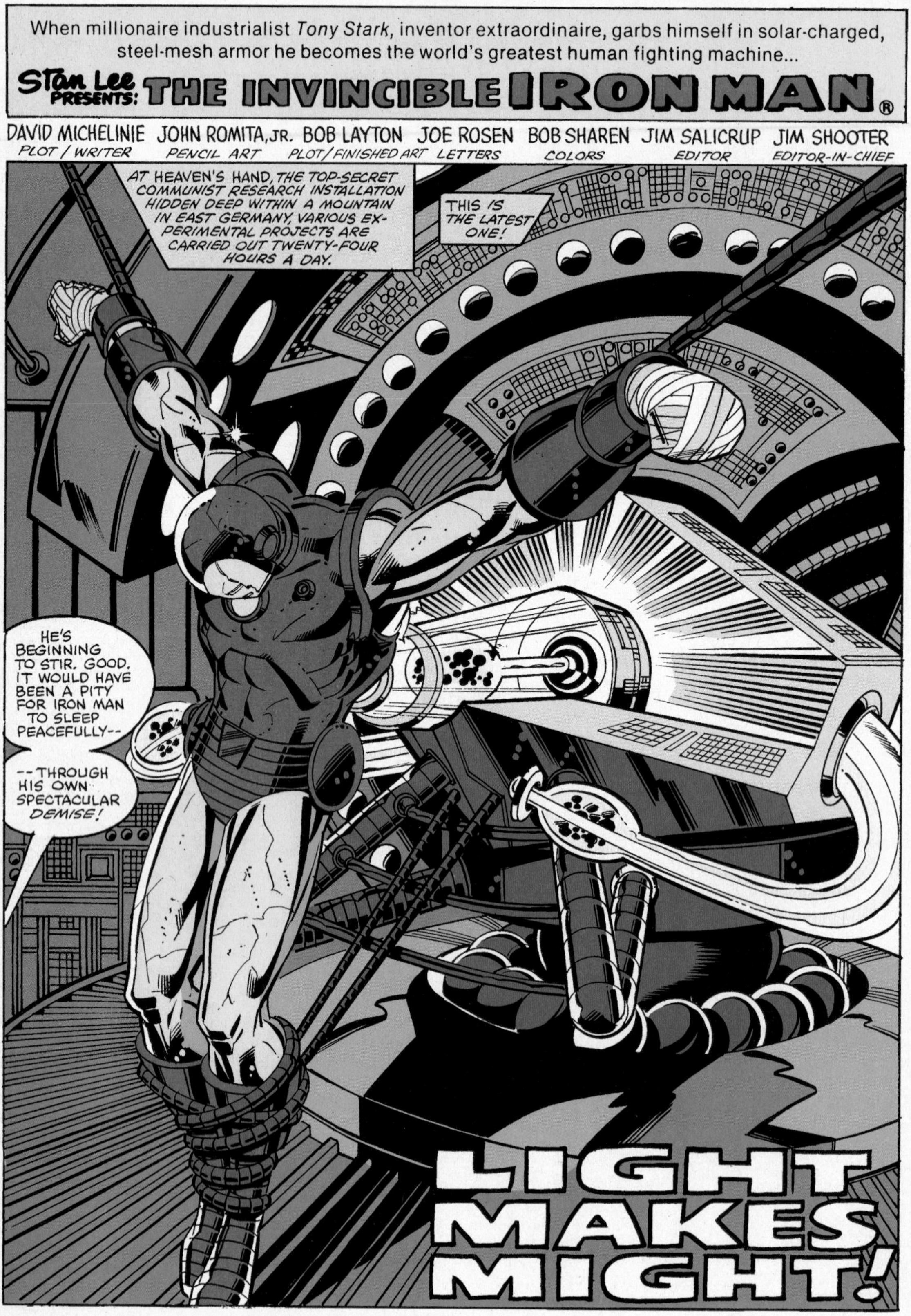
When millionaire industrialist Tony Stark, inventor extraordinaire, garbs himself in solar-charged, steel-mesh armor he becomes the world's greatest human fighting machine...
Stan Lee PRESENTS: THE INVINCIBLE IRON MAN®
DAVID MICHELINIE PLOT / WRITER JOHN ROMITA, JR. PENCIL ART BOB LAYTON PLOT/FINISHED ART JOE ROSEN LETTERS BOB SHAREN COLORS JIM SALICRUP EDITOR JIM SHOOTER EDITOR-IN-CHIEF
AT HEAVEN'S HAND, THE TOP-SECRET COMMUNIST RESEARCH INSTALLATION HIDDEN DEEP WITHIN A MOUNTAIN IN EAST GERMANY, VARIOUS EXPERIMENTAL PROJECTS ARE CARRIED OUT TWENTY-FOUR HOURS A DAY.
THIS IS THE LATEST ONE!
HE'S BEGINNING TO STIR. GOOD. IT WOULD HAVE BEEN A PITY FOR IRON MAN TO SLEEP PEACEFULLY--
--THROUGH HIS OWN SPECTACULAR DEMISE!
LIGHT MAKES MIGHT!

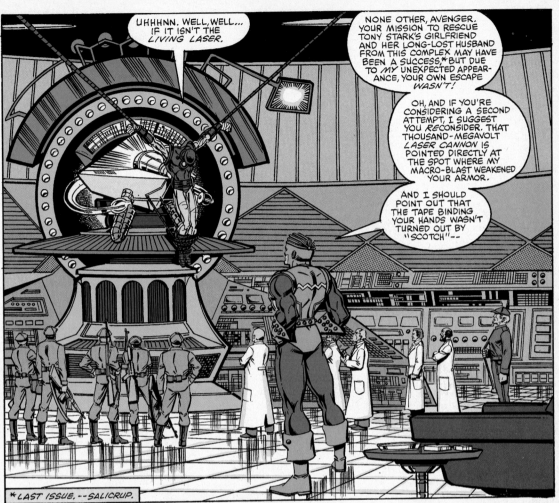

UHHHNN. WELL, WELL... IF IT ISN'T THE *LIVING LASER.*

NONE OTHER, AVENGER. YOUR MISSION TO RESCUE TONY STARK'S GIRLFRIEND AND HER LONG-LOST HUSBAND FROM THIS COMPLEX MAY HAVE BEEN A SUCCESS,* BUT DUE TO *MY* UNEXPECTED APPEARANCE, YOUR OWN ESCAPE *WASN'T!*

OH, AND IF YOU'RE CONSIDERING A SECOND ATTEMPT, I SUGGEST YOU *RECONSIDER.* THAT THOUSAND-MEGAVOLT *LASER CANNON* IS POINTED DIRECTLY AT THE SPOT WHERE MY *MACRO-BLAST* WEAKENED YOUR ARMOR.

AND I SHOULD POINT OUT THAT THE TAPE BINDING YOUR HANDS WASN'T TURNED OUT BY "*SCOTCH*"--

*LAST ISSUE. --SALICRUP.

--IT'S *AVIATION TAPE,* OF THE SORT USED TO ATTACH WINGS TO AIRCRAFT--

--AND AS SUCH, IS STRONG ENOUGH TO RESIST EVEN THE FLEXING OF *YOUR MIGHTY PINKIES.*

SO THAT ACTIVATING YOUR MUCH-VAUNTED RE-PULSOR RAYS WOULD RESULT ONLY IN BLOWING YOUR OWN FINGERS OFF! AND IF YOU'RE THINKING OF *YANKING* THOSE CABLES LOOSE--

--DON'T. OTHERS CONNECT YOUR FEET TO THE CANNON'S TRIGGER, AND THE SLIGHTEST MOVEMENT WOULD... BUT I'M SURE YOU GET THE PICTURE.

I DO -- GRAPHICALLY! IT'S GOING TO TAKE A STROKE OF GENIUS TO GET OUT OF THIS !

SO I'D BETTER KEEP THE LASER BUSY WHILE I START STROKING!

121

YOU'VE ALWAYS BEEN A CROOK, LASER, A THIEF. SO WHY TURN POLITICAL NOW?

I HAVEN'T. I'M HERE BECAUSE--

--ⵌAHEMⵌ THIS BUSINESS IS OF A PRIVATE NATURE, GENTLEMEN. IF YOU'LL EXCUSE US...?

I AM SORRY, HERR PARKS, BUT WE MUST REMAIN, OUR ORDERS SAY--

YOU NOW HAVE OTHER ORDERS!

SZZARASH

"MINE!"

Y-YAWHOL! W-WE HAVE NEW ORDERS, DON'T WE, HEINZ?

S-SOUNDS GOOD TO ME, ERICH!

W-WE WILL WAIT OUTSIDE, YA?

EXCELLENT. NOW, I MIGHT AS WELL MAKE MYSELF COMFORTABLE. MY STORY IS A FASCINATING ONE--

--AND I'D LIKE TO ENJOY IT AS MUCH AS I'M SURE YOU WILL.

AS YOU WELL KNOW, I WAS BORN *ARTHUR PARKS*, AND LIVED THE HUMBLE EXISTENCE OF A RESEARCH SCIENTIST--

--UNTIL MY BRILLIANT DISCOVERIES IN LASER TECHNOLOGY LED ME TO MORE FULFILLING, AND REWARDING, PURSUITS.

READ THAT: *CRIME!*

BUT LIFE HAS A *CRUEL* STREAK--

--AND SEEMS TO GENERATE AS MANY SUPER-POWERED *HEROES* AS IT DOES *VILLAINS...*

"WHICH IS WHY I AGREED WHEN *COUNT NEFARIA* OFFERED TO *DOUBLE* MY POWER IN EXCHANGE FOR MY HELP IN DEFEATING THE *AVENGERS.**

SEE AVENGERS #164-166.--J.S.

"FOR AWHILE IT WORKED. I HELD MY OWN AGAINST THEM ALL--

"--UNTIL SUDDENLY, MY AUGMENTED ABILITIES *FADED...*AND I REALIZED I'D BEEN TRICKED!

"NEFARIA'S POWER BOOST HAD BEEN A TEMPORARY RUSE BY WHICH HE CREATED ENERGY TEMPLATES OF MY CELLULAR STRUCTURE, GUIDES HE USED TO INCREASE HIS *OWN* STRENGTH!

"BUT THE EXPERIMENT ULTIMATELY *FAILED*-- WE WERE BOTH DEFEATED! AND I WAS LUCKY TO ESCAPE ALIVE. OR RATHER--

"--*BARELY* ALIVE! FOR I SOON DISCOVERED THAT MY METABOLISM HAD BEEN ALTERED, AND THAT I WAS ABSORBING ENERGY CONSTANTLY AND INVOLUNTARILY FROM ANY SOURCE OF LIGHT!

"I COULD RELEASE SMALL AMOUNTS IN THE FORM OF LASER-BLASTS, BUT NEVER ENOUGH TO FORESTALL AN INEVITABLE, AND *DEADLY*, OVERLOAD!

"IT WAS THEN THAT I WAS APPROACHED BY EAST GERMAN AGENTS. THEIR INTELLIGENCE NETWORK HAD LEARNED OF MY PLIGHT, AND THEY OFFERED ME AN ALTERNATIVE.

"IT SEEMS THAT RUSSIA HAD PUT A NUMBER OF *FAÇADE* SATELLITES IN ORBIT OVER THE LAST FEW YEARS, DESIGNATED AS 'COMMUNICATIONS APPARATUS'--

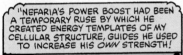

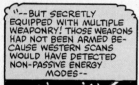

"--BUT SECRETLY EQUIPPED WITH MULTIPLE WEAPONRY! THOSE WEAPONS HAD NOT BEEN ARMED BECAUSE WESTERN SCANS WOULD HAVE DETECTED NON-PASSIVE ENERGY MODES--"

"--BUT ONCE THE SATELLITES HAD BEEN ACCEPTED BY THE WORLD COMMUNITY, THE RUSSIANS PLANNED TO ARM THEM BY TRANSMITTING MASSIVE AMOUNTS OF LASER ENERGY TO ONBOARD RECEPTORS."

"AND SINCE I AM, QUITE LITERALLY, A *LIVING LASER*, THE SCIENTISTS HERE THOUGHT TO DRAIN THAT ENERGY FROM ME, ACTIVATING THEIR WEAPONS--"

--AND, INCIDENTALLY, SAVING MY LIFE!

AND THE THOUGHT OF BETRAYING YOUR OWN COUNTRY DOESN'T BOTHER YOU?

IT DOES, A BIT.

BUT THE THOUGHT OF *DYING* BOTHERS ME A GREAT DEAL MOR--

--EH? THE METAL TAPE BINDING YOUR HANDS! IT'S--

...MELTING?!

VERY OBSERVANT, PARKS!

WHILE YOU WERE SPOUTING OFF--

--I WAS CYBERNETICALLY CHANNELING ELECTRIC HEAT TO THE EXTERIOR SURFACES OF MY GAUNTLETS! YOUR SUPER-TAPE IS DISSOLVING, COMING APART! AND JUST GUESS WHO'S GOING TO BE--

CHRRRIP

CH-CHP

CHK

--NEXT!

SHRAK SHRAK

GOT TO ANGLE MY REPULSOR RAYS JUST RIGHT, SEVER THESE STEEL CABLES--

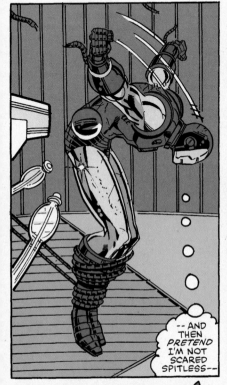

-- AND THEN *PRETEND* I'M NOT SCARED SPITLESS--

--WHILE I TRY TO PULL MYSELF INTO A QUICK-TUCK POSITION--

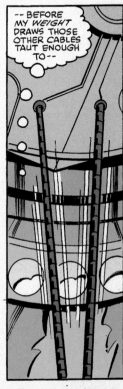

--BEFORE MY *WEIGHT* DRAWS THOSE OTHER CABLES TAUT ENOUGH TO--

FRRAK--

⸢ WHEW ⸣

--KRRROW

HEAVEN'S HAND TREMBLES...

125

...WHILE MILES DISTANT, THE RUMBLING ENGINES OF A VERTICAL TAKE-OFF AND LANDING VEHICLE SOFTEN--

--AS THAT UNIQUE CRAFT BEGINS ITS DESCENT TOWARDS STARK INTERNATIONAL'S WEST BERLIN AIRFIELD--

--UNDER THE EXPERT HAND OF MR. STARK'S PRIVATE PILOT, JIM RHODES...

IT'S A GOOD THING I RADIOED AHEAD FOR AN EMERGENCY TEAM, BETH--

--THIS GUY'S IN BAD SHAPE! JUST WHO IS HE, ANYHOW? HE SURE DON'T LOOK LIKE ONE O' YOUR MERCS!

HE'S NOT.

HE'S THE REASON I LET MYSELF BE TAKEN TO HEAVEN'S HAND IN THE FIRST PLACE, AND THE REASON I HIRED THOSE MERCENARIES TO BREAK US OUT, HE'S MY HUSBAND.

OH, WELL THAT EXPLAINS--

-- SAY WHAT?!

YOU MEAN ALL THE TIME YOU BEEN KEEPIN' COMPANY WITH THE BOSS, YOU'VE BEEN MARRIED? JUST WHAT KINDA GAMES YOU PLAYIN', LADY?

LOOK, RHODEY, I THOUGHT ALEX WAS DEAD! HOW WAS I SUPPOSED TO KNOW HE'D BEEN KIDNAPPED BY--

--OH, BLAST IT, WE DON'T HAVE TIME FOR THIS! WE'VE GOT TO GET ALEX TO THE INFIRMARY AND--

I'M SORRY, MS. CABE, BUT THIS MAN IS SUFFERING FROM EXTREME EXHAUSTION AND MALNUTRITION.

HE NEEDS A HOSPITAL.

BUT TAKING HIM TO A GERMAN HOSPITAL WOULD LEAVE HIM TOO VULNERABLE!

RHODEY, YOU'VE GOT TO FLY US BACK TO THE STATES! I HAVE CONNECTIONS THERE AND--

HOLD ON, LADY! I TAKE ORDERS FROM ONE MAN-- TONY STARK!

AND HE TOLD ME TO GET YOU TO SAFETY-- ONLY YOU! SO UNTIL I HEAR DIFFERENT, I'M--

RHODEY!

PLEASE?

THE MOMENT STRETCHES-- TENSE, SILENT AND ANGRY--

--UNTIL...

AW, SHOOT. GO ON AN' GET 'IM ON BOARD.

JUST DON'T EXPECT THE "FRIENDLY SKIES" TREATMENT, Y'HEAR?

LEASTWAYS NOT 'TIL I'VE HAD A LONG TALK WITH THE BOSS!

I FEEL TERRIBLE.

BUT I CAN WORRY ABOUT CONVALESCENCE LATER! THE LASER'S STUNNED--

--AND I'VE GOT TO PULL MYSELF FREE OF THESE CABLES BEFORE THOSE SOLDIERS HE SENT AWAY DECIDE TO--

ACHTUNG!

NUTS.

THE AMERIKANISCH WARRIOR! HE HAS ESCAPED!

ATTACK! QUICKLY! WE MUST RECAPTURE HIM!

SORRY, KAMERADEN--

EYIGE!

HURENSOHN!

VAS DER TEUFEL--?!

--BUT I CAN'T ALLOW THAT!

128

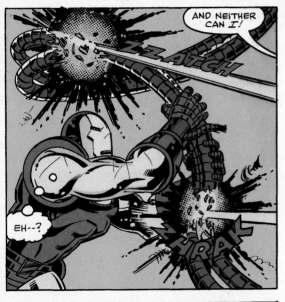

AND NEITHER CAN *I*!

EH--?

YOU'RE *MINE*, AVENGER!

FAKAM

MY ARMOR HAS LIMITED *LASER RESISTANCE*-- I CAN PROBABLY TAKE ANYTHING PARKS DISHES OUT, SHORT OF A *DIRECT HIT!*

BUT LET'S SEE IF HE CAN SAY THE SAME FOR A *REPULSOR BLAST!*

UNFORTUNATELY, WITH THE AID OF A *COUNTER-FREQUENCY LASER SHIELD*--

--HE *CAN!*

YOUR WEAPONS ARE *WORN*, IRON MAN--

--AND THEY'RE *TIRED!*

BUT I'VE *EXPANDED* THE VISTAS OF MY LASER CAPABILITIES!

FOR EXAMPLE: THE HUMAN *EYE* PERCEIVES OBJECTS BY THE *LIGHT* THEY REFLECT--

--SO BY USING LASER ENERGY TO *BEND* LIGHT AROUND ME, I CAN DO--

--*THIS!*

HE'S VANISHED! OR AT LEAST, HE *APPEARS* TO HAVE VANISHED!

BUT THAT'S ONLY TO THE *HUMAN EYE!*

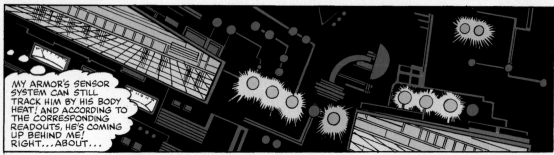

MY ARMOR'S SENSOR SYSTEM CAN STILL TRACK HIM BY HIS BODY HEAT! AND ACCORDING TO THE CORRESPONDING READOUTS, HE'S COMING UP BEHIND ME! RIGHT...ABOUT...

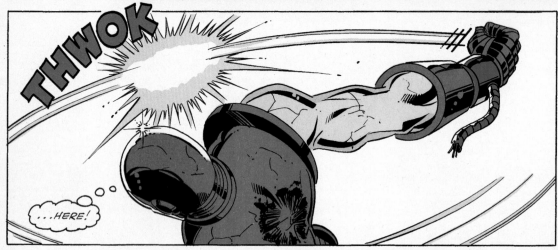

THWOK

...HERE!

WHHHAKASH

THE LASER DIDN'T EXPECT THAT!

I'VE GOT TO PRESS THE ADVANTAGE, USE MY BOOT SKATES TO MOVE IN FOR--

--EH?

YOU'VE MADE A GRAVE MISTAKE, IRON MAN, IN THINKING ME AN *EASY* OPPONENT! MY LASER LIGHT CAN SHEAR THROUGH TILE, THROUGH CONCRETE, EVEN SOLID STEEL!

MUCH LIKE THE COMPONENTS OF THIS FLOOR!

OR HADN'T YOU--

"--NOTICED!"

KRABASH

FRAGILE

AND NOW THE COUP DE GRACE! BY USING LIGHT ENERGY TO EXCITE ELECTRONS IN THE VERY AIR, I CAN MAKE THEM MOVE FASTER! ENOUGH TO CREATE--

--FIRE!

THESE FLAMES WON'T HURT ME--NOT IF I SLIDE THE PLEXIGLASS SHIELDS OVER MY EYE AND MOUTH SLITS, AND TURN ON MY INTERIOR OXYGEN SUPPLY!

BUT THIS INSTALLATION'S *WORK FORCE* COULD BE IN REAL DANGER!

HAVE TO OVERRIDE MY SAFETY CIRCUITS, BUILD UP PRESSURE IN THE FIRE EMERGENCY DUCTS OF MY CUFFS AND EPAULETS--

--SO THAT WHEN I FINALLY RELEASE THE FLAME-RETARDANT FOAM THAT'S STORED IN THEM--

--IT'LL SPRAY OVER A WIDE ENOUGH AREA TO DAMPEN THIS MAN-MADE HOLOCAUST!

GOOD! IT'S WORKING!

NOW TO CUT THAT RAVING LIGHT-MASTER DOWN TO SIZE--

--BY SENDING OUT A BEAM OF INTENSE *MAGNETISM* FROM MY CHEST-MOUNTED LENS SYSTEM--

"--ONE STRONG ENOUGH TO BRING DOWN A BIG SECTION OF THE *FLOOR* FROM THE ROOM ABOVE! HOPEFULLY--

WHA--?!

"--THE SECTION THE LIVING LASER IS *STANDING* ON!"

KERRASH

IT'D SERVE THAT LUNATIC RIGHT IF I STARTED A FIRE AROUND *HIM!*

BUT I GUESS I'LL HAVE TO SETTLE FOR--

132

GRRREAARRGH

WHAT THE BLOODY--

PRRUNCH

SHRAK

WHATEVER THAT IS, I'VE GOT TO HIT IT WITH A QUICK REPULSOR BLAST, BUY SOME TIME TO--

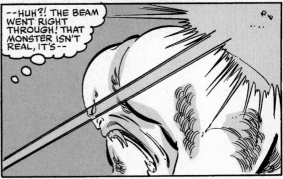

--HUH?! THE BEAM WENT RIGHT THROUGH! THAT MONSTER ISN'T REAL, IT'S--

BY NOW YOU'VE PROBABLY GUESSED THAT MY "COHORT" IS MERELY A HOLOGRAM--

--CREATED BY LASER LIGHT AS A DIVERSION TO HELP ME END THIS CONFLICT SWIFTLY! SO TELL ME, AVENGER, HOW DOES IT FEEL TO BE--

--BLIND!

PHASH

WHNG?!

I WOULDN'T KNOW, PARKS!

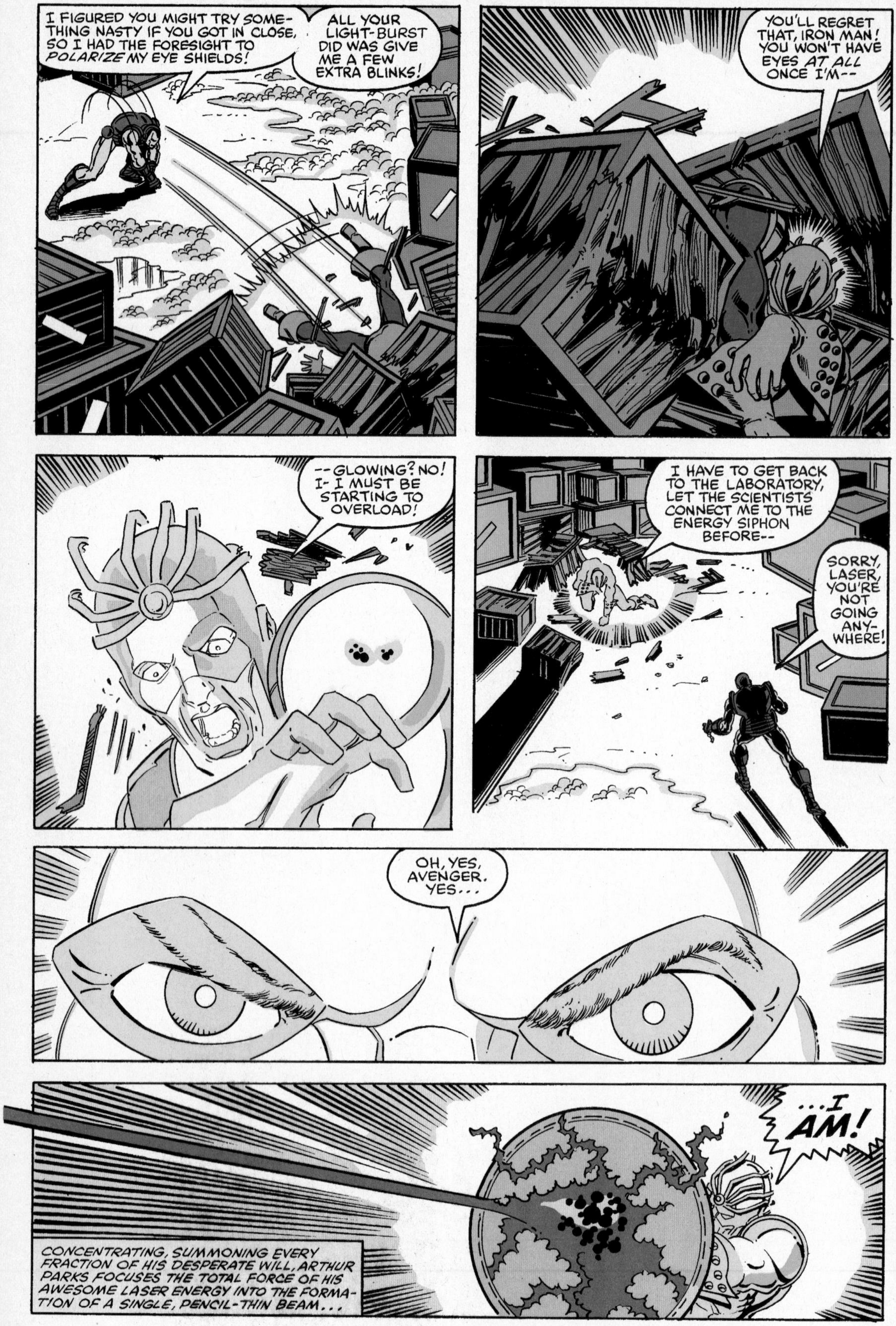
I FIGURED YOU MIGHT TRY SOMETHING NASTY IF YOU GOT IN CLOSE, SO I HAD THE FORESIGHT TO *POLARIZE* MY EYE SHIELDS!
ALL YOUR LIGHT-BURST DID WAS GIVE ME A FEW EXTRA BLINKS!
YOU'LL REGRET THAT, IRON MAN! YOU WON'T HAVE EYES *AT ALL* ONCE I'M--
--GLOWING? NO! I- I MUST BE STARTING TO OVERLOAD!
I HAVE TO GET BACK TO THE LABORATORY, LET THE SCIENTISTS CONNECT ME TO THE ENERGY SIPHON BEFORE--
SORRY, LASER, YOU'RE NOT GOING ANYWHERE!
OH, YES, AVENGER. YES...
...I *AM!*
CONCENTRATING, SUMMONING EVERY FRACTION OF HIS DESPERATE WILL, ARTHUR PARKS FOCUSES THE TOTAL FORCE OF HIS AWESOME LASER ENERGY INTO THE FORMATION OF A SINGLE, PENCIL-THIN BEAM...

...ONE THAT SHOCKINGLY, PAINFULLY, CUTS THROUGH IRON MAN'S ARMOR--

--AS WELL AS THE MAN WITHIN!

AAAAAAAAAAA--!

N-NOT HURT... BADLY. LASER BEAM CAUTERIZED ...ITS OWN WOUND, B-BUT... SO DIFFICULT... TO MOVE!

HURRY! I MUST GET INTO THE SIPHON CHAMBER!

BUT THAT'S IMPOSSIBLE! THE SCHEDULE--!

BLAST IT, MAN, THIS COMPLEX HOUSES A NUCLEAR REACTOR!

AND IF I EXPLODE LIKE A GOD-CURSED ROMAN CANDLE, THAT REACTOR IS GOING TO--

HURRY! YOU MUST GET INTO THE SIPHON CHAMBER!

A WISE DECISION, HERR DOKTOR...

THAT BEAM HIT MY NERVOUS SYSTEM... LIKE AN ELECTRIC SHOCK!

NO PERMANENT DAMAGE... BUT ÷WHEW÷ I FEEL LIKE I'VE SPENT FIVE WEEKS... IN A CUISINART! C-CAN'T HARDLY... STAND!

BUT I'VE GOT TO DO *SOMETHING!* IF I HEARD RIGHT...

...THOSE *KILLER SATELLITES*...ARE ABOUT TO BE ARMED!

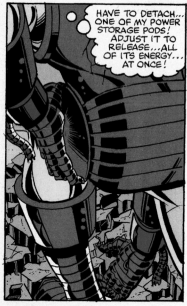

HAVE TO *DETACH*...ONE OF MY *POWER STORAGE* PODS! *ADJUST* IT TO *RELEASE*...ALL OF ITS *ENERGY*...AT *ONCE!*

THEN I'LL *SET* IT...FOR *TEN SECONDS*...AND --

--*THROW!*

SKEK

KEK

KEK

THE *TOSS* IS MADE -- A *CUMBERSOME* COMBINATION OF *CUNNING, HOPE* AND *LUCK.*

MOSTLY, LUCK...WAS--?

A-A *BOMB?!*

RUN!

K-PLAK

PHALOOOOM

MOTHER!

THE SIPHONING PROCESS! I-IT'S BEEN STOPPED-- BEFORE IT EVEN STARTED!

THIS IS IRON MAN'S DOING!

BLAST! THE LASER'S HEADING THIS WAY! AND EVEN WITH MY STRENGTH RAPIDLY RETURNING, MY RIGHT ARM'S STILL USELESS!

THIS COULD BE IT, SHELL-HEAD...

HOWEVER...

PLEASE! I-I'M STARTING TO FUSE! TO ERUPT! Y-YOU'VE GOT TO--

--HELP ME!

I... I CAN'T, PARKS. IT'S TOO LATE.

WHAT YOU SAID ABOUT THE DANGER OF THE NUCLEAR REACTOR WAS TRUE.

AND I'M AFRAID THAT LEAVES ME LITTLE CHOICE.

WH- WHAT--?!

I'M SORRY.

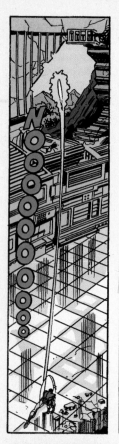

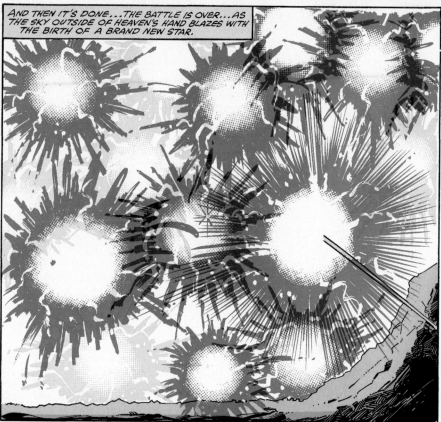

AND THEN IT'S DONE...THE BATTLE IS OVER...AS THE SKY OUTSIDE OF HEAVEN'S HAND BLAZES WITH THE BIRTH OF A BRAND NEW STAR.

WHILE BELOW, A GRIM, GOLDEN AVENGER WATCHES, AND REGRETS. FOR SPECTACULAR AS IT MAY BE--

...DEATH IS NEVER PRETTY.

WITHIN MOMENTS, THE NIGHT TURNS DARK ONCE MORE, AND AN UNSTEADY IRON MAN MOVES OUT TO JOIN IT, FUNCTIONING AT HALF POWER, FLYING SKYWARD...

...WESTWARD...

...HOMEWARD.

EPILOGUE: THIRTY-SIX HOURS LATER, AT A PRIVATE HOSPITAL IN BETHESDA, MARYLAND...

THE DOCTORS SAY ALEX IS GOING TO BE FINE, AND I'M GLAD.

FOR HIM.

BUT A LOT OF THINGS HAVE CHANGED SINCE I PLAYED THE DOCILE HOUSEWIFE. I'M A DIFFERENT WOMAN, I LIVE A DIFFERENT LIFE, AND THEN, OF COURSE, THERE'S --

BETH?

--TONY!

HI, HOW'S ALEX?

OH, DOING PRETTY WELL. HOW'S YOUR ARM?

GOOD.

GETTING BETTER.

UH...

UM...

BLAST.

I CAN'T PLAY THIS GAME, BETH. COME HOME WITH ME.

NO, TONY. ALEX IS STILL MY HUSBAND, LEGALLY, AND HE NEEDS ME.

ESPECIALLY NOW.

BUT I NEED YOU!

I KNOW!

PLEASE, TRY TO UNDERSTAND. ALEX WAS DISTURBED, HOOKED ON PILLS, AND I LEFT HIM.

IF I'D STAYED, IF I'D TRIED TO HELP HIM MORE, WELL... MAYBE NONE OF THIS WOULD HAVE HAPPENED.

I KNOW...

BUT, BETH, YOU'RE JUST FEELING GUILTY! AND THERE'S A BIG DIFFERENCE BETWEEN THAT AND LOVE!

I KNOW WHAT LOVE FEELS LIKE, TONY. YOU OF ALL PEOPLE SHOULD REALIZE THAT. SO PLEASE...

...DON'T MAKE THIS ANY HARDER THAN IT ALREADY IS.

WELL, I GUESS THAT'S IT, THEN. LISTEN, UM, DON'T HESITATE TO CALL ME IF YOU NEED ANYTHING, OKAY? I MEAN ANYTHING AT ALL.

I WON'T, TONY. THANK YOU.

GOOD-BYE.

AND SO HE TURNS, HIS BROW FROZEN IN FURROW, HIS MIND SHUTTING OUT THE MEMORY OF A LAST GENTLE SIGH.

OUTSIDE, HIS CHAUFFEUR-DRIVEN LIMOUSINE WAITS TO RETURN HIM TO LONG ISLAND, TO THE HOME OFFICES OF STARK INTERNATIONAL--

--WHERE HE OVERSEES THE RECONSTRUCTION OF RECENTLY-DAMAGED RESEARCH FACILITIES.

HE PUTS IN A FULL DAY.

A LONG DAY.

AND THROUGHOUT THAT DAY, HE SPEAKS NOT ONCE OF THE HOLLOWNESS IN HIS HEART, OF THE CONFUSION THAT CHOKES HIS VERY SOUL.

SOME WOULD CONSIDER THAT A SIGN OF GREAT STRENGTH; OTHERS, A SIGN OF WEAKNESS.

BUT TONY STARK MERELY CONSIDERS IT A NECESSITY, A WAY OF GETTING TO THE NEW LIFE HE MUST START TOMORROW--

--AND OF GETTING THROUGH THE LONG, LONG NIGHT THAT LIES AHEAD...

THE END.

MARVEL

$1.25
200
NOV
02454

APPROVED
BY THE
COMICS
CODE
AUTHORITY

IRON MAN

TONY STARK
IS
IRON MAN!

SPECIAL
DOUBLE-
SIZED
200TH
ISSUE--
FEATURING
THE LONG-
AWAITED
CLASH
WITH THE
MAN WHO
STOLE
**STARK
INTER-
NATIONAL!**

OBADIAH STANE
IS
IRON-MONGER!

THIS IS THEIR FINAL BATTLE!

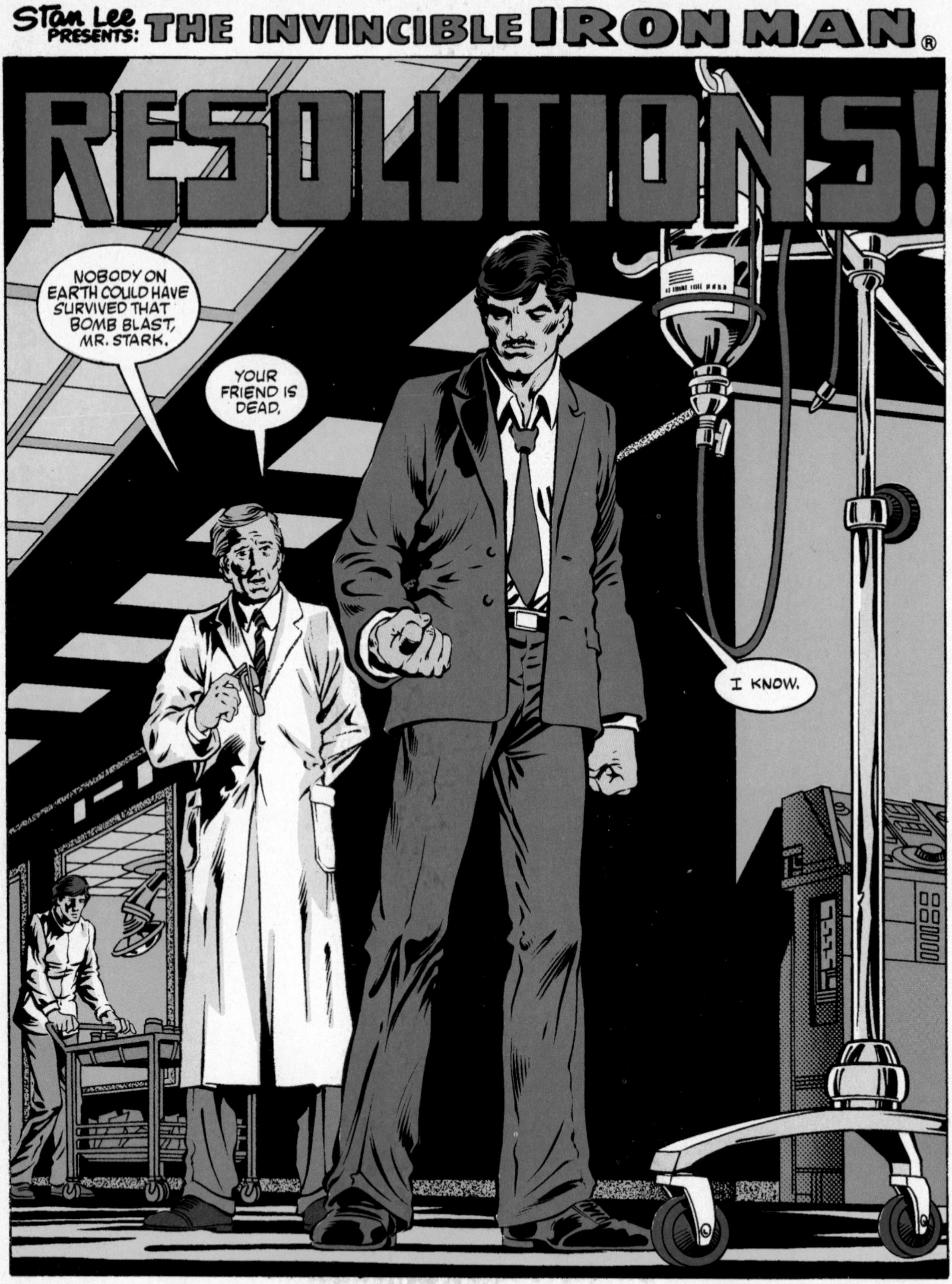
STAN LEE PRESENTS: THE INVINCIBLE IRON MAN®
RESOLUTIONS!
NOBODY ON EARTH COULD HAVE SURVIVED THAT BOMB BLAST, MR. STARK.
YOUR FRIEND IS DEAD.
I KNOW.

DENNY O'NEIL WRITER · **MARK BRIGHT** PENCILER · **AKIN & GARVEY** INKER · **RICK PARKER** LETTERER · **BOB SHAREN** COLORIST · **MARK GRUENWALD** EDITOR · **JIM SHOOTER** EDITOR IN CHIEF

THE RAIN BEGAN ABOUT SIX HOURS AGO, AT MIDNIGHT. IT SWEPT INTO SILICON VALLEY FROM THE NORTH, DRIVEN BY WINDS FROM THE MOUNTAINS.

TONY STARK HAD ARRIVED NEARLY SIX HOURS BEFORE THAT AND HAD WAITED WHILE HIS OWN WOUNDS WERE TENDED, THEN WAITED MORE WHILE THE DOCTORS DEALT WITH THE INJURIES OF HIS CLOSEST FRIENDS.

ONE OF THEM WAS BEYOND HELP.

HE IS NOT AWARE OF LEAVING THE HOSPITAL, NOR OF THE FOUL WEATHER OUTSIDE, AT THIS MOMENT, HIS WORLD IS FILLED WITH A MEMORY THAT BLOTS OUT EVERYTHING ELSE --

-- THE MEMORY OF AN EXPLOSION THAT DESTROYED THE DOME THAT HAD BEEN HIS HOME THESE PAST FEW MONTHS.

HE HAD SEEN THE PITIFUL MANGLED THING THAT WAS ONCE A MAN TAKEN FROM THE ACRID WRECKAGE --

-- AND HAD WATCHED THE PARAMEDIC REMOVE CLYTEM-NESTRA ERWIN FROM THE REMAINS OF THE CAR SHE HAD BEEN DRIVING.

HIS REVERIE IS INTERRUPTED BY--

HEY, TONY.

YOU'RE GETTIN' WET, MAN. YOU OUGHTTA SCORE AN UMBRELLA SOMEPLACE.

YOU WANNA CATCH PNEUMONIA?

HOW ARE YOU, JIM?

I'VE FELT BETTER. WAY BETTER. BUT I'M NOT COMPLAININ'. I'M ALIVE.

IF I HADN'T BEEN OUT BEHIND THE DOME AT THE TIME OF THE BIG BANG, I WOULDN'T BE.

FUNNY... I DON'T EVEN REMEMBER WHAT I WAS DOING THERE.

HOW'S CLY?

THEY'RE FINISHED.

LAST I SAW THE DOCS WERE STILL WORKING ON HER.

ARE YOU OKAY?

NO! AND DON'T TOUCH ME--

--DON'T COME NEAR ME!

WHY ARE YOU MAD AT TONY?

BECAUSE IF IT WEREN'T FOR HIM, MY BROTHER WOULD BE ALIVE!

I DON'T UNDERSTAND!

OH, YES YOU DO. YOU KNEW THAT SOONER OR LATER *OBADIAH STANE* WOULD STRIKE OUT AT YOU *AGAIN*... AND KNOWING THAT, YOU *HAD* TO KNOW THAT *SOME INNOCENT PERSON* MIGHT GET HURT.

SOMEBODY LIKE MORLEY.

YOU *COULD* HAVE STOPPED HIM. YOU COULD HAVE BECOME IRON MAN AND GONE AFTER HIM AND... AND *STOPPED* HIM!

CLY, WE AREN'T *SURE* STANE IS BEHIND THIS.

DON'T BE A *FOOL*, RHODEY.

SHE'S RIGHT, JIM.

IT WAS STANE. IT HAD TO BE.

I WAS AFRAID. NOT OF STANE... OF MYSELF. OF MYSELF AS IRON MAN. I FEARED THAT IF I PUT ON IRON MAN'S ARMOR, I'D BECOME WHAT I WAS... WHAT I FOUGHT SO HARD TO *STOP* BEING...

A DRUNK.

DON'T CALL ME IRON MAN-- THAT'S WHAT I'VE BEEN SAYING, FOR MONTHS. I'VE DENIED ANY CONNECTION TO THAT IDENTITY.

EVEN WHEN I PUT ON A METAL SUIT, I REFUSED TO LET YOU CALL ME THAT NAME.

I'VE BEEN A FOOL. OR A COWARD. OR BOTH.

"MY FRIEND IS DEAD... OTHERS MAY HAVE BEEN CAPTURED, TAKEN WHO KNOWS WHERE BEFORE IT GOT TO THIS POINT.

"I COULD HAVE STOPPED HIM BEFORE IT GOT TO THIS POINT. BUT I DIDN'T."

BUT I WILL. I'LL ACCEPT THE RESPONSIBILITY THAT GOES WITH WHO I AM AND I WILL STOP OBADIAH STANE.

NOW YOU'RE *TALKING*, BUDDY! I GOT THE ARMOR RIGHT HERE--

YOU KEEP IT.

BUT WITH THIS BUSTED LEG, I WON'T BE ABLE TO WEAR IT... TO *HELP*.

I APPRECIATE YOUR CONCERN, RHODEY, BUT I CAN DO THIS ALONE.

WHERE YOU GOIN'?

TO LOS ANGELES.

I'VE KNOWN THAT MAN FOR A LOTTA YEARS... AND I'VE *NEVER* SEEN AS *INTENSE* AS HE IS NOW.

I ALMOST FEEL SORRY FOR STANE.

I DON'T.

AT THAT MOMENT IN NEW YORK...

STANE INTERNATIONAL

BUT I DO NOT UNDERSTAND WHY YOU DID NOT KILL TONY STARK, OBADIAH.

BECAUSE THEN HE COULD NOT REALIZE THAT I HAD DEFEATED HIM. IT IS FAR MORE SATISFYING TO LET AN ENEMY *LIVE*-- WITH THE KNOW-LEDGE OF HIS HUMILIATION.

THAT IS WHY I ARRANGED THE BOMB TO EXPLODE WHEN HIS *FRIENDS* WERE IN THE DOME.

I CAN READ ANTHONY STARK LIKE A BOOK. HE WILL BLAME HIMSELF FOR ERWIN'S DEATH AND HE WILL RETURN TO THE BOTTLE.

WITHIN A MONTH, HE WILL AGAIN BE IN THE GUTTER!

WHAT ABOUT HER?

MADAME MASQUE? WE MAY FIND A USE FOR HER LATER.

YOU DON'T RESENT WHAT I'VE DONE TO YOU?

NO. I ADORE YOU.

AS YOU ONCE ADORED STARK?

YES!

THAT AFTERNOON, AT THE LOS ANGELES HEADQUARTERS OF THE AVENGERS...

TONY! GOOD TO SEE YOU.

BEEN A WHILE. HOW ABOUT WE SHOOT A GAME OF POOL AND CHEW THE FAT?

GET OUT OF MY WAY, HAWKEYE.

WHAT'S WITH *HIM*? I'VE SEEN FRIENDLIER BARRACUDA.

BEATS ME! HE'S GOING INTO THE LAB--

"--SO I GUESS HE'S ANXIOUS TO FINISH WORK ON THAT *NEW ARMOR* HE'S BEEN DESIGNING."

UNKNOWN TO THE BOWMAN, TONY STARK *HAS* FINISHED IT.

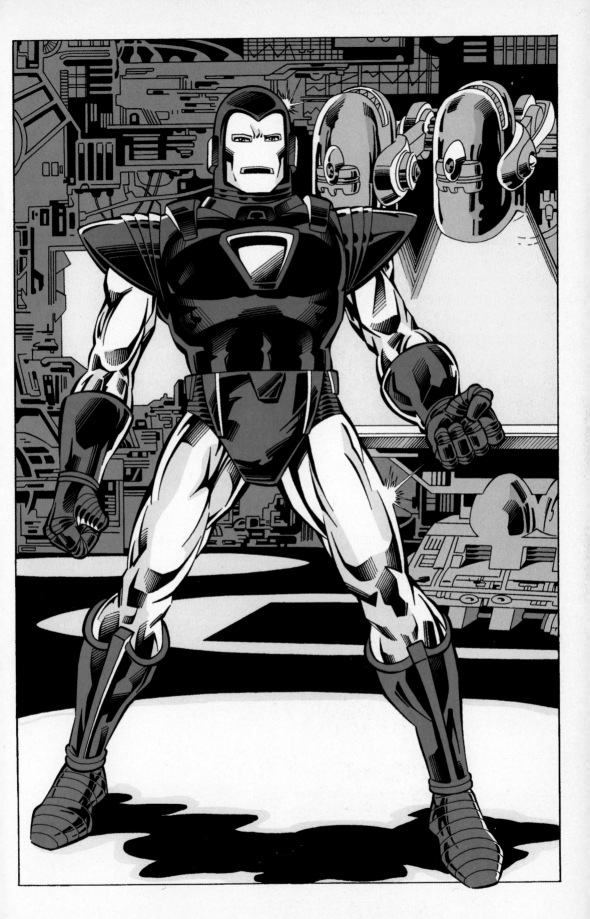

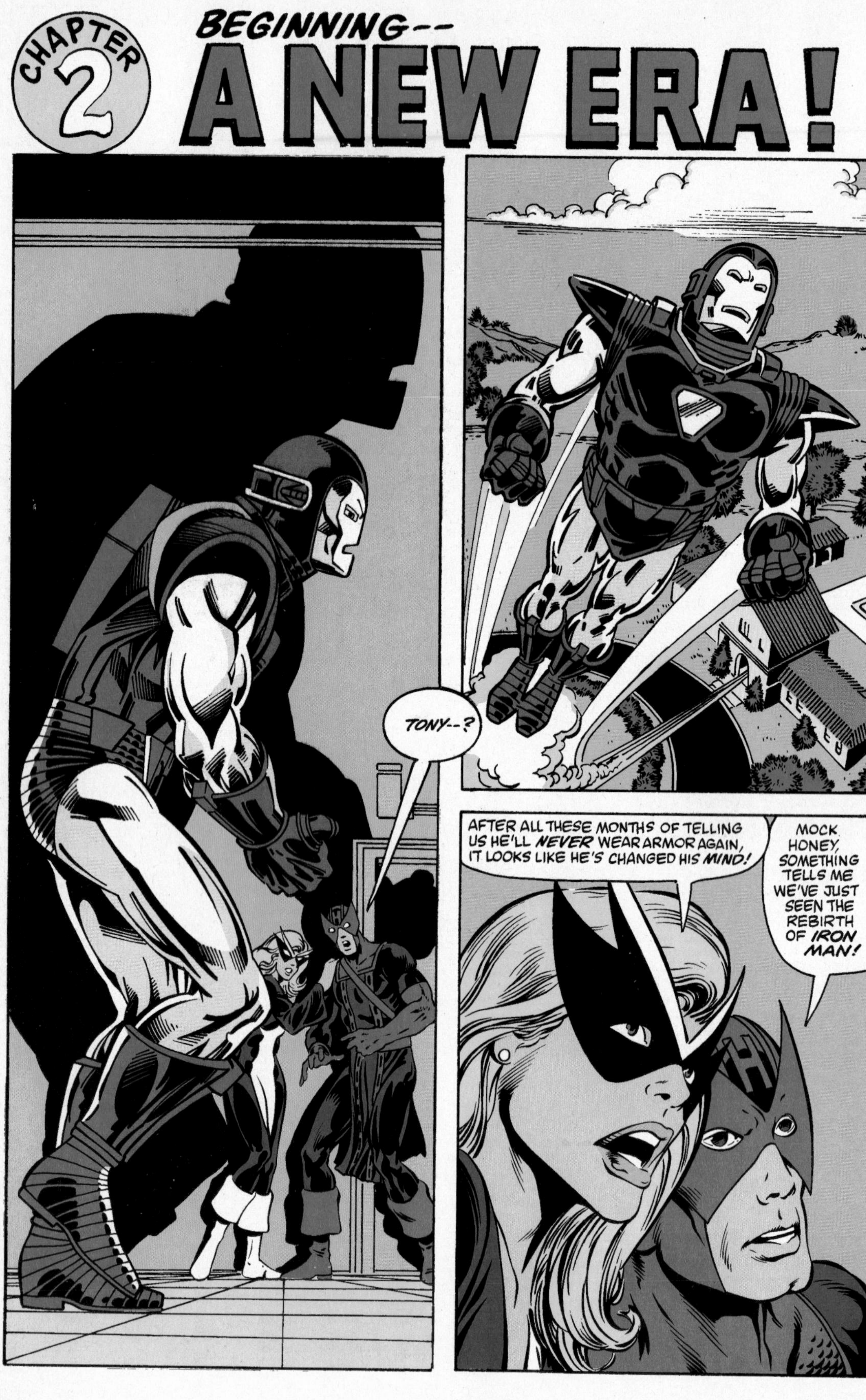
CHAPTER 2
BEGINNING--
A NEW ERA!
TONY--?
AFTER ALL THESE MONTHS OF TELLING US HE'LL NEVER WEAR ARMOR AGAIN, IT LOOKS LIKE HE'S CHANGED HIS MIND!
MOCK, HONEY, SOMETHING TELLS ME WE'VE JUST SEEN THE REBIRTH OF IRON MAN!

| INTO THE UPPER REGIONS WHERE THE AIR THINS AND IT IS ALWAYS COLD, HE SOARS-- | --UNTIL *200 MILES* ABOVE THE EARTH, AT THE APEX OF HIS FLIGHT, HE PAUSES FOR A MOMENT... | THEN, HE AIMS HIMSELF DOWN-- | --AND PLUMMETS; THE OUTER COATING OF HIS ARMOR PROTECTING HIM FROM THE TERRIBLE HEAT OF HIS RE-ENTRY. | HE STARTED IN CALIFORNIA-- HE ENDS IN NEW YORK. IT HAS TAKEN HIM TWENTY MINUTES. |

151

EVERYTHING'S A GO SO FAR--DUAL SOURCE PROPULSION SYSTEM WORKS WELL BOTH IN AND OUT OF THE ATMOSPHERE--

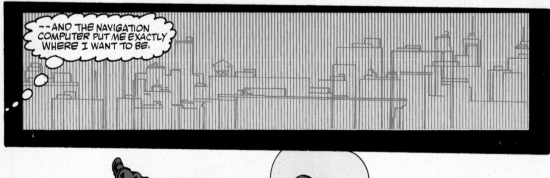

--AND THE NAVIGATION COMPUTER PUT ME EXACTLY WHERE I WANT TO BE.

I WISH I HAD TIME TO TEST THE WEAPONS SYSTEMS...BUT THE PEOPLE STANE KIDNAPPED MAY BE IN GREAT DANGER.

I CAN'T AFFORD TO WASTE A SECOND.

MEANWHILE, AT STANE INTERNATIONAL, LONG ISLAND...

I DID NOT KNOW THERE WAS A LEVEL THIS FAR BELOW THE SURFACE, OBADIAH.

INDEED. AND I HAVE *ANOTHER* SURPRISE FOR YOU!

I AM NOT CERTAIN I CAN *STAND* ANOTHER SURPRISE.

THERE IS YOUR DARLING DR. ATLANTA -- BUSY AS ALWAYS.

HE IS REFINING HIS *PSYCHE IMPRINT* PROCESS. AN EARLY VERSION OF IT WON HIM A NOBEL PRIZE.

THEN HE EXPERIMENTED ON *HIMSELF* AND SOMETHING WENT WRONG AND...

PLEASE, SPARE ME THE DETAILS.

THAT IS WHY YOU FOUND HIM IN A MENTAL HOSPITAL?

AN INSANE ASYLUM.

WHATEVER.

I AM STILL SO CONFUSED FROM WHAT YOU DID TO ME. I LOVE YOU FOR IT, BUT...

DO NOT SPEAK OF IT, MY DEAR. AS TIME PASSES, SO WILL YOUR CONFUSION.

NOW, FOR THE SURPRISE I PROMISED YOU.

AND WHAT IS THE *PURPOSE* OF YOUR SPLENDID PROJECT?

I CALL THIS *PROJECT IRONMONGER!*

HERE, YOU SEE HALF-A BILLION DOLLARS WORTH OF COMPUTERS, TEST RIGS-- ALL MANNER OF SCIENTIFIC EQUIPMENT.

THE MEN AND WOMEN ARE THE BEST SCIENTISTS AND TECHNICIANS I COULD FIND.

AS YOU KNOW, STANE INTERNATIONAL WAS ONCE *STARK* INTERNATIONAL. WHEN STARK MOVED OUT, HE LEFT SOME STRANGE THINGS BEHIND... THINGS HE UNDOUBTEDLY FORGOT.

AMONG THEM WAS *THIS*...

...A NOTEBOOK WITH A FEW SCRIBBLINGS DEALING WITH IRON MAN'S ARMOR.

THESE PEOPLE, THIS EQUIPMENT-- FOR MONTHS IT HAS BEEN PUT TO DECIPHERING THOSE SCRIBBLINGS... CLARIFYING THEM, IMPROVING THE DESIGNS THEY SUGGEST.

THE RESULT?

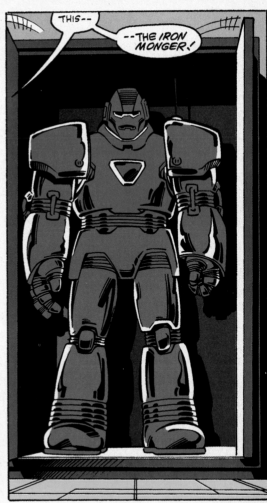

THIS--

--THE *IRON MONGER!*

A VARIANT OF IRON MAN'S ARMOR?

ARMOR FAR *BETTER* THAN IRON MAN'S. *PERFECT* ARMOR. THE *PINNACLE* OF TECHNOLOGY!

ITS POSSIBILITIES ARE ENDLESS. I CAN SELL IT TO ANY NATION ON EARTH FOR MORE MONEY THAN ANYONE HAS EVER *DREAMT* OF POSSESSING.

OR I COULD BUILD *THOUSANDS* OF DUPLICATES-- *HUNDREDS* OF THOUSANDS--AND OUTFIT MY OWN ARMY.

THEN, I COULD *TAKE* ANY NATION ON EARTH!

THAT LAST POSSIBILITY IS *MOST* APPEALING!

IF I WERE A GRATEFUL SORT, I WOULD *THANK* THAT POOR WRETCH STARK!

SOMEWHERE ABOVE...

CHARLIE... THE RADAR'S SHOWING SOMETHING.

RIGHT OVERHEAD.

Stone INTERNATIONAL

HEY...IT'S GONE!

RIGHT OFF THE SCREEN. LET'S DO A VISUAL CHECK.

YEAH...UP THERE, TO THE LEFT.

LOOKS LIKE A MAN!

WHERE'D IT GO?

I TELL YA, CHARLIE, THESE LATE NIGHTS HAVE GOTTA STOP!

YOU AIN'T WRONG!

THE *DETECTION UNIT* IN MY NEW HELMET INDICATES THAT THEY'RE USING *RADAR*, BUT THE COATING ON MY ARMOR IS DOING WHAT IT'S SUPPOSED TO DO--ABSORB THE SIGNAL SO IT DOESN'T BOUNCE BACK TO THEIR SCREEN.

I WAS PRETTY SURE IT WOULD.

I WASN'T CERTAIN THAT THE CHAMELEON EFFECT WOULD WORK, BUT IT IS. *SCANNERS* ARE REGISTERING THE SKY AND CLOUDS--AND A HOLOGRAM PROJECTOR IS MAKING ME BLEND IN WITH THEM.

NO BUGS IN THE ARMOR YET.

I'LL CIRCLE THE ENTIRE PLANT FOR A FEW MINUTES--

-- AND HOPE MY SENSORS CAN DETECT WHERE STANE IS HIDING THE KIDNAP VICTIMS.

HOWEVER--

DR. ATLANTA!

I *TOLD* YOU THERE WOULD BE NO EXPERIMENTING UNTIL I ORDERED IT.

THERE, THERE, DOCTOR...YOU'LL GET YOUR CHANCE!

16

OH, HE HAS ALREADY *HAD* HIS CHANCE. HE HAS DONE SOMETHING *VERY* INTERESTING TO THEM.

AT THAT MOMENT--

NO SIGN OF MY FRIENDS. I'LL HAVE TO TRY A *DIRECT* APPROACH!

I'LL DEMAND TO SEE STANE--

--AND I WON'T BOTHER TO KNOCK!

KRASH

OH, MY GAWD--!

TELL OBADIAH STANE IRON MAN'S HERE.

D-DO YOU HAVE AN A-A-APPOINTMENT, SIR?

GOOD QUESTION, LADY.

I THINK THE ANSWER IS YES. I'VE HAD AN APPOINTMENT WITH OBADIAH STANE FOR A LONG TIME!

I'LL T-T-TELL HIM.

YOU DO THAT.

AND MS. ? YOU SHOULDN'T GET SO FLUSTERED. YOU COULD TAKE LESSONS FROM A WOMAN NAMED *MRS. ARBOGAST.*

THEN--

HE IS WHAT?

OBADIAH! WHAT IS WRONG?

IF IT IS TRUE--

YES IT IS!

IRON MAN? BUT HE LOOKS DIFFERENT.

OH, THE ARMOR IS DIFFERENT BUT THE MAN INSIDE IS NOT.

I KNOW IT IN MY BONES:

HE IS NOT DESTROYED. HE IS NOT VANQUISHED. HE IS NOT GROVELING IN THE GUTTER.

HE IS HERE. HE IS DEMANDING A CONFRONTATION!

WILL NOTHING RID ME OF HIM?

159

MAYBE A *CIRCUITS-BREAKER* WILL RID ME OF HIM!

IN A DISTANT QUARTER OF THE CAMPUS, A PROTOTYPE OF THE AUTOMATED DESTRUCTION MACHINE IS LAUNCHED...

WWWW

FWOOSH!

DETECTION SCANNER INDICATES I'M UNDER ATTACK--

--MISSILES AIMED FROM ABOVE.

I CAN'T LET THEM HIT THE BUILDING. INNOCENT PEOPLE MAY BE INSIDE IT.

ANOTHER OF STANE'S NASTY TOYS... LIKE THE ONE JIM AND I DEALT WITH A FEW DAYS AGO.*

-- SHOULD THOROUGHLY CONFUSE THEM--!

RIGHT ON THE MONEY!

THE GUIDANCE SYSTEMS IN THOSE MISSILES ARE FAIRLY PRIMITIVE. A SIMPLE *DISRUPTOR FIELD*--

* IRON MAN #198.

NEXT ON STANE'S AGENDA-- A *THERMAL RAY!* ONE OF THOSE TURNED MY INTERIM ARMOR TO SCRAP DURING THE EARLIER ENCOUNTER-- *WOULD* HAVE *FRIED ME* IF JIM HADN'T SAVED ME.

BUT INSIDE *THIS* ARMOR, I'M COOL AS DECEMBER!

MAY AS WELL USE THIS OPPORTUNITY TO TEST THE SUIT'S *MUSCLE*--!

KHRASH

STILL ON THE MONEY!

YOU DID NOT REALLY EXPECT IT TO STOP HIM?

BE QUIET.

WILL MY *CHESSMEN* RID ME OF HIM?

FROM A NEARBY DORMITORY--

CHESSMEN! I WONDER IF *THOSE* MEN ARE THE ONES I FOUGHT WHEN I *FIRST* BECAME AWARE OF STANE!*

THEY GAVE ME A FEW VERY HARD MINUTES... NEARLY *BEAT* ME!

*SEE ISSUES #163-166.

THEY PLAY A ROUGH GAME... WITH A *PERMANENT* CHECKMATE!

I'LL SWITCH ON MY SPEAKER SO THEY CAN HEAR ME.

LISTEN, KNIGHTS AND BISHOP... YOU CAN TURN AROUND NOW AND SAVE YOURSELVES GRIEF.

OKAY! I *DID* WARN YOU!

I OUGHT TO LET YOU HIT THE GROUND--

-- AND BOUNCE!

BUT I'LL GIVE YOU THE BENEFIT OF THE DOUBT AND ASSUME YOU'RE NOT AS BAD AS YOUR BOSS!

HE ALWAYS *DID* HAVE THAT UNFORTUNATE STREAK OF MERCY.

THE BREAKER FAILED. THE CHESSMEN FAILED.

NO ONE WILL RID ME OF HIM! NO ONE!

THEN I MUST DO IT *MYSELF!*

OBADIAH... WHERE ARE YOU *GOING?*

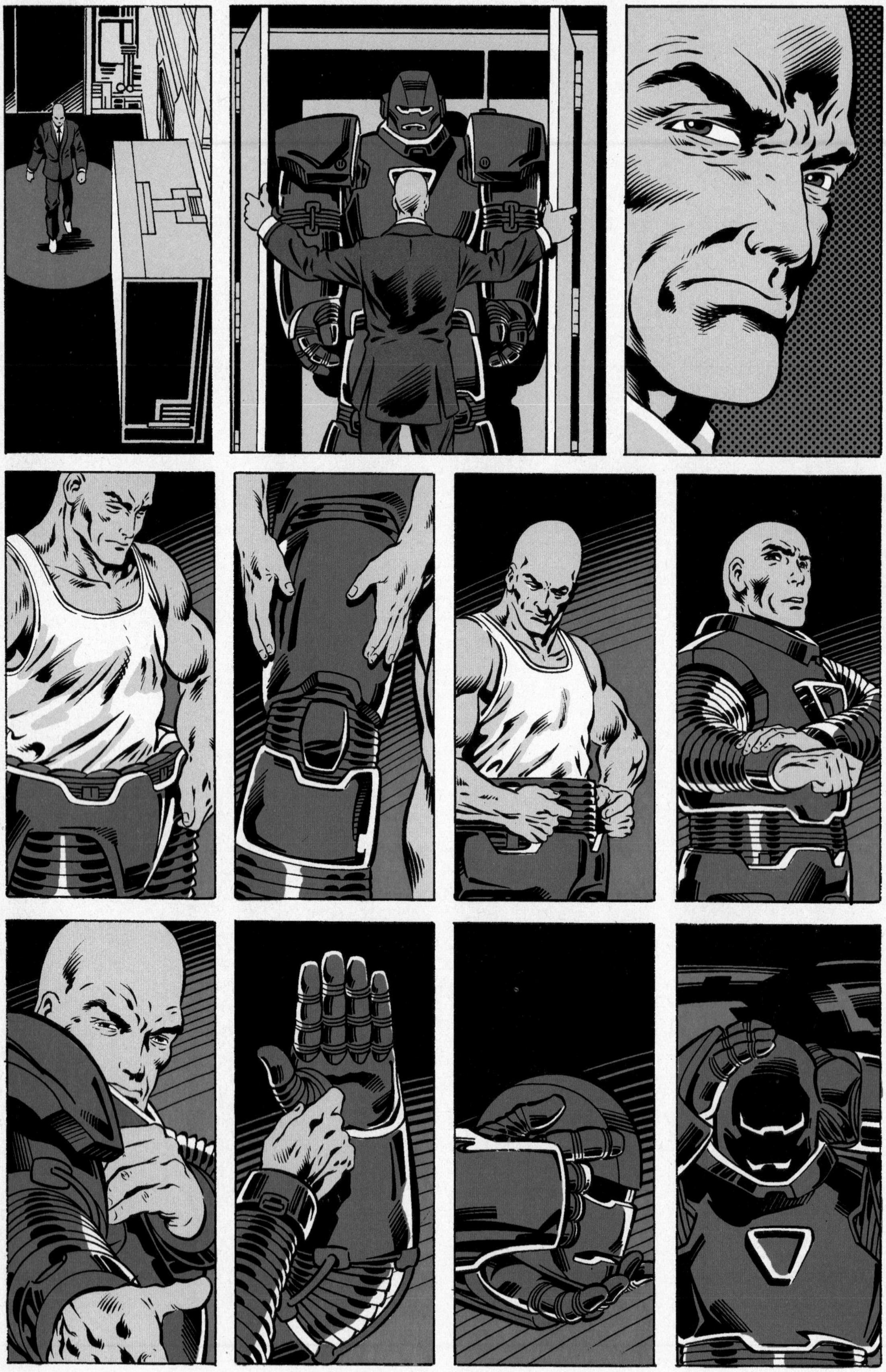

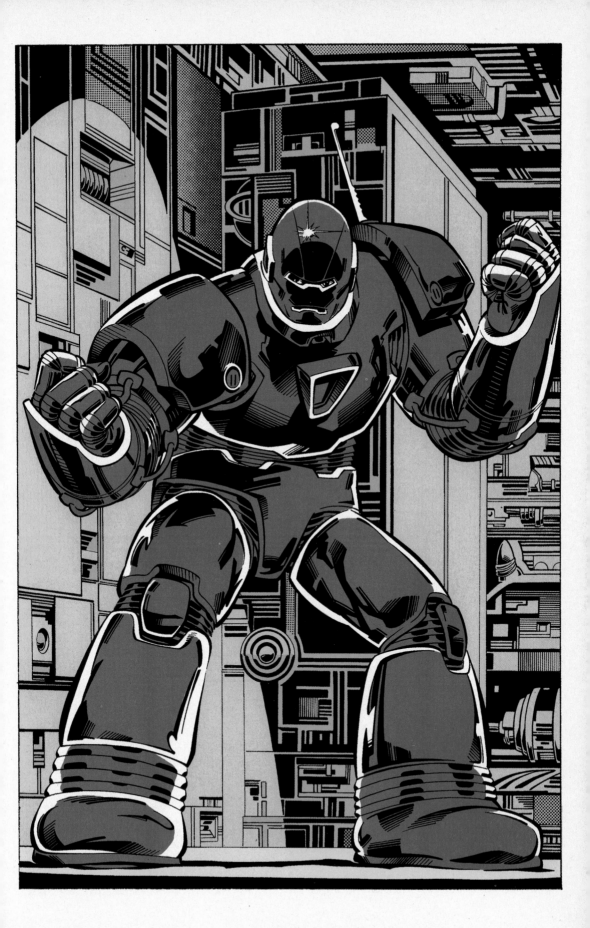

MR. *STANE* IS IN THAT ARMOR? I NEVER KNEW *HE* WANTED TO WEAR IT.

HE *HAS* BEEN IN ON ALL THE TESTS...

Stane has always wanted to win at any cost...

DO YOU KNOW WHO I AM?

YES.

SO IT HAS COME TO THIS.

STARK!

TWO WAYS WE CAN PLAY IT, STANE. YOU CAN SHED THE METAL AND AGREE TO LET THE LAW SETTLE THE DIFFERENCES BETWEEN US.

THAT'LL TAKE A LONG TIME, BUT I'M IN NO HURRY.

AND THE OTHER WAY--

--IS THIS!

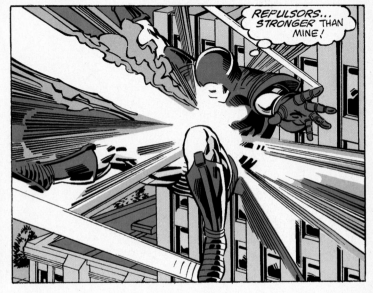

REPULSORS... STRONGER THAN MINE!

FRAT-WA-SK!

DO YOU REALIZE WHAT JUST *HAPPENED?*

A GUY IN ARMOR JUST CRASHED THROUGH THE ROOF!

NO, TO OUR *EXPERIMENT!*

HE RUINED OUR *SAFETY* DEVICES, THAT FUSE COULD SET OFF THE EXPLOSIVES ANY *SECOND!*

THIS WHOLE PLACE COULD BLOW *SKY HIGH!*

AND, ABOVE...

NICE *ATTACK,* STANE -- FOR AN AMATEUR. OF COURSE, IT DIDN'T *HURT* ME.

NOR DID I *EXPECT* IT TO. THAT WAS JUST A *SAMPLING* OF WHAT IS IN STORE FOR YOU.

I DELAYED MEETING YOU IN COMBAT FOR *MONTHS,* FOR *YEARS!*

I WAS FOOLISH. THE FEELING OF POWER IS, IS...

EXQUISITE.

NOW-- A **SECOND** BLAST!

NOT THIS TIME, STANE. THIS TIME, I'M **READY!**

I'VE ACTIVATED MY FIELD... IT ONLY FUNCTIONS FOR A MAXIMUM OF SIX SECONDS, BUT THAT WILL BE LONG ENOUGH.

HIS ARMOR IS BUILT FROM MY OLD BASIC DESIGN... WITH A LOT OF MODIFICATIONS.

ONE OF THOSE MODIFICATIONS MUST ACCOUNT FOR THE ODD ELECTRO-MAGNETIC TRANSMISSIONS I'M PICKING UP.

YOU WITHSTAND THE REPULSORS? THEN THE **LASER**--!

I'VE GOT AN EVEN **NEATER** ANSWER TO THAT--

--THE OUTER FABRIC OF MY SUIT CAN **ABSORB** ANY FORM OF ENERGY, INCLUDING HEAT--

-- AND **RETURN** IT... WITH **INTEREST!**

HE'S *VIBRATING*...

...TOTALLY LOST CONTROL...

KRA-AZH!

HE'S RECOVERED... BUT IT SHOULDN'T HAVE HAPPENED IN THE FIRST PLACE.

THAT ARMOR'S NOT EXACTLY WHAT I *THINK* IT IS!

FREEP FREEP FREEP

THESE PEOPLE ARE IN A *PANIC!* THAT ALARM--

-- WHEN I WAS BOSS AROUND HERE, IT MEANT IMMINENT *DANGER!*

WRENKK

170

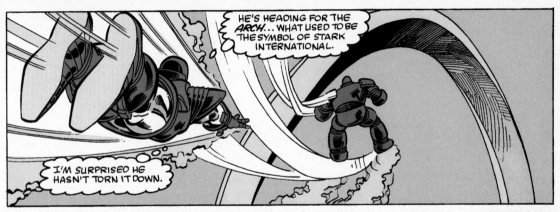

HE'S HEADING FOR THE *ARCH*... WHAT USED TO BE THE SYMBOL OF STARK INTERNATIONAL.

I'M SURPRISED HE HASN'T TORN IT DOWN.

STRONGARM TACTICS DIDN'T WORK A SECOND AGO. WHAT MAKES YOU THINK THEY'LL WORK *NOW?*

RENCH!

THIS IS NOT FOR *YOU--*

--IT IS FOR *THEM!*

AT LEAST SIX OF THOSE PEOPLE WILL BE CRUSHED... AND THE ANGLE IS WRONG FOR MY REPULSORS.

I'VE HESITATED TO USE MY *PULSE-BOLTS--*

THEY'VE NEVER BEEN TESTED AND I DON'T HAVE ANY IDEA HOW *POWERFUL* THEY ARE.

BUT AT THE MOMENT, THEY'RE ALL I'VE *GOT--!*

NOW I KNOW.

THEY'RE *VERY* POWERFUL!

STANE'S STUNT WITH THE ARCH WAS OBVIOUSLY A PLOY TO GAIN TIME... HE'S HEADING FOR *SOMETHING!*

HIS ARMOR'S *FAST*--BUT MINE IS A LOT *FASTER!*

YOU CAN'T OUTRUN ME, STANE!

MY RECEIVER'S PICKING UP THAT ODD STATIC AGAIN--!

I'M PASSING OVER THE BUILDING I SMASHED INTO EARLIER--

BAW- WVOOMF!

172

I HOPE EVERYBODY GOT OUT OKAY!

STANE INTERNATIONAL

ME TOO! *NOBODY* COULD HAVE LIVED THROUGH THAT EXPLOSION.

HOWEVER--

NASTY! WASN'T QUITE UP TO NUCLEAR STRENGTH...BUT NOT FAR FROM IT!

I CAN'T DETECT ANYBODY TRAPPED ANYWHERE--

-- SO I'M FREE TO PURSUE STANE WITH A CLEAR CONSCIENCE.

HE DUCKED IN HERE --

-- BUT THERE'S NO SIGN OF HIM.

I OKAYED THE PLANS FOR THIS BUILDING MYSELF, BACK WHEN IT WAS PART OF STARK INTERNATIONAL, STANE *CAN'T* BE HIDING.

UNLESS--

-- HE MODIFIED IT SOME WAY.

I'LL PUT MY HELMET OPTICS ON ENERGY DETECTION MODE--

BINGO! THERE ARE ELECTRICAL CABLES IN THE WALLS AND FLOOR WHERE THERE *SHOULDN'T* BE! AND THERE'S STILL JUICE FLOWING THROUGH THEM OR THEY WOULDN'T SHOW UP ON MY SCAN.

STANE BUILT A SUB-BASEMENT.

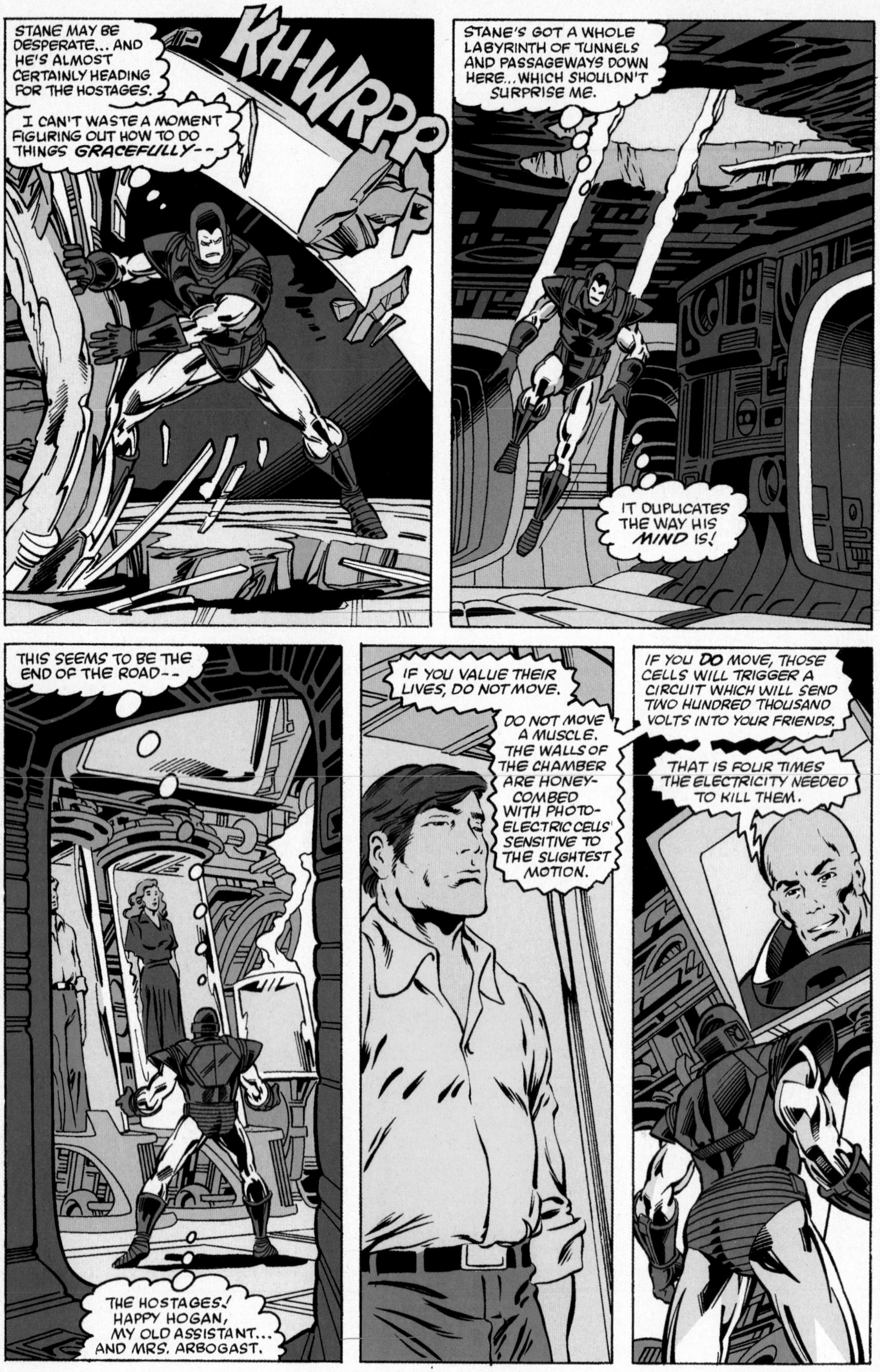
STANE MAY BE DESPERATE... AND HE'S ALMOST CERTAINLY HEADING FOR THE HOSTAGES.
I CAN'T WASTE A MOMENT FIGURING OUT HOW TO DO THINGS GRACEFULLY--
KH-WRPP
STANE'S GOT A WHOLE LABYRINTH OF TUNNELS AND PASSAGEWAYS DOWN HERE... WHICH SHOULDN'T SURPRISE ME.
IT DUPLICATES THE WAY HIS MIND IS!
THIS SEEMS TO BE THE END OF THE ROAD--
THE HOSTAGES! HAPPY HOGAN, MY OLD ASSISTANT... AND MRS. ARBOGAST.
IF YOU VALUE THEIR LIVES, DO NOT MOVE.
DO NOT MOVE A MUSCLE. THE WALLS OF THE CHAMBER ARE HONEY-COMBED WITH PHOTO-ELECTRIC CELLS SENSITIVE TO THE SLIGHTEST MOTION.
IF YOU DO MOVE, THOSE CELLS WILL TRIGGER A CIRCUIT WHICH WILL SEND TWO HUNDRED THOUSAND VOLTS INTO YOUR FRIENDS.
THAT IS FOUR TIMES THE ELECTRICITY NEEDED TO KILL THEM.

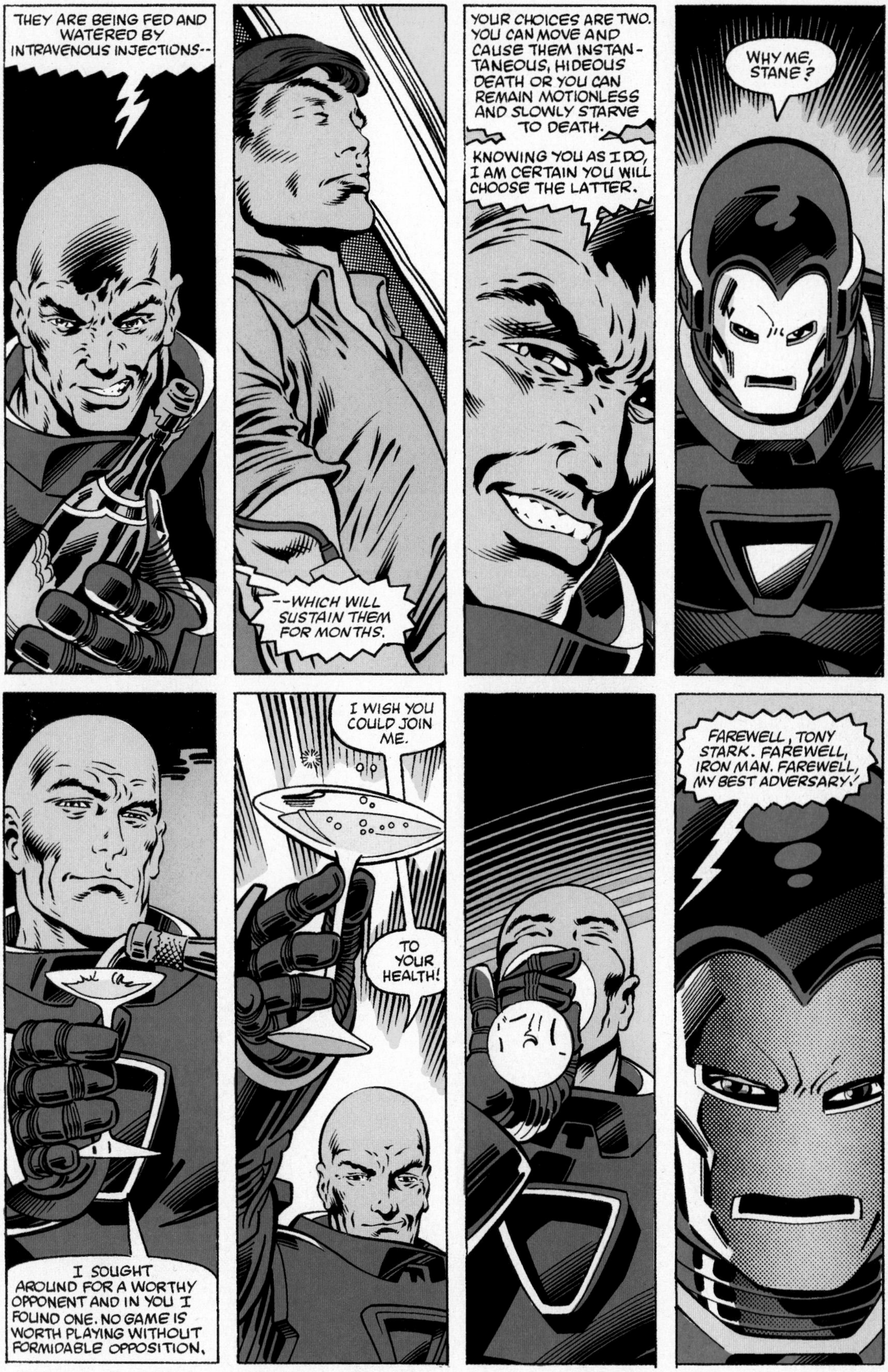
THEY ARE BEING FED AND WATERED BY INTRAVENOUS INJECTIONS--
--WHICH WILL SUSTAIN THEM FOR MONTHS.
YOUR CHOICES ARE TWO. YOU CAN MOVE AND CAUSE THEM INSTAN-TANEOUS, HIDEOUS DEATH OR YOU CAN REMAIN MOTIONLESS AND SLOWLY STARVE TO DEATH.
KNOWING YOU AS I DO, I AM CERTAIN YOU WILL CHOOSE THE LATTER.
WHY ME, STANE?
I SOUGHT AROUND FOR A WORTHY OPPONENT AND IN YOU I FOUND ONE. NO GAME IS WORTH PLAYING WITHOUT FORMIDABLE OPPOSITION.
I WISH YOU COULD JOIN ME.
TO YOUR HEALTH!
FAREWELL, TONY STARK. FAREWELL, IRON MAN. FAREWELL, MY BEST ADVERSARY!

DON'T COUNT ME OUT YET.

ENERGY SCAN THE ROOM...

-- DIRECTLY IN LINE WITH MY CHEST PLATE.

THAT GIVES ME A SHOT!

THE CABLE FEEDING THE HOSTAGES' APPARATUS IS BEHIND THE FAR WALL --

FZZSST

DID IT! I BURNED THROUGH THE WALL AND THE CABLE. THAT TAKES CARE OF STANE'S ELECTROCUTION PLOY --

-- AND THIS SHOULD TAKE CARE OF EVERYTHING ELSE.

SHRIPPPF!

EXACTLY 30 SECONDS LATER--

WH-WHERE AM I?

WHO ARE *YOU*? ARE YOU *IRON MAN*? YOU DON'T *LOOK* LIKE IRON MAN!

APPEARANCES CAN BE DECEIVING, OLD FRIEND!

HE *SOUNDS* LIKE IRON MAN.

I'LL EXPLAIN EVERYTHING SOON. MEANWHILE, YOU'D ALL BETTER STAY PUT. YOU'RE SEVERAL HUNDRED FEET UNDERGROUND --

"-- AND THERE'S AN INFERNO RAGING ABOVE."

I'LL RETURN FOR YOU SHORTLY.

THE WIRING FOR THE TELEVISION SCREEN LEADS IN THIS DIRECTION. STANE SHOULD BE AT THE END OF IT.

NO. HE MUST REALIZE I BEAT HIS TRAP... AND HE'S RUN-- *AGAIN!*

LONG PASSAGEWAY--

--LEADS TO AN EXIT BEYOND THE STANE INTERNATIONAL CAMPUS.

YOU HAVE *HOUNDED* ME.

YOU WILL *NOT* STAY DEFEATED!

THAT'S RIGHT.

I WILL TELL YOU THE SECRET OF MY SUCCESS, IT IS THIS: IN EVERY GAME I PLAY, I HAVE ALTERNATIVE TACTICS.

IF ONE DOES NOT WORK, I USE ANOTHER. I CONTINUE UNTIL I HAVE WON.

THIS--THIS INFANT IS THE INSTRUMENT OF MY *FINAL* TACTIC... AND IT WILL *NOT* FAIL!

ARE YOU CERTAIN?

YES! EITHER YOU REMOVE YOUR HELMET, OR I WILL CRUSH THIS FRAIL FLESH TO PULP BETWEEN MY PALMS.

178

IT IS NOW, THIS MOMENT, THIS SMALL SLIVER OF A SECOND, THAT HE FINALLY, FULLY BECOMES IRON MAN--

--ACTS WITHOUT CONSCIOUS THOUGHT--

--SENDS BOLTS OF ENERGY BLASTING DOWNWARD--

-- WITH IMMEDIATE AND DEVASTATING EFFECT--

KA- THOM

HIS ARMOR'S SEIZED UP. HE'S FROZEN!

I WAS RIGHT. THAT ODD NOISE I GOT ON MY RECEIVER WHEN-EVER WE WERE NEAR THE BUILDING I DESTROYED-- IT WAS A TRANSMISSION FROM A COMPUTER!

STANE'S ARMOR WAS COMPUTER-CONTROLLED!

MAKES SENSE... STANE HAD NO EXPERIENCE. THE COMPUTER GAVE HIM THE EDGE HE ALWAYS INSISTED ON...

... OR HE THOUGHT IT DID.

HIS ARMOR WAS MADE FROM MY BASIC DESIGN. THAT DESIGN WOULD CAUSE IT TO FREEZE IF IT WERE CON-TROLLED FROM AN OUTSIDE SOURCE.

179

I'LL EASE STANE TO A SOFT LANDING WITH MY REPULSORS AND--

TAKE GOOD CARE OF THIS KID, MISTER. TAKE *REAL* GOOD CARE!

STANE'S FINALLY RECOVERED... HE'S UNFROZEN THE ARMOR TRYING TO ESCAPE--

--BUT HE CAN'T HANDLE IT!

END OF THE LINE, STANE.

NOT QUITE, TONY.

OH, YOU NEED NOT WORRY THAT I WILL CONTINUE TO FIGHT WITH YOU.

I CONCEDE YOUR SUPERIORITY AT THAT GAME, TONY.

YOU DO NOT MIND MY USING YOUR FIRST NAME, DO YOU?

BUT HAVE YOU WON, TRULY? I THINK NOT. FOR I HAVE ALWAYS BELIEVED THAT THE ESSENTIAL PART OF WINNING IS TO ENJOY YOUR OPPONENT'S HUMILIATION AT LOSING.

THAT IS THE REAL REWARD OF THE GAME.

OF THAT, I CAN DEPRIVE YOU.

THAT IS WHAT MY FATHER DEPRIVED EVERYONE OF. HE SAW THE WORLD AS HIS OPPONENT AND AT THE LAST HE REALIZED HE COULD NOT WIN.

IF HE HAD NOT DONE IT THAT NIGHT, HE WOULD HAVE DONE IT ANOTHER.

WHAT ARE YOU TALKING ABOUT?

THIS, TONY.

STANE... NO!

40

WHAT HAPPENED?

SOMEBODY LOST.

END

182

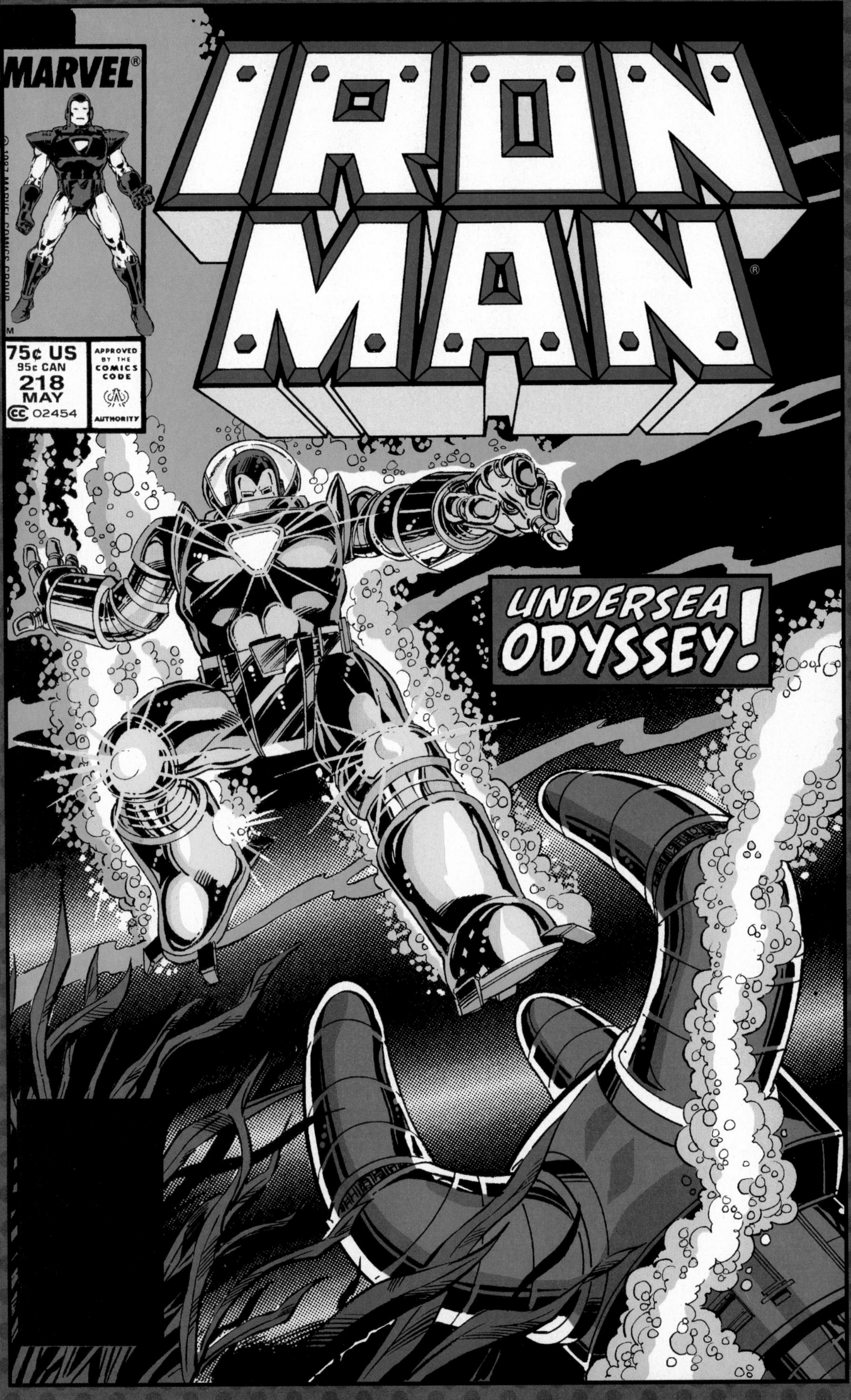
MARVEL
IRON MAN
75¢ US
95¢ CAN
218
MAY
02454
APPROVED BY THE COMICS CODE AUTHORITY
UNDERSEA ODYSSEY!

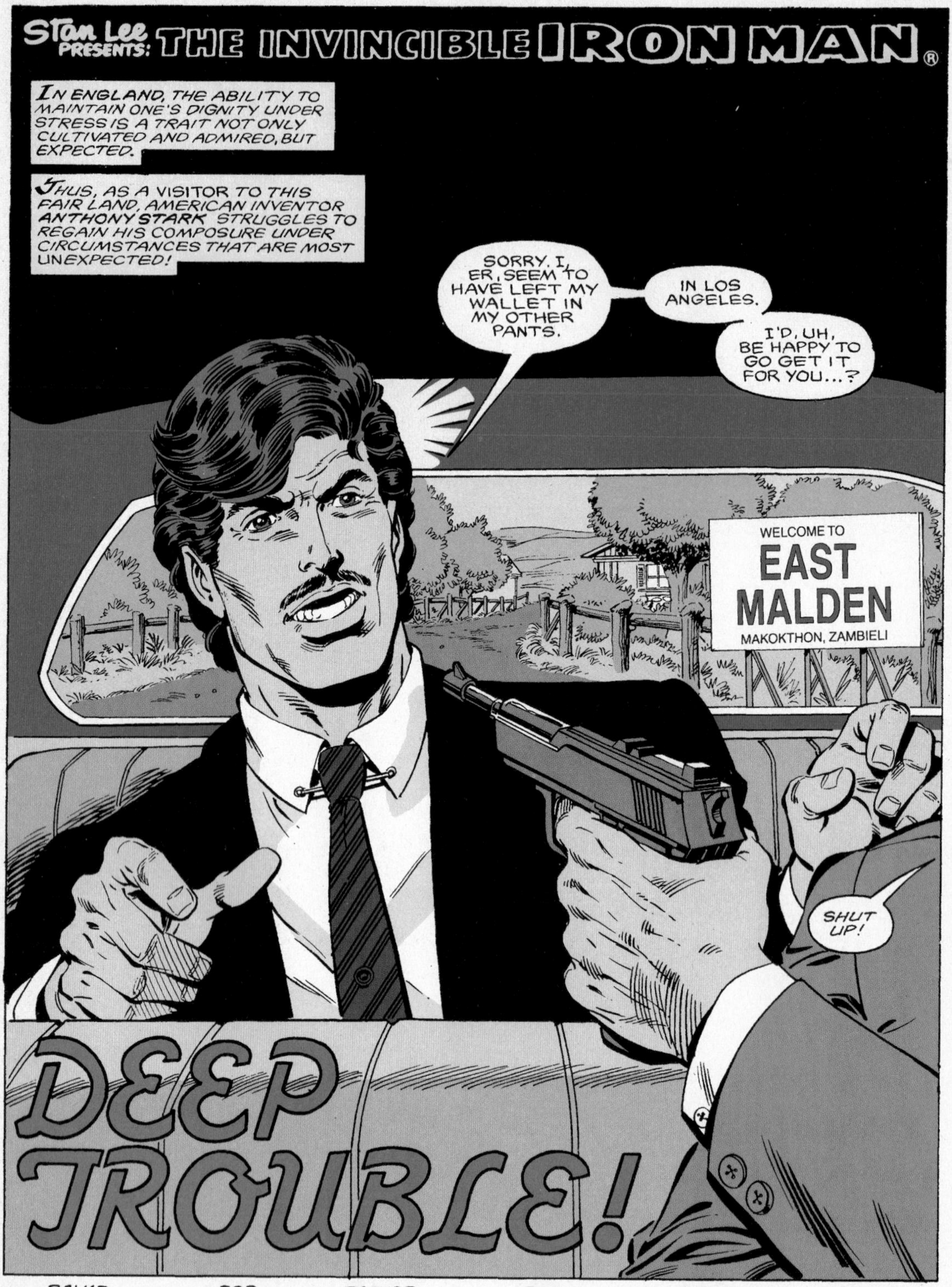
Stan Lee PRESENTS: THE INVINCIBLE IRON MAN®
IN ENGLAND, THE ABILITY TO MAINTAIN ONE'S DIGNITY UNDER STRESS IS A TRAIT NOT ONLY CULTIVATED AND ADMIRED, BUT EXPECTED.
THUS, AS A VISITOR TO THIS FAIR LAND, AMERICAN INVENTOR ANTHONY STARK STRUGGLES TO REGAIN HIS COMPOSURE UNDER CIRCUMSTANCES THAT ARE MOST UNEXPECTED!
SORRY. I, ER, SEEM TO HAVE LEFT MY WALLET IN MY OTHER PANTS.
IN LOS ANGELES.
I'D, UH, BE HAPPY TO GO GET IT FOR YOU...?
WELCOME TO EAST MALDEN MAKOKTHON, ZAMBIELI
SHUT UP!
DEEP TROUBLE!

DAVID MICHELINIE PLOT/SCRIPT • BOB LAYTON PLOT/ART • JANICE CHIANG LETTERS • BOB SHAREN COLORS • MARK GRUENWALD EDITOR • JIM SHOOTER EDITOR IN CHIEF

YA NO MORE THINK WE'RE *CROOKS* THAN WE THINK YOU'RE A *TOURIST*, MATE! SO JUST GET OUT'N THE CAR--

--AN' FOLL... THAT *PATH* LI... BRIGHT BO...

ALAS... WE... S...

I *THOUGHT* SOMETHING WAS ODD WHEN THOSE ''SECURITY AGENTS'' WHO MET ME AT THE AIRPORT BROUGHT ME OUT TO THE COUNTRY, INSTEAD OF INTO LONDON. THEY *SAID* IT WAS A ''PRECAUTION''.

15 K SOUTH BRIDGE

I'LL BET THE *REAL* MINISTRY OF DEFENSE DELEGATES ARE STILL AT HEATHROW LOOKING FOR ME. I ONLY HOPE THEY DON'T END UP FINDING ME--

--IN THE *OBITUARIES!*

GOOD AFTERNOON, MR. STARK. I AM *IRINA TARASOVA*, AND BEFORE YOU CONSIDER ANYTHING FOOLISH, LET ME ASSURE YOU THAT MY FRIEND HERE IS NOT REACHING FOR A PACK OF *CIGARETTES!*

YOU ARE WISE ENOUGH TO KNOW WHOM I *REPRESENT*--

-- JUST AS YOU ARE WISE ENOUGH TO KNOW THAT MY PEOPLE CANNOT ALLOW YOU TO *SUCCEED* IN YOUR MISSION HERE.

SO BE A SMART CAPITALIST, EH? GO HOME. AND HOPE, AS I DO, THAT ONE DAY WE CAN MEET AGAIN ... ON *FRIENDLIER* TERMS.

THIS ROAD IS NOT WELL TRAVELED. BUT YOU SHOULD BE ABLE TO FIND TRANSPORTATION EVENTUALLY.

DOSVEDONYA!

HOWEVER, AS THE BOGUS GOVERNMENT LIMO SPEEDS AWAY...

I'LL FIND TRANSPORTATION, ALL RIGHT.

BUT NOT THE SORT MS. K.G.B. HAD IN MIND!

WITH MOTIONS WORN SMOOTH BY FAMILIARITY, SOPHISTICATED THUMBPRINT LOCKS ARE DEACTIVATED.

A CUSTOM-DESIGNED HIGH-TECH BRIEFCASE SPRINGS OPEN.

AND IN THE SPAN OF TIME IT TAKES TO CHANGE A SUIT OF CLOTHES--

--THE INVINCIBLE IRON MAN SOARS HIGH OVER THE PLAINS OF RURAL ENGLAND!

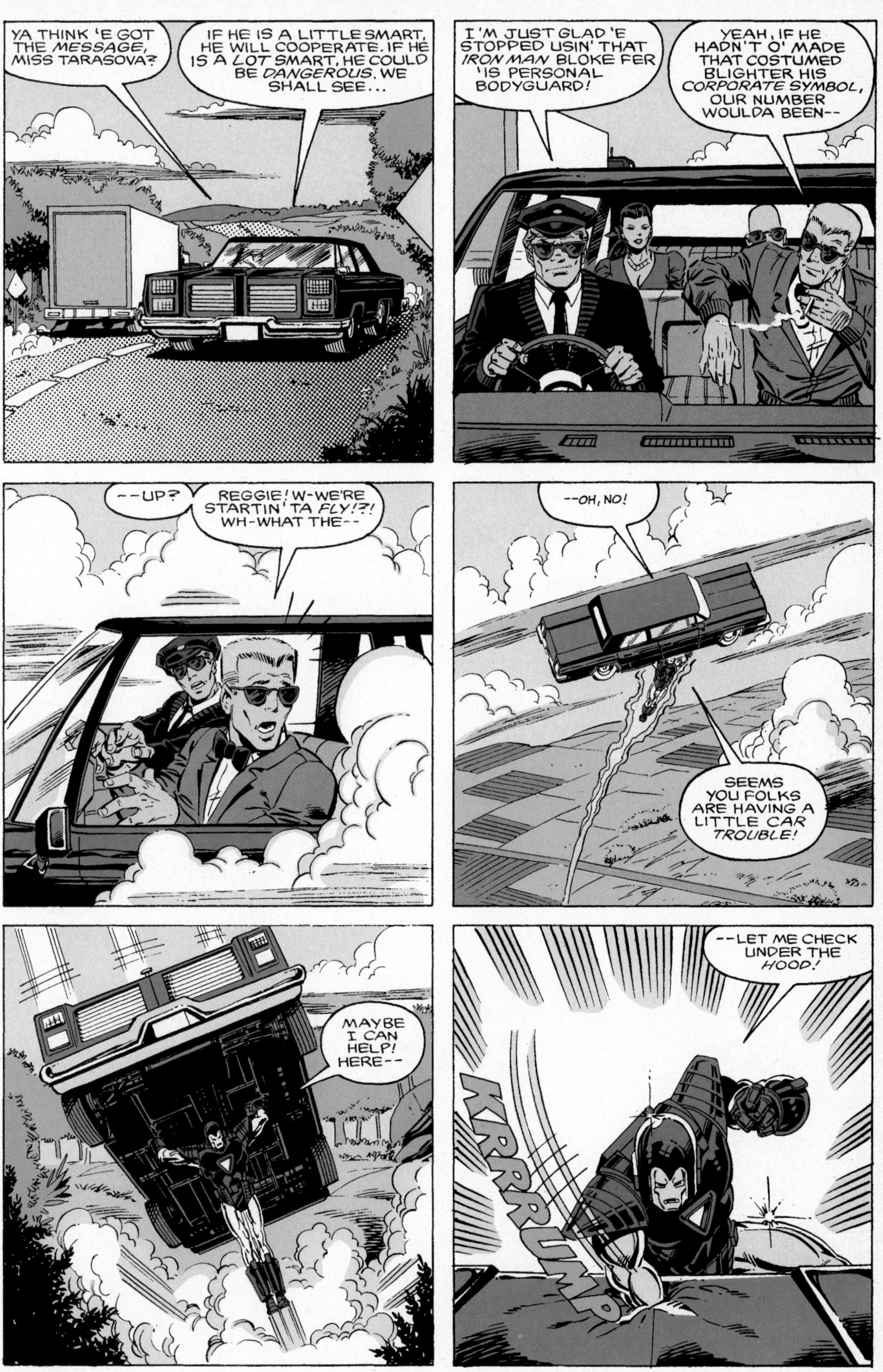
YA THINK 'E GOT THE MESSAGE, MISS TARASOVA?
IF HE IS A LITTLE SMART, HE WILL COOPERATE. IF HE IS A LOT SMART, HE COULD BE DANGEROUS. WE SHALL SEE...
I'M JUST GLAD 'E STOPPED USIN' THAT IRON MAN BLOKE FER 'IS PERSONAL BODYGUARD!
YEAH, IF HE HADN'T O' MADE THAT BLIGHTER COSTUMED HIS CORPORATE SYMBOL, OUR NUMBER WOULDA BEEN--
--UP?
REGGIE! W-WE'RE STARTIN' TA FLY!?! WH-WHAT THE--
--OH, NO!
SEEMS YOU FOLKS ARE HAVING A LITTLE CAR TROUBLE!
MAYBE I CAN HELP! HERE--
--LET ME CHECK UNDER THE HOOD!
KRRRUMP

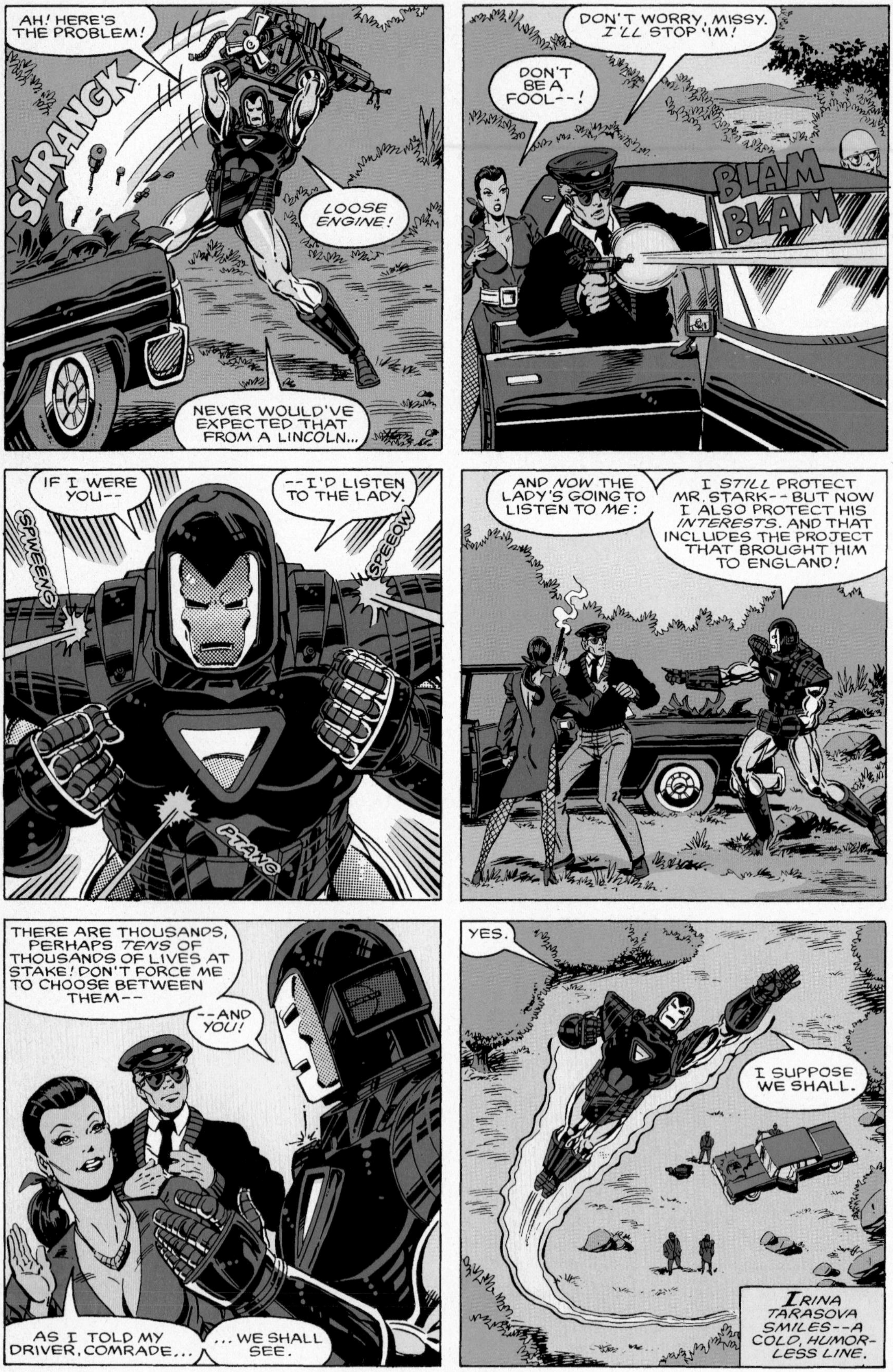

AH! HERE'S THE PROBLEM!
SHRANGK
LOOSE ENGINE!
NEVER WOULD'VE EXPECTED THAT FROM A LINCOLN...
DON'T WORRY, MISSY. I'LL STOP 'IM!
DON'T BE A FOOL--!
BLAM
BLAM
IF I WERE YOU--
--I'D LISTEN TO THE LADY.
SPWEENG
SPEEOW
PTANG
AND NOW THE LADY'S GOING TO LISTEN TO ME:
I STILL PROTECT MR. STARK--BUT NOW I ALSO PROTECT HIS INTERESTS. AND THAT INCLUDES THE PROJECT THAT BROUGHT HIM TO ENGLAND!
THERE ARE THOUSANDS, PERHAPS TENS OF THOUSANDS OF LIVES AT STAKE! DON'T FORCE ME TO CHOOSE BETWEEN THEM--
--AND YOU!
AS I TOLD MY DRIVER, COMRADE...
...WE SHALL SEE.
YES.
I SUPPOSE WE SHALL.
IRINA TARASOVA SMILES--A COLD, HUMORLESS LINE.

AND MOMENTS LATER, AFTER IRON MAN HAS RETRIEVED HIS ARMOR TOTE AND HIS CIVILIAN CLOTHING...

I FIGURED IT WOULD COME TO THIS, SOMEHOW.

I GUESS I'VE KNOWN IT FROM THE MOMENT IT ALL STARTED THREE DAYS AGO--

"--AT STARK ENTERPRISES HEADQUARTERS IN SOUTHERN CALIFORNIA..."

HOW MAY I HELP YOU, MR. KUTTNER?

AS YOU ARE AWARE, MR. STARK, THE STATE DEPARTMENT HAS SENT ME HERE ON A MATTER OF EXTREME CONFIDENTIALITY. A SPECIAL LOW-LIGHT PHOTOGRAPHY SYSTEM YOU DEVELOPED WAS USED IN THE RECENT EXPLORATORY SEARCH OF THE SUNKEN VESSEL, TITANIC, WAS IT NOT?

WHY, YES. WAS THERE A PROBLEM?

OH, NO, MR. STARK. THE EQUIPMENT PERFORMED SPLENDIDLY.

WHICH, UNFORTUNATELY, HAS LEAD TO SOMETHING OF A CRISIS IN NATIONAL SECURITY!

THIS PHOTOGRAPH SHOWS HERETOFORE UNSEEN DEBRIS ON THE OCEAN FLOOR NEAR THE TITANIC.

THAT CENTRAL CANISTER WAS SOMETHING OF A MYSTERY UNTIL RECENTLY--

--WHEN ITS SERIAL NUMBER WAS FINALLY TRACED TO A FILE PREDATING WORLD WAR I. IT WAS APPARENTLY ASSOCIATED WITH AN ANGLO-AMERICAN TEAM WORKING ON THE DEVELOPMENT OF--

--CHEMICAL WEAPONS!

CHEMICAL--! BUT MR. KUTTNER, THIS CANISTER LOOKS LIKE IT'S STARTING TO--

--DECOMPOSE!

YES. THE *PARAFFIN COATING* IS ERODING, AND THE ONLY PERSON WHO CAN TELL US THE SPECIFIC *CONTENTS* OF THAT CANISTER--

--IS THE SOLE SURVIVING MEMBER OF THE *RESEARCH TEAM:*

CARTER HASTINGS. THE OLD COOT'S A RECLUSE NOW, AN ECCENTRIC. HAS A NEUROTIC FEAR OF GOVERNMENT, WON'T TALK TO *ANYONE.*

MR. KUTTNER.

HE'LL TALK TO *ME!*

"I PROMISED I'D DO MY BEST--"

--AND I HAVE. BUT THE EQUATION'S *CHANGED.* WHEN I CONTACTED *THE MINISTRY OF DEFENSE* A FEW MINUTES AGO VIA MY HELMET RADIO TO LET THEM KNOW I'D GET HASTINGS ON MY OWN--

--I TOLD THEM THERE WAS A *LEAK* IN THEIR SECURITY.

AND I DOUBT I'VE SEEN THE *LAST* OF MS. TARASOVA!

Nevertheless...

SO, THIS IS HASTINGS' HIDEAWAY. CERTAINLY DOESN'T *LOOK* VERY--

--DANGEROUS?

G-GET OFFA MY PROPERTY -⁺K-KOFF⁺- YA PARLIAMENT PUP! L-LESS'N YA WANNA BE *BURIED* HERE! -⁺KOFF⁺-

WHOA, OLD TIMER! I'M NOT EVEN *BRITISH!*

DON'T MATTER! I- I CAN SMELL AUTHORITY A MILE AWAY! ⊰WHEEZE⊱

G-GET OUT!

IF YOU'D JUST READ THIS LETTER OF *INTRODUCTION* FIRST...?

WON'T DO NO GOOD! I'VE READ MORE *SUMMONSES* THAN YOU COULD--

--⊰GASP⊱-A-A PERSONAL REQUEST FROM *HER MAJESTY*?!? Y-YA MEAN, YOU *KNOW*--?

⊰AHEM⊱ WON'T YOU COME IN?

*M*OMENTS LATER...

THE POOR FELLOW'S FRAIL, OBVIOUSLY IN *ILL HEALTH*. I'LL HAVE TO BE GENTLE.

YOU SAY YOU WERE ACTUALLY ABOARD THE *TITANIC* ON HER TRAGIC VOYAGE, MR. HASTINGS?

AYE. THAT I WAS ⊰KOFF⊱

CARE FOR A BIT OF *FORTITUDE* WITH THAT, SONNY?

NO, THANKS. PLAIN TEA'S FINE.

PLEASE, GO ON.

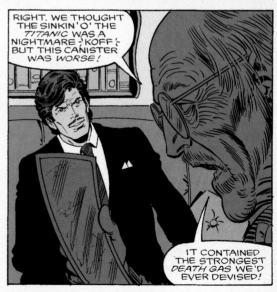

RIGHT. WE THOUGHT THE SINKIN' O' THE *TITANIC* WAS A NIGHTMARE ⊰KOFF⊱ BUT THIS CANISTER WAS *WORSE*!

IT CONTAINED THE STRONGEST *DEATH GAS* WE'D EVER DEVISED!

WHEN IT SANK TO THE BOTTOM OF THE *ATLANTIC*, I THOUGHT THINGS WAS OVER.

BUT THROUGH THE YEARS ⁻KOFF⁻ I'VE SOMEHOW KNOWN THAT SOME-DAY... I'D BE *PUNISHED*.

PUNISHED?

AYE. Y'SEE, I WAS ACCOMPANYIN' THAT CANISTER TO AMERICA FOR FURTHER *TESTIN'*. ⁻KOFF⁻. BUT WHEN I WAS RESCUED, I TOLD MY SUPERIORS THAT FURTHER CALCULATIONS SHOWED THE GAS WASN'T *EFFECTIVE* AFTER ALL.

THE PROJECT WAS *SCRUBBED*.

BUT THOSE CALCULATIONS *REALLY* PROVED ⁻KOFF KOFF⁻ THAT THE GAS WOULDN'T *DISSIPATE*, THAT IT'D LINGER FOR DAYS, WEEKS, CUTTIN' A PATH O' HORROR WHEREVER THE WIND TOOK IT!

I COULDN'T HAVE THOSE *CIVILIAN DEATHS* ON MY CONSCIENCE.

BUT NOW, IF THE GAS ESCAPES THAT RUPTURIN' CANISTER--! MR. STARK, Y-YA'VE *GOT* TO STOP IT! YA MUST ⁻KOFF K-KOFF⁻

TAKE IT EASY, MR. HASTINGS. I PROMISE I'LL DO EVERYTHING--

--I CAN.

THAT "BUG" YA PLANTED IN THE YANK'S POCKET WHEN YA WAS SMARMIN' UP TO 'IM WORKS GREAT, IRINA! WE KIN HEAR *EVERYTHING* THEY SAY!

DA. AND THE WORDS WE'VE HEARD ARE MORE IMPORTANT THAN YOU COULD *POSSIBLY* IMAGINE!

OPEN THE *CLANDESTINE BROADCAST FREQUENCY,* FULL SCRAMBLE! I MUST SPEAK WITH THE HEAD OF OUR OCEANIC OPERATIONS!

AT ONCE!

THE SEAS ARE CALM, THE CLOUDS DARK AND LOW, TWO DAYS LATER--

--AS A CUSTOM-DESIGNED STARK ENTERPRISES VESSEL BOBS GENTLY ON THE SURFACE OF THE NORTH ATLANTIC...

THE EXPLORATORY SUB HAS RETURNED, *COMMANDER.* THE LATEST DATA IS BEING FED INTO MY DIVER'S COMPUTER--

BETHANY

--AFTER WHICH IT WILL BE PASSED ALONG TO YOUR *FRIGATE'S SENSOR INPUTS,* AS PER OUR PLAN. JUST REMEMBER, IF THOSE SENSORS DETECT THE *SLIGHTEST* TRACE OF *TOXICITY* IN THE WATER...

DON'T WORRY, WE'LL *SHAG OUT* OF HERE FASTER THAN *MARCOS* LEFT *MANILA!*

GOOD LUCK.

"LUCK"? LUCK HAS VERY LITTLE TO DO WITH IT.

EVER SINCE MY BATTERY OF INDIVIDUALIZED ARMOR WAS DESTROYED IN A PANIC MOVE TO MAKE SURE THEY WOULDN'T FALL INTO THE WRONG HANDS--*

*IN IM #174-175.

-- I'VE KNOWN THERE WOULD BE SPECIAL SITUATIONS--

--WHICH WOULD REQUIRE SPECIALIZED CAPABILITIES.

THAT IS WHY I BUILT THIS EXPERIMENTAL DEEP SEA ARMOR, MY REGULAR IRON MAN SUIT CAN GO UNDERWATER--

--BUT NOT FOR MILES, OR STAY DOWN FOR HOURS!

THIS SUIT, ON THE OTHER HAND, UTILIZES THE MOST RECENT INNOVATIONS IN UNDERSEA TECHNOLOGY, AND WAS BUILT SPECIFICALLY TO WITHSTAND THE UNIQUE CONDITIONS OF A DEEP SEA ENVIRONMENT.

SURE WISH I'D HAD TIME TO TEST IT FIRST...!

PLOOSH

I'LL NEVER GET OVER HOW MAGNIFICENT THE UNDERWATER WORLD IS. IT'S AS BEAUTIFUL AS OUTER SPACE. AND--

--JUST AS *DEADLY!* I'D BETTER RUN A QUICK *SYSTEMS CHECK.*

GOOD. ACCORDING TO THE READOUTS IN MY *OUTER HELMET,* EVERYTHING'S FUNCTIONING PERFECTLY: OXYGEN FLOW, ELECTRICAL RELAYS, AQUATIC PROPULSION JETS.

I BUILT EVERY *SAFEGUARD* I COULD THINK OF INTO THIS SUIT, TRIED TO CONSIDER EVERY *CONTINGENCY.*

EVEN SO, I CAN'T HELP FEELING AWESOMELY... AND UTTERLY...

...ALONE.

*H*E DIVES.

*S*TRAIGHT DOWN.

*I*NTO LIQUID EBONY.

*T*HE OCEAN PRESSES TIGHT--

--LIKE A CLOSING HAND.

195

UNTIL AT LAST, TWO MILES DOWN, A HALOGEN LAMP BEAM SWEEPS ACROSS FADED PAINT ON RUSTING METAL.

AND INSIDE THE MASSIVE SUIT OF ULTRA-PRESSURIZED ARMOR, TONY STARK SHUDDERS SLIGHTLY.

THE SEARCH BEGINS.

TROUBLE, SIR?

NO, NOT AS LONG AS THEY STAY WHERE THEY ARE.

MOST OF OUR OPEN SEA OPERATIONS ARE SHADOWED BY RUSSIAN "TRAWLERS".

THEY'RE GENERALLY NO PROBLEM, AS LONG AS THEY KEEP THEIR DISTANCE. BUT STILL...

...IT MIGHT BE WISE TO GET MR. STARK ON THE HORN.

RIGHT AWAY, SIR!

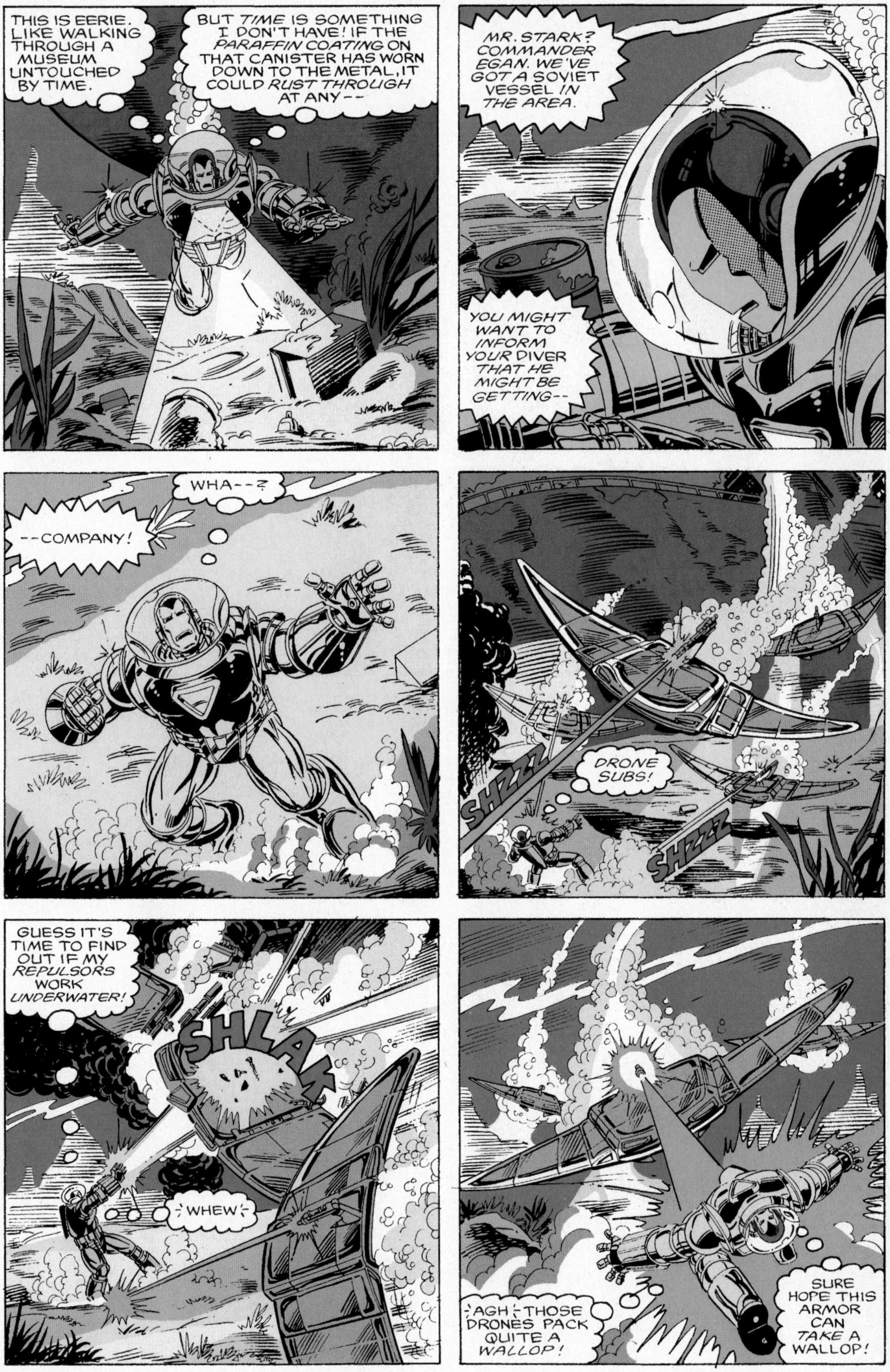
THIS IS EERIE. LIKE WALKING THROUGH A MUSEUM UNTOUCHED BY TIME.
BUT TIME IS SOMETHING I DON'T HAVE! IF THE PARAFFIN COATING ON THAT CANISTER HAS WORN DOWN TO THE METAL, IT COULD RUST THROUGH AT ANY--
MR. STARK? COMMANDER EGAN. WE'VE GOT A SOVIET VESSEL IN THE AREA.
YOU MIGHT WANT TO INFORM YOUR DIVER THAT HE MIGHT BE GETTING--
WHA--?
--COMPANY!
DRONE SUBS!
SHZZZ
SHZZZ
GUESS IT'S TIME TO FIND OUT IF MY REPULSORS WORK UNDERWATER!
SHLAK
WHEW
AGH--THOSE DRONES PACK QUITE A WALLOP!
SURE HOPE THIS ARMOR CAN TAKE A WALLOP!

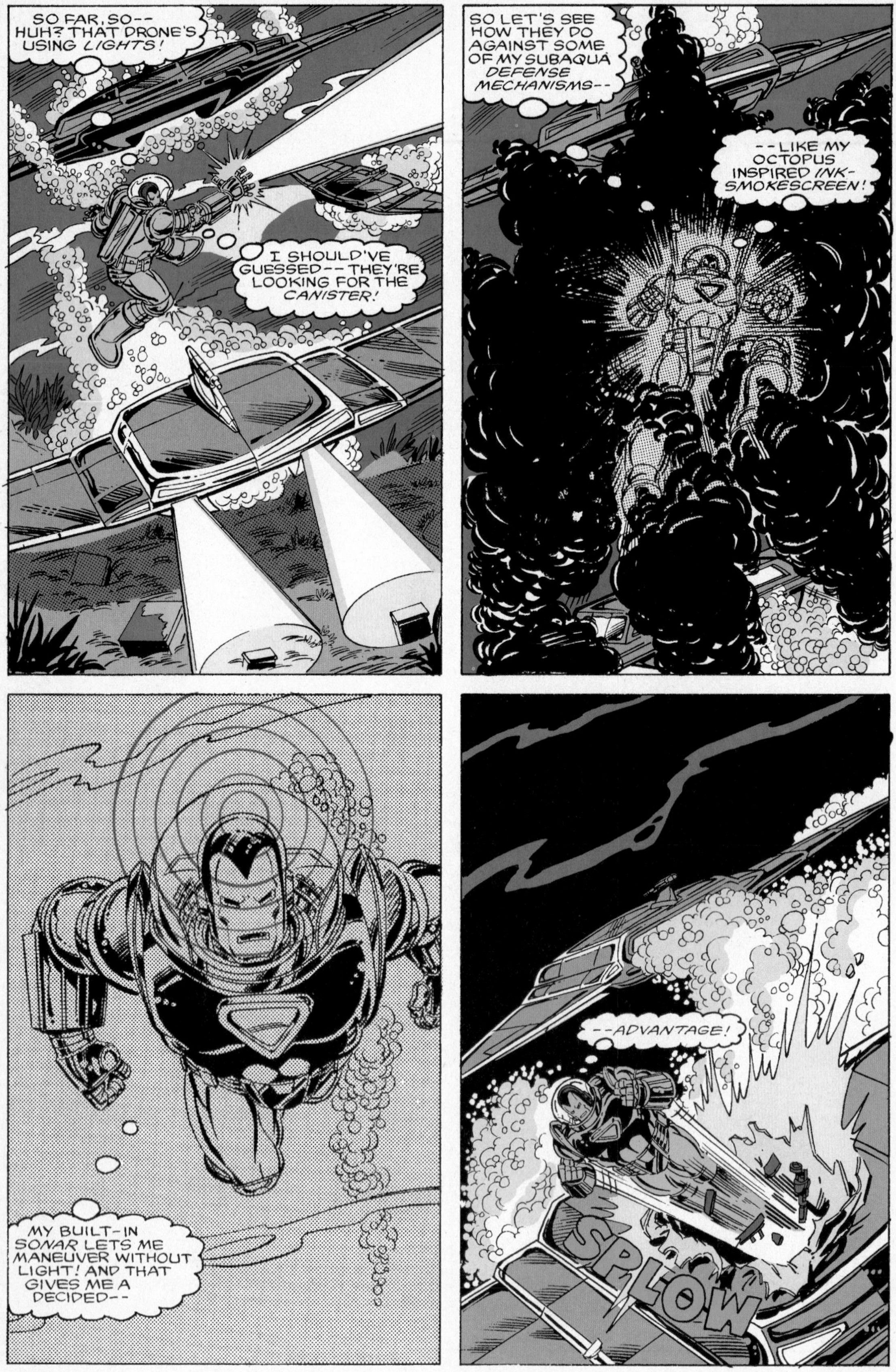
SO FAR, SO-- HUH? THAT DRONE'S USING *LIGHTS*!
I SHOULD'VE GUESSED-- THEY'RE LOOKING FOR THE *CANISTER*!
SO LET'S SEE HOW THEY DO AGAINST SOME OF MY SUBAQUA *DEFENSE MECHANISMS*--
--LIKE MY OCTOPUS INSPIRED *INK-SMOKESCREEN*!
MY BUILT-IN *SONAR* LETS ME MANEUVER WITHOUT LIGHT! AND THAT GIVES ME A DECIDED--
--*ADVANTAGE*!
SPLOW

SHZZZ

SHZZOK

UH-OH. INK CLOUD'S *DISPERSING!* DRONES ARE ATTACKING AGAIN!

MAYBE IT'S TIME TO TRY SOME OF THE *OFFENSIVE* WEAPONRY I DERIVED FROM SEA CREATURES!

LIKE THE UNIQUE ASSAULT CAPABILITIES--

--OF THE *ELECTRIC EEL!*

THAT WAS EASY. *TOO* EASY. WHOEVER SENT THOSE DRONES AFTER THE CANISTER EITHER DIDN'T WANT IT *BADLY* ENOUGH--

--OR THEY WERE JUST *SETTING ME UP* FOR--

--AGGH!

WH-- WHAT THE--?

THRUB

199

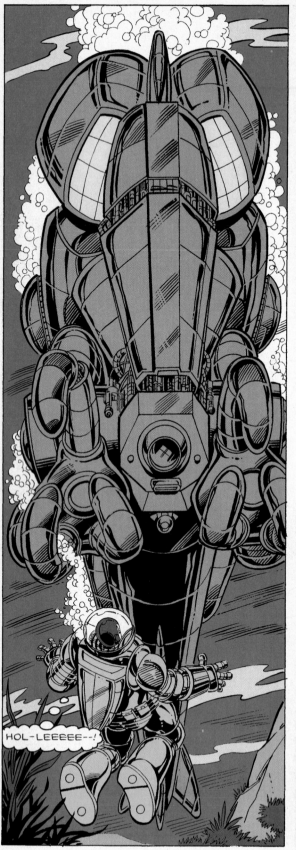

HOL-LEEEEE--!

YOUR EMPLOYER SHOULD HAVE LISTENED TO ME, COMRADE IRON MAN! IF HE HAD--

--YOU MIGHT HAVE LIVED!

THAT VOICE--!

ABOARD THE "TRAWLER...

DA, COMRADE. I CONTROL THE ROBOT LEVIATHAN, JUST AS IT NOW CONTROLS YOU!

AND IN THE DIFFICULT GAME WE BOTH PLAY, CONTROL MEANS EVERYTHING!

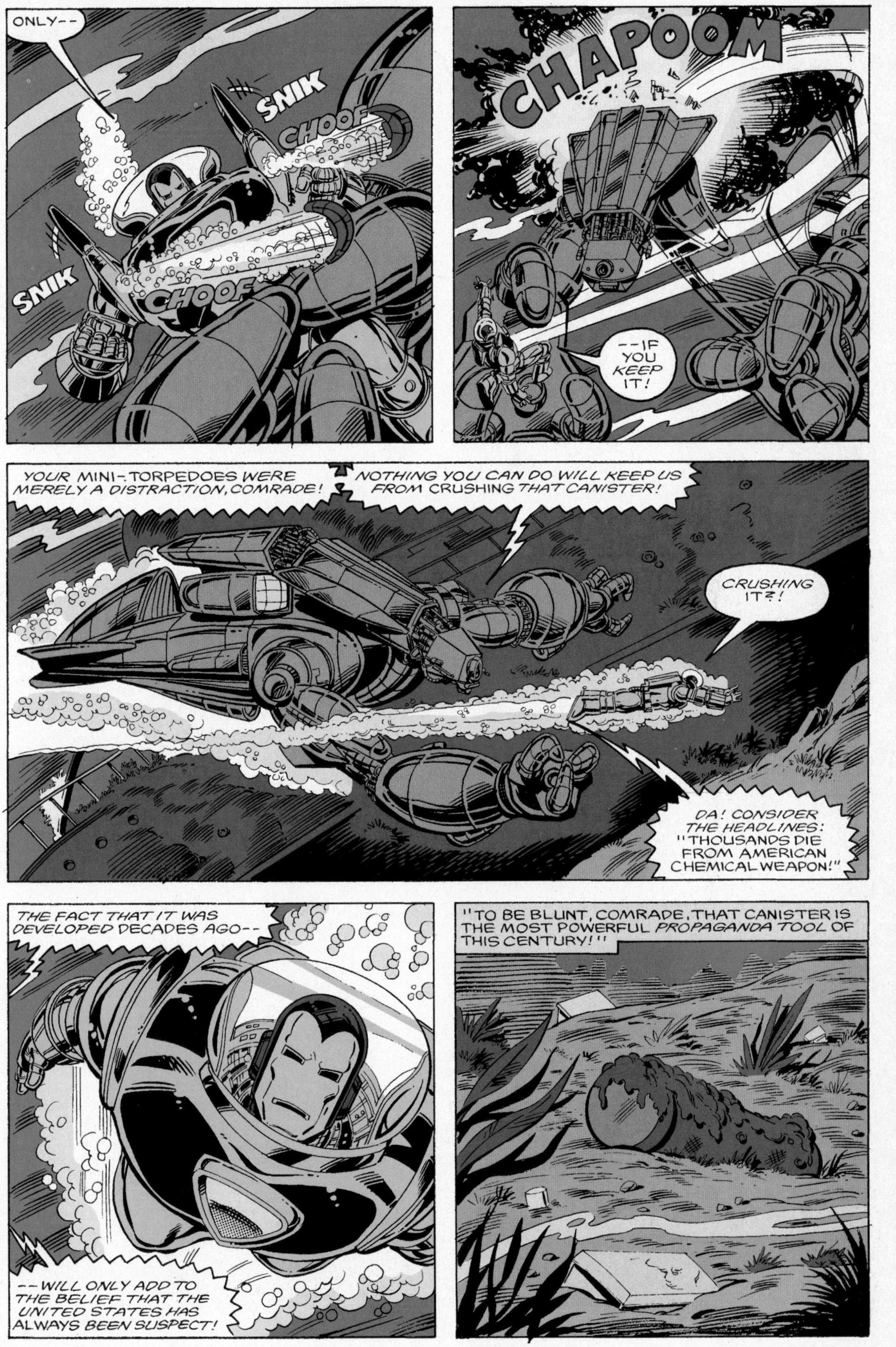
ONLY--
SNIK
CHOOF
SNIK
CHOOF
CHAPOOM
--IF YOU KEEP IT!
YOUR MINI-TORPEDOES WERE MERELY A DISTRACTION, COMRADE!
NOTHING YOU CAN DO WILL KEEP US FROM CRUSHING THAT CANISTER!
CRUSHING IT?!
DA! CONSIDER THE HEADLINES: "THOUSANDS DIE FROM AMERICAN CHEMICAL WEAPON!"
THE FACT THAT IT WAS DEVELOPED DECADES AGO--
--WILL ONLY ADD TO THE BELIEF THAT THE UNITED STATES HAS ALWAYS BEEN SUSPECT!
"TO BE BLUNT, COMRADE, THAT CANISTER IS THE MOST POWERFUL PROPAGANDA TOOL OF THIS CENTURY!"

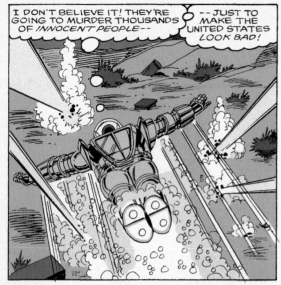

I DON'T BELIEVE IT! THEY'RE GOING TO MURDER THOUSANDS OF *INNOCENT PEOPLE*--

--JUST TO MAKE THE UNITED STATES *LOOK BAD!*

LEVIATHAN'S FASTER THAN ME! MORE *POWERFUL!* MY ONLY SURE CHANCE FOR SURVIVAL--

--IS TO GET *OUT* OF HERE!

BUT MY ONLY SURE CHANCE TO *STOP* THAT THING--

--IS TO GRAB THE CANISTER, SLOW DOWN--

--AND USE MYSELF AS *BAIT!*

UGK H-HE TOOK IT, ALL RIGHT!

AND HE'S SQUEEZING! T-TRYING TO *POP* ME LIKE A HUMAN BALLOON!

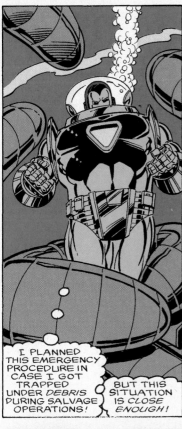

I PLANNED THIS EMERGENCY PROCEDURE IN CASE I GOT TRAPPED UNDER *DEBRIS* DURING SALVAGE OPERATIONS!

BUT THIS SITUATION IS *CLOSE* ENOUGH!

MY INNER SUIT IS STRONG ENOUGH TO WITHSTAND THE *PRESSURE* AT THIS DEPTH, BUT ONLY FOR A COUPLE OF *MINUTES!*

HAVE TO PRAY THAT'S LONG ENOUGH!

BECAUSE I *ALSO* TOOK STEPS TO INSURE THAT *SCAVENGERS* COULDN'T GET HOLD OF MY ABANDONED ARMOR --

-- BY SEEING THAT THE EMERGENCY ESCAPE SEQUENCE AUTOMATIC- ALLY TRIGGERED --

WHRAPOWM

--A MASSIVE *SELF- DESTRUCT* CHARGE!

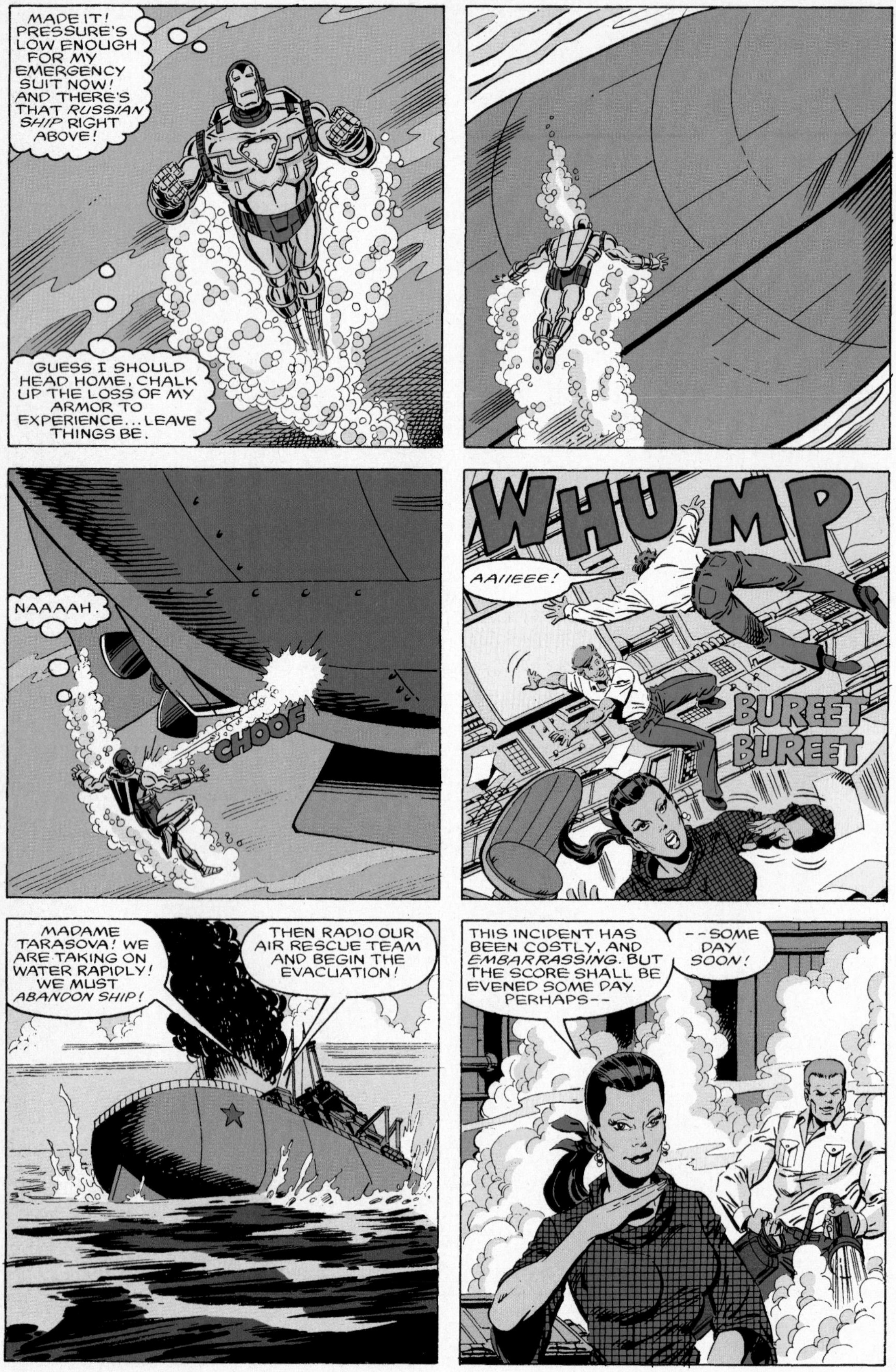
MADE IT! PRESSURE'S LOW ENOUGH FOR MY EMERGENCY SUIT NOW! AND THERE'S THAT RUSSIAN SHIP RIGHT ABOVE!
GUESS I SHOULD HEAD HOME, CHALK UP THE LOSS OF MY ARMOR TO EXPERIENCE... LEAVE THINGS BE.
NAAAAH.
CHOOF
WHUMP
AAIIEEE!
BUREET BUREET
MADAME TARASOVA! WE ARE TAKING ON WATER RAPIDLY! WE MUST ABANDON SHIP!
THEN RADIO OUR AIR RESCUE TEAM AND BEGIN THE EVACUATION!
THIS INCIDENT HAS BEEN COSTLY, AND EMBARRASSING. BUT THE SCORE SHALL BE EVENED SOME DAY. PERHAPS--
--SOME DAY SOON!

EPILOGUE! DAYS LATER, AT OUR BLESSED LADY HOSPITAL IN A SUBURB OF LONDON...

THE DOCTOR SAYS HE'S DYING.

OUR BLESSED LADY HOSPITAL

THE STRAIN WAS TOO MUCH FOR HIS AGE AND CONDITION. THEY DON'T EXPECT HIM TO LAST THE NIGHT.

MR. HASTINGS?

Y... YOU ⸮IS K-KOFF⸮ IS IT...?

IT'S IN GOOD HANDS, SIR. IT WILL BE DISPOSED OF SAFELY.

TH-THANK ⸮KOFF⸮ HEAVEN! NOW ⸮KOFF⸮ AT LAST ⸮KOFF⸮ KOFF⸮ I CAN...

...SLEEP.

SLEEP WELL, MR. HASTINGS.

IN PEACE.

AND MAY THE NEXT WORLD--

--BE A LITTLE LESS MAD THAN THIS ONE.

THE END

205

THE MANY ARMORS OF IRON MAN: With Bob Layton

Perhaps no other artist is as creatively attuned to a Marvel character as Bob Layton is to Iron Man. During two seminal stretches in the '70s and '80s, Bob, along with co-writer David Michelinie, plotted, wrote and drew the Iron Man, getting to know his way around the high-tech armor that Tony Stark dons in his pursuit of adventure. There have been many armors in the long history of Iron Man — some good, some great, and some not-so-wonderful — but Bob graciously joined us to pick out a few of his favorites to riff on, and we think you'll enjoy his insightful commentary!

**Iron Man Legend
Bob Layton**

"The original Iron Man armor as portrayed in *Tales of Suspense #39* was to leave a lasting impression on me as a child. Not because it was a superior design, per se, but because of what it represented in the sense of comic history. Anthony Stark would be the first mainstream character who relied on the very technology that gave him superhuman abilities to stay alive. As with many of Stan Lee's creations, Tony Stark was a beautifully flawed character, whose weaknesses originated from within and not from a lump of radioactive material from his home planet. Regardless of who drew that original "gray armor," it always felt like you could hear it clanging down the hallway coming towards you with its huge, lumbering, metallic feet. I think most of us who grew up reading *Iron Man* have an affinity for this original design because of its lasting impression on our young minds that this character was destined to be unique in comic history. I knew it — and so did you!"

Original Gray Armor. Design by Don Heck, circa *Tales of Suspense #39* (1963), art by Adi Granov.

"One of the editorial policies back in the early days of Marvel was that going into outer space should always be a "big deal." So, when David Michelinie and I were concocting the Sunturion/Roxxon storyline, it gave us the opportunity to come up with a design specifically for the requirements and rigors of operating in Zero-G. In approaching this design, I basically took the elements of the original Red-and-Gold Armor and modified it for the task at hand. Specifically, since weight was no longer an issue, we could bulk it up a bit to accommodate extra fuel and additional armaments. We also decided to remove any access areas where the armor could be breached, foremost — the mouthpiece. Because of the vacuum of space, it seemed ridiculous for him to have a mouthpiece to begin with. Most notable about this particular design, it was the *very first* of many variant armors to come. No matter what design appeared in the future, they would all owe their genesis to this humble beginning. It's one of the things that I brought to the series that I am mosof."

Original Space Armor. Design and art by Bob Layton, circa *Iron Man #142* (1981).

"The Silver Centurion Armor was an important landmark in the *Iron Man* series, mainly because it was the first time that Marvel deviated from the original Red-and-Gold design. Not only did we change the color scheme, but we also altered the basic, recognizable features that Iron Man had displayed for decades. Ironically, I wasn't the artist on the series at the time Mark Gruenwald commissioned me to create this new design for Iron Man. He told me that he was looking for something that looked slightly samurai in nature. Mark wanted to present the Iron Man armor as more warrior-like in appearance than in previous incarnations. After several designs, the Silver Centurion was the one that we settled on and turned out to be one of the most popular versions of the character. On a personal level, it was my least favorite of the armors I designed, only because of my personal philosophy that the Iron Man armor should always become more streamlined as it evolves."

Silver Centurion Armor. Design and art by Bob Layton, circa *Iron Man #200-230* (1985-1987).

"**T**his is one of the few versions that I've never drawn. At the time this design was created, I was Editor-in-Chief and Senior Vice President of Valiant Comics and had little or no time to even read the series. But, what I love about this concept is that it incorporates my philosophy on variant armors into one, single design. Instead of a lone, integrated suit, this design was based on a modular component concept. I believe it's a great idea to have a single armor that had the versatility and capability of multitasking. And I also like the streamlined look of the basic under-armor configuration."

Modular Armor. Design and art by Tom Morgan, circa *Iron Man #314*

Man design, he's also improved and upped me on a couple of those, as well. Most notable is the fact that this armor looks like it could be totally functional. In fact, since we've seen it walking around in the clips from the Iron Man movie, it seems Stan Winston *has* made it completely functional! Kudos to Adi.

"In addition, the basic design harkens back to the classic Red-and-Gold armor that is near and dear to every Iron Man fan's heart. Where it breaks the rules is a matter of taste. Again, I reiterate my creative imperative to make each design more streamlined and sleek as the technology evolves. Unfortunately, although functional, it does look a bit clunky on occasion. Additionally, I'm a big fan of very, very shiny metal. The brushed metal look is simply not as appealing to me as the once-highly-reflective surfaces. There are times where it looks more like plastic than metal. That's really my only criticism of what is otherwise a well-thought-out and executed design."

The Many Armors of Iron Man TPB cover (1992) by Mark Chiarello & Mark Bright

Current Iron Man Armor. Design and art by Adi Granov, circa *Iron Man #314* (1995)